THE
NRA

THE NRA

The Unauthorized History

Frank Smyth

FLATIRON
BOOKS
NEW YORK

THE NRA. Copyright © 2020 by Frank Smyth. All rights reserved.
Printed in the United States of America. For information, address Flatiron Books,
120 Broadway, New York, NY 10271.

www.flatironbooks.com

Designed by Steven Seighman

The Library of Congress Cataloging-in-Publication Data is available upon request.

ISBN 978-1-250-21028-9 (hardcover)
ISBN 978-1-250-21029-6 (ebook)

Our books may be purchased in bulk for promotional, educational, or business
use. Please contact your local bookseller or the Macmillan Corporate and
Premium Sales Department at 1-800-221-7945, extension 5442, or by email at
MacmillanSpecialMarkets@macmillan.com.

First Edition: March 2020

10 9 8 7 6 5 4 3 2 1

For Peter L. Mazzarella

CONTENTS

Introduction   1

Part One—A Hundred Years

1. With an Eye Toward Future Wars   15
2. The "Royal" NRA   25
3. The Promiscuous Toting of Guns   41
4. A High Plane of Honest, Frank Discussion   53
5. Public Opinion Demands Some Control   65

Part Two—The Shift

6. The Awakening   83
7. A Great Religion   101

Part Three—The Focus

8. The Politburo   125
9. The Business Model   153
10. Hidden Hands   173
11. A Family Sport   194
12. The Creed   217

Acknowledgments   239
Notes   241
Index   280

INTRODUCTION

The National Rifle Association of America has an exquisite heritage. It could be argued that the NRA is America's strongest civic organization, if not also its most enigmatic. Few other nonprofit groups in the United States have lasted as long. Few founded before or since are so large in membership: today the NRA claims over 5 million members. And no other nonprofit group in the United States has wielded comparable influence on so many levels or enjoyed such extraordinary success in its aims.

The NRA is as old as "Major League" baseball, older than the American Red Cross, older than the Boy Scouts. It was founded in New York during Reconstruction, on the eve of America's Gilded Age, with the mission to improve military preparedness in anticipation of future wars. For much of the twentieth century, the NRA's primary activity was hosting competitive shooting matches for National Guard, military, and civilian shooters, financed by government money and run by the NRA on its ranges. For decades the NRA also supported the regulation of firearms, from the first major federal gun law in 1934 to the second in 1968.

A few years later the NRA "shifted [its] focus," to borrow the words of David Keene, who in 2013 became the first NRA president to give a speech in a major foreign power's capital, in Moscow. This shift, whose implications would have profound consequences in American life, can in fact be dated to the NRA's 1977 annual meeting in Cincinnati—an event still known in NRA lore as the "Cincinnati Revolt." Before Cincinnati, the nonprofit Association had a basic transparency to both the public and its membership. After Cincinnati, it became an organization of secrecy, where information is shared on a need-to-know basis and is concentrated at the top.

This closed culture has led the modern Association's leadership to rewrite the NRA's own history, crafting a new narrative that has served the organization's shifted focus. Many groups, like many people, tweak their past to polish their image in the present. But the NRA does this to an unusual degree. The Association's modern leaders have buried the very same history that their predecessors used to celebrate. The NRA's own two founding fathers, both famous men in their day (each of whom, as it happens, left a permanent stamp on New York City), are little celebrated by the group now, their accomplishments rarely evoked. To take another example from its forgotten history: just six years after the organization was chartered, the NRA became rifle champions of the world, beating the Irish champions on its home range outside New York City. The NRA's legacy, as will be seen in these pages, is rich in events that one might think it would burnish. But it doesn't.

Why wouldn't the modern NRA want to celebrate all those things? Why would the modern Association wish to leave buried so much of the treasure of its own rich history? Is it because to do so would be to say too much about the many leaders who helped shape the Association and lead to uncomfortable questions about what those leaders would think of today's NRA? Perhaps the NRA cannot afford the risk of opening the door to its own past lest the exhumation reveal how far the modern NRA has strayed from its origins.

* * *

One prominent NRA leader in the twentieth century was a man named Milton A. Reckord. A lieutenant general and a highly decorated veteran of three foreign wars, Reckord lived a long life. He served as executive vice president of the NRA, a title even more impressive than it sounds, as traditionally the EVP has essentially been the CEO of the Association. For a span of more than twenty-three years—apart from a five-year leave of absence to serve during World War II—he stood at the Association's helm. In fact, General Reckord's tenure leading the NRA was surpassed only in 2014 by the Association's current CEO, Executive Vice President Wayne LaPierre.

At age ninety-four Reckord was interviewed in his home in Maryland over two days for an official NRA oral history. In it, the general explained many things he'd seen and been involved in, including how the NRA had negotiated a compromise with lawmakers to establish the nation's first "sane, reasonable and effective" gun control law.

This NRA oral history was never published. And the NRA— which today runs a multimillion-dollar multimedia empire—has in fact never digitized its storied flagship magazine, the *American Rifleman*. However, back issues of this and other NRA monthly magazines—once also available in optional leather binders—are traded on eBay. Large collections spanning decades are rare, but some date back over a century.

Thumbing through the *American Rifleman*'s pages is illuminating. Take two ongoing columns, launched sixty-nine years apart.

"The Dope Bag" is a regular column nearly a century old. To this day, this column still answers members' questions about "target and hunting small arms, hunting licenses, game guides, and kindred subjects," as it said upon the column's launch in 1922. "The Fox gun you mention is one of the best duck guns made," began one early reply to a reader's query. Today vintage issues of NRA magazines, especially with articles like "Backwoods Gunsmithing" and "Handloading Ammunition," are coveted by collectors.

"Standing Guard" is a very different column. It has been penned by current NRA CEO Wayne LaPierre in the *American Rifleman* since 1991, when LaPierre—after a long, stormy voyage—finally secured the helm of the organization, which he had quietly sought for some time. In this column LaPierre has offered such views as "There is no difference" between Democrats and Socialists "any longer." The same Democrats are threatening "the bedrock values of our society," so "to preserve our values and protect our freedom, America needs the good guys to step up like never before." These are sentiments one would struggle to find in issues from a much earlier era.

* * *

An aura of mystery surrounds the NRA and its leadership today. No other major nonprofit group in America is so cloaked in the dark. The modern NRA has long concealed its operations and spending, along with information about its bylaws and board. Its leaders have tightly managed the Association's elections, much like a communist politburo, to choose who is eligible to appear on the ballot, preempting potential internal challenges for control.

And this penchant for secrecy is borne out in the literature about the NRA. While there are hundreds of books addressing gun violence, gun control, and gun rights in the United States, few have ever dealt directly with the NRA. The modern Association limits access for journalists and academics. In fact, there are only two book-length histories of the NRA that have been published to date. Each one happens to have been authorized by the NRA itself.

NRA: An American Legend is the most recent official account of the Association, published in 2002 in collaboration with the NRA and its staff. An oversized coffee-table book of 304 glossy pages, its foreword was written by the late spy thriller author Tom Clancy. The book is now out of print.

Americans and Their Guns: The National Rifle Association Story Through Nearly a Century of Service to the Nation was the organization's first official history, published in 1967 with a copyright to the National Rifle Association of America (the group's legal name since 1876). Today there is no sign of this NRA book on the Association's website or among the displays at its Firearms Museum or annual meetings, and it too is out of print.

In the pages that follow, the story of this remarkable organization will be told, and it will be told for the first time by a writer unbeholden to the organization.

* * *

I am a gun owner. And I don't hunt. I keep a so-called assault weapon—a Glock 19, an Austrian-designed 9 mm semiautomatic pistol. This is a tactical, high-capacity weapon that has minimal recoil and rarely jams, and for these very same reasons it is now the sidearm of choice for most police and other law enforcement professionals across this country. I have long believed that the Second Amendment protects my right to keep arms in my home.

I have also long believed that having my weapon registered by its serial number under my name, in my home state of New Jersey, after I'd undergone not one but two criminal and mental health background checks along with being fingerprinted twice, is a reasonable requirement that does not infringe on my Second Amendment rights at all—a view that America's courts have upheld, at least so far.

For decades now within American gun circles, gun activists who take what LaPierre has called an "absolutist" stand on gun rights have derided fellow gun owners who fail to share their views as "Fudds," a smear derived from the name of the hapless hunter Elmer Fudd in the baby-boomer-era Bugs Bunny cartoons. A Fudd is a gun owner like me who supports gun regulations, especially when it comes to tactical, semiautomatic firearms. (I am a paradox because I am a Fudd who owns a signature non-Fudd gun.)

Guns have long been a part of my life. But I first became interested in the NRA more than a quarter of a century ago. It was the early 1990s, and Congress was debating the crime bill. Prison reform advocates warned that many nonviolent first-time drug offenders, instead of being offered a chance at rehabilitation, were already being sentenced to decades in jail.

I wrote a piece for *The New Republic* about followers of the Grateful Dead—then the top-grossing live musical act in America, touring seasonally in venues around the nation—who were being arrested for trafficking LSD and being sentenced to long jail terms. In my reporting, I stumbled upon the fact that the NRA was quietly behind a number of TV ads in key districts across the country. These ads claimed that Congress was planning to let tens of thousands of drug dealers out of prison—without mentioning that they were nonviolent first-time offenders. The NRA-funded ads made no mention of guns either, and would seem at first glance to have little to do with the NRA's stated aims. Why was the NRA quietly spending money on ads that never mentioned guns? I decided to begin examining this seemingly inscrutable organization.

In the mid-1990s, while writing for the *Village Voice*, I managed to gain access to an NRA board meeting, and I witnessed what, much to my surprise, was the start of an epochal struggle for power. I saw legendary NRA leaders in action, many of whom are septuagenarians or octogenarians by now but who remain redoubtable board directors. I watched as a few of these same leaders, including Wayne LaPierre, navigated shrewdly between competing sides. I also learned to expect the unexpected, as I personally went from being shunned by top NRA leaders for having documented the secrets of their internal power struggles to soon seeing the same leadership distribute to other reporters photocopies (in violation of my and the paper's joint copyright) of my opinion piece from the *The Washington Post*—when it served their internal power machinations.

By the 2000s, that power struggle was finally brought to an end through the inspired decision by LaPierre to recruit the legendary Hollywood actor Charlton Heston for the post of NRA president. And I moved on to other matters in my reporting. Then Sandy Hook happened. In the wake of the unbearable carnage of the Sandy Hook Elementary School shooting in Newtown, Connecticut, before the winter holidays in 2012, I wondered how the NRA—which had remained silent after almost every other high-profile mass shooting— might respond.

Seven days later, Wayne LaPierre told the nation during a live, nationally televised press conference, "The only thing that stops a bad guy with a gun is a good guy with a gun." At this point I was surprised not that he said it, but only that he finally said it out loud to a national audience.

It was after Sandy Hook that I set out again to learn as much as I could about the NRA. A rich body of NRA materials, including the unpublished NRA oral history, the out-of-print first authorized history, and issues of the *American Rifleman* and its progenitors and sister publications, along with official NRA board, foundation, and financial documents found in university archives and tax records, leaves a long trail of trends, figures, and facts.

In 2018 I also joined the NRA myself as a regular member at the discounted rate of $30 for one year, and I renewed my membership for $35 the following year. Back during the rise of the Cold War, the NRA had a loyalty test, as prospective members were required to affirm that they were not anti-government subversives as a condition of membership. But the modern NRA—which has long been in endless fundraising mode—requires no loyalty pledge of any kind to join, just payment. I used my membership card to gain access to NRA conventions and events, including recent board meetings where the most contentious power struggle since the 1990s came to a head after breaking out in the press and on the convention floor.

I never quote here any members with whom I interacted. I have respected both their privacy and the presumption of privacy surrounding those same conversations. Nor do I rely on anonymous sources. Instead, as can be seen in my endnotes, I have obtained NRA documents and NRA official journals, as the organization has long called its own members-only magazines, and combined these with other archival material dating back more than a century and a half and with my first-person reporting.

Taken together, what I have found allows me to document a story that is not widely known—including by most members of the NRA. It will be told here in full.

* * *

In learning about any organization, one of the crucial strands to follow is the money. As the NRA's membership has risen from 3.3 million people in 1994 to a claimed more than 5 million people as of this writing, the NRA has steadily expanded its lobbying wing, and today has an army of paid representatives in Washington and in every state capital. Perhaps the most formidable of these is a petite great-grandmother in Florida, Marion P. Hammer. An octogenarian raised in South Carolina by a family of subsistence hunters and farmers after her father died serving in Okinawa during World War II, Hammer remains as pivotal to the NRA's future today as she was more than a quarter century ago. With her profile rising again during the Association's latest internecine war, Hammer is by any measure no Fudd.

The U.S. gun industry has sustained the organization's growth since its founding, through ads in NRA magazines along with donations and other forms of support. Together, the gun industry and the NRA have produced the largest civilian gun market in the world.

While, as will be seen, the NRA advances gun manufacturers' aims, the industry's direct lobby is the National Shooting Sports Foundation in Newtown, Connecticut, located three miles from Sandy Hook Elementary School. Also in Newtown lived an NRA board member and women's smallbore shooting champion named Patti Clark. In a sign of how closely the NRA and the industry are tied, she chaired the NRA board's Nominating Committee, which included George K. Kollitides II, the CEO of Freedom Group—the same firm that made the rifle the shooter used that day in Newtown.

* * *

The NRA at the center of this debate has long been a politically cautious organization, especially when it comes to choosing allies. For a long time it was loath to favor one party over another, supporting both Democrats and Republicans who embraced its point of view. But in recent years this too has changed. The NRA has never before so fully embraced any politician as it has President Donald J. Trump.

The NRA has been plagued by scandal, including allegations of financial impropriety and connections with Russian agents. The year 2019 saw an internecine war break out between CEO LaPierre and former NRA president Oliver North and spill into public view to an unusual degree. The NRA's second-in-command, Chris Cox, the young gun from Tennessee who for the past seventeen years had been the NRA lobbying chief, was accused of conspiring with North and was forced out by LaPierre. Lately, too, more dues-paying NRA members are wondering how their dues are being spent. Wayne LaPierre, known jokingly throughout the Association as a lousy shot, was found to have billed the NRA for a private jet in the Bahamas, a rack of custom-tailored Italian suits, and a summer of rent for his intern. Meanwhile, nearly half of Americans now see the organization in a negative light.

The latest war for power at the top is the most tumultuous internal struggle the NRA has seen in more than forty years. But it resembles several previous leadership fights. Indeed, since the shift, NRA leaders have been slinging accusations at each other, sometimes embellishing if not inventing facts in order to more effectively smear their rivals for power.

The NRA since 1977 has rewritten the history of its own genesis and development and, as will be seen, has attempted to rewrite key periods of American and world history. Recently, the NRA has crafted and circulated fresh narratives about both Reconstruction and the Holocaust, which entire canons of historical scholarship had previously somehow missed. For decades the NRA has preserved its own historical treasures in a "climate controlled room with restricted access" logged to the "central computer" of its National Firearms Museum at its headquarters in Fairfax, Virginia, that no one—neither NRA members nor the public—has ever seen.

Today the NRA has its back against the wall for the first time since the Cincinnati Revolt, resulting from the combination of its own internecine wars and a rising tide of gun violence and corresponding outrage across the nation. Yet at the same time, never before has its fate been so entwined with a political party, and as of this writing, that party controls the presidency and the Senate. The NRA has embedded itself in the organization and planks of the Republican Party, and the NRA's annual meetings have become one of the biggest annual forums for both current and emerging leaders within the GOP. From the late 2000s through the early 2010s, the erstwhile Fox News star Glenn Beck was the most frequent keynote speaker at the NRA's annual conventions. In 2017 the convention was addressed by the sitting president of the United States for the first time since 1983, when President Ronald Reagan addressed it. And both President Donald Trump and Vice President Mike Pence have spoken at each NRA annual meeting since.

* * *

The story of the NRA tracks the life of the nation over the past century and a half and provides a window on the American experience. The NRA has been a major actor through nearly every period of American history since Reconstruction. The NRA, not unlike organized baseball, has touched the lives of countless Americans over generations. Like baseball and its legends, the NRA and its legacies are woven deeply into the fabric of the nation. What that fact says about this country, and what it means for the people who live in it—who each day go to schools and workplaces, who attend religious services, who go to shopping malls, restaurants, movie theaters, and concerts with their families—are questions that this book will attempt to illuminate, but cannot answer.

PART ONE

A HUNDRED YEARS

The NRA does not advocate an "ostrich" attitude toward firearms legislation. We recognize that the dynamism and complexities of modern society create new problems which demand new solutions. Accordingly, the National Rifle Association has come forth with a positive, specific and practical program for reasonable and proper firearms controls. In this spirit, we offer them to the Congress and to the people of the United States.

—Franklin L. Orth, executive vice president,
The National Rifle Association of America,
Washington, D.C., April 10, 1967

One

WITH AN EYE TOWARD FUTURE WARS

The National Rifle Association was formed in New York City by a group of former Union Army officers six years after the end of the Civil War. Nearly all of these men were still on active duty in the New York National Guard. Most had commanded men in what remains America's costliest war.

They met, crowded into the small office of a military journal in lower Manhattan, with an eye toward future wars. In Europe, Prussia, a small power, had recently defeated Austria and France, two larger empires, in no small part due to better rifles and better marksmanship. The men meeting in New York expected the United States to one day be drawn into wars involving Europe, and they felt compelled to act.

The year was 1871, the height of Reconstruction. The Civil War had drastically expanded the federal government and boosted industrial production. Over the thirty years to come, an economic boom would transform the nation. Railroads, banking, mining, agriculture, and steel would see massive growth. The Native American population would be decimated. Immigrants from Europe, Asia, and other regions would journey to America to work.

The men who met in New York City had seen almost unimaginable carnage. At least 360,000 Union and 258,000 Confederate men fell over five years in battle. Far more died of disease. An unrecorded number survived as amputees. No other war since has claimed so many American lives, and its toll on American forces remained more than that of all other wars combined until World War II.

It had been a long war. In the words of William Conant Church, a special correspondent for *The New York Times* who was embedded with Union commanders during the Peninsula Campaign in southeastern Virginia, "Each day has been an era; each hour an epoch."

The battle for Gettysburg was the war's costliest for both sides. A Union private deployed there with the 22nd Regiment of the New York National Guard, George W. Wingate, was promoted to sergeant during the fighting in Carlisle nearby. He would later write down his observations of that day:

> *At times it seemed doubtful whether the incessant uproar was really the bombardment of a quiet village; for, during the momentary pauses of the cannonade, the chirp of the katydid, and the other peaceful sounds of a country summer night, were heard as though nature could not realize that human beings had sought that quiet spot to destroy each other.*

By 1871, George Wood Wingate and William Conant Church were in their thirties and living in Brooklyn, New York, when together they founded the National Rifle Association at Church's offices across the East River at 192 Broadway.

* * *

These two New Yorkers brought complementary skills to the fledgling organization. Wingate by this point was an expert marksman, a rifle trainer, and a writer without peer. Church was the most respected military writer of his age, as well as one of the top newspaper and literary editors and publishers of his generation.

Neither of these is a name that elicits recognition today. Nor are they featured much at all in materials produced by today's NRA. But once they were famous men. William Church was a lifetime member and director of the New York Zoological Society, and a founding "fellow in perpetuity" of the Metropolitan Museum of Art. George Wingate left an even deeper mark on New York City. To this day, Wingate is a neighborhood in Brooklyn near Crown Heights. At its center is Wingate Park, a six-acre recreation and sporting complex. There was until recently a George W. Wingate High School in Brooklyn. Wingate also served as cofounder and first president of the New York Public Schools Athletic League. "In addition to the muscular development coming from its athletic exercises, the League endeavors in every way to inculcate good habits," he wrote, "and in particular 'square dealing.'" Today the league still has an award in his name, honoring the top athlete in each sport for boys as well as girls in New York City every year. The PSAL under Wingate began offering sports to girls in 1905.

Wingate was born in 1840 in New York. Little is known about his father, Charles Wingate, except that he was from rural Vermont. George Wingate's mother, Mary Phelps Robinson, was born in Ireland. Wingate studied law at the New York Free Academy, which later became the City University of New York, and was admitted to the New York bar. But he soon responded, as so many others did, to President Abraham Lincoln's call for able-bodied men to join the Union cause. Enlisting in the New York guard's 22nd Regiment, Wingate soon proved to be the best shot in his company. The 22nd was deployed in Pennsylvania and helped defend Harrisburg before engaging Confederate troops in Carlisle during the Gettysburg campaign.

Wingate returned to New York months later, and the year before the war ended he cofounded a law firm, Wingate & Cullen, in Brooklyn. Over one hundred and fifty years later, after a modern merger, the firm still bears his name as Wingate, Kearney & Cullen, LLP.

George Wingate taught countless men and boys how to shoot. He would eventually author *The Manual for Rifle Practice*, which went through multiple editions. The first was commissioned by William Conant Church to run in the *Army and Navy Journal and Gazette of the Regular and Volunteer Forces*, which Church edited and owned with his brother.

Wingate was a hunter too. He embodied a conservationist ethic and respect for wildlife that would remain strong within the NRA over the ensuing century:

> *I jumped off my horse and got my rifle ready, but [four antelope] were then six hundred yards off and going like swallows through the air, and it was useless to shoot. I have heard friends describe how they kill running antelope at six hundred yards, but I know I cannot perform such a feat, and therefore prefer to save my ammunition for something I feel I have a reasonable chance of hitting.*
>
> *It was beautiful, however, to watch these graceful creatures as they sailed along over fallen trees and scarcely seemed to touch the earth in their flight.*

Of the two NRA cofounders, Wingate was the man of action, and Church the public intellectual. Church was born in 1836 in Rochester, New York, along Lake Ontario, the eldest surviving son of a Baptist preacher who teetered between prosperity and poverty. Billy, as his family called him, had an itinerant childhood and never finished high school. But he still benefited from having been raised within a literary family, who had sent him to Boston Latin, an elite secondary school, until his father took ill and could no longer afford the tuition. By age sixteen Church was working on his own in Boston as an errand boy and handyman before landing a job in a bookstore in Beacon Hill on "Booksellers' Row." From there he was soon hired by a nearby publishing house specializing in schoolbooks. In 1853, with his employers' blessing, he went to New York at the age of seventeen to find work with other publishers.

"In leaving us," his employers wrote to him, "it may be gratifying to you, and assist you in placing yourself in a place of greater responsibility if we . . . testify to the uniform honesty and integrity of purpose, with which you have discharged your duties while in our service."

William Conant Church always had an engaging personality and presence. His biographer would later write about Church: "He was as much at home talking before John D. Rockefeller Jr.'s Bible class . . . as he was lecturing on Swedenborg before the convicts in Sing Sing" or "spending 'an evening at Pfaff's' in Brooklyn, where he met Walt Whitman," or "addressing a large audience of veterans" at a reunion.

Church grew enamored with the world of New York journalism. By the time he was nineteen, he had cofounded with his father—who by then had recovered his health—a weekly newspaper called the *New York Chronicle*. In 1860, on the eve of the Civil War, the twenty-four-year-old Church negotiated with the New York *Sun*, one of the city's big penny papers, to be its European correspondent. After the war broke out, he cut his time in Europe short and took a steamer back to report as a special correspondent, as war reporters were then called, for the *Evening Post*, *The Sun*, and *The New York Times*.

Church was eventually detailed to the Army of the Potomac, and his dispatches ran under the single-name pseudonym "Pierrepont," for the street he lived on in Brooklyn. Church quit reporting after just thirteen months to join the Union Army himself, negotiating an officer's commission through his contacts. Made a brevet lieutenant colonel, meaning he had the title but not necessarily the salary, Church was put in charge of organizing the volunteer militia to defend Washington in case of a possible Confederate advance.

But he did not last long in Washington, either. Church was recruited to run a professional journal of military affairs to support the Union effort. In June 1863 he resigned his military commission and moved to New York. Within ten weeks the first issue of the *Army and Navy Journal and Gazette of the Regular and Volunteer Forces* was released.

Showing his depth and range, Church after the Civil War helped establish and edit with his brother a literary magazine, *The Galaxy*, intended to compete with *The Atlantic* in Boston. *The Galaxy*'s contributors included Henry James, Walt Whitman, Helen Hunt, and Mark Twain. But after two years it folded, absorbed by the *Atlantic*, and Church turned his attention again to the *Army and Navy Journal* and other matters.

* * *

Wingate and Church first met a year later, in the summer of 1869, while Church was still running the *Journal* and Wingate was heading his Brooklyn law firm. They took to each other. Each man had seen firsthand the appalling lack of marksmanship on both sides in the Civil War. Both had seen fellow officers more focused on improving marching drills than rifle accuracy. Both were supportive of an active role after the war for state national guards.

Wingate himself had a commission in the New York National Guard, where he had been promoting rifle practice, with mixed success. But the unexpected deaths of three guardsmen during the Orange Riot in Manhattan in 1871 lent more urgency to the effort, as the guardsmen found themselves in need of better riflery.

It was the shifting balance of power overseas in Europe that most captured Church and Wingate's attention. France had dominated the continent since the beginning of the nineteenth century. After much fanfare in Paris, France invaded Prussia in 1870, expecting an easy victory. But Prussia repelled the invasion and defeated France in little more than six months. The Germans had used breech- or rear-loading rifles that were superior in range, firepower, and reloading speed to the kind of rifled, front-loading muskets used by French troops.

For centuries, infantrymen had stood elbow to elbow, firing simultaneously on command, without necessarily aiming at any particular target among the mass of enemy coats facing them in the opposing line. But in the Prussian campaigns against first Austria and then France, infantrymen in the line suddenly found themselves easy prey for German sharpshooters reloading and firing at will from beyond their range.

By the summer of 1871, Church's *Journal* made the case to form a rifle practice group: "An association should be organized in this city to promote and encourage rifle shooting on a scientific basis. The National Guard [of New York] is today too slow in getting about this reform. Private enterprise must take up the matter and push it into life."

* * *

Wingate and Church convened a group of sixteen men. There were six generals, three colonels (including Church), three majors, one captain (Wingate), and three civilians. Nearly all came from the New York City and Brooklyn divisions of the New York National Guard. They packed themselves into the *Army and Navy Journal*'s cramped offices at 192 Broadway, near John Street.

They met during a time of immense change. Construction of the transcontinental railroad had started during the Civil War, and rail lines now connected the land from coast to coast. A man named Rockefeller had just formed what would become the largest oil company in the world. The first black man was elected to Congress, a

Republican named Hiram Rhodes Revels, representing Mississippi. The last holdout state of the Confederacy, Georgia, rejoined the Union, as the Confederated States of America, already defeated, officially dissolved. The Fifteenth Amendment, which prohibited denying citizens the right to vote based on their "race, color, or previous condition of servitude," had been unanimously ratified by the nation's thirty-seven states. The 1871 Indian Appropriation Act meant the federal government no longer treated recognized Native American tribes as sovereign nations.

The men meeting in 192 Broadway were prominent and capable. Major General Alexander Shaler was a Union commander decorated with the nation's highest award, the Medal of Honor, a former prisoner of war who would later become the New York City fire commissioner. Major John N. Partridge had been wounded leading his company of Massachusetts volunteers in a Union charge, and would later serve as New York's superintendent of public works.

German-born General Franz Sigel had commanded a brigade of Missouri volunteers, and, much like Church, had frequently clashed with senior Union officers. Colonel Watson C. Squire had raised a company of Ohio volunteers soon known in the Union as "Squire's Sharpshooters," and "he was given the gold leaf in his straps" for "distinguished gallantry." He married into the family that owned Remington Arms and would eventually move to Seattle, where he would be elected governor of Washington Territory and later a senator representing Washington State.

Colonel Henry J. Cullen was Wingate's law partner and, like him, was an officer who had held both command and oversight posts in the New York National Guard. He happened to live on Pierrepont Street in Brooklyn, like Church, and by then was their district's elected representative in Albany.

A man "of medium height, rather stout, and with a face that may be properly described as Napoleonic," Cullen was, like the others at the NRA's first meeting, a redoubtable man. Take this odd vignette from years later in Europe. One night in Austria on the steps of the Vienna Opera House, Cullen happened to "conflict" with a former American secretary of state, James G. Blaine. "I had engaged a *valet de place* to carry my overcoat, and, when I reached the Opera House, I bade him toss it to me," Cullen told *The New York Times*. Secretary Blaine thought it his and "began staring at me and the coat." He then made "a very lively effort to deprive me of my property, and the scene was reaching a climax when one of his daughters tripped down the stairs, and, at once divining what had happened, said, 'Papa, that is not your overcoat.'"

Also present that day on lower Broadway was David W. Judd, who had been elected to the New York State Assembly to represent Richmond County (now known as Staten Island). He was a Republican, like most of the men in the room. Alfred W. Craven was the chief engineer for one of New York's largest aqueducts, which carried water from the Croton River in Westchester to reservoirs in the city, and was one of the founders of what is now the American Society of Civil Engineers.

These men, under the direction of Church and Wingate, drafted a certificate of incorporation, and ten months later, on November 17, 1871, received a charter from the state of New York. Thus was the National Rifle Association born. Its mission was documented in the group's first surviving statement, called "The National Rifle Association: What It Was Organized For, Who Compose It, What It Proposes to Do, and What It Has Done," an edited version of which later ran in *Harper's Weekly*:

> [F]or not only the conflict between Prussia and Austria, but the more
> recent French and Prussian contest, have demonstrated that the very
> accuracy and rapidity of fire which renders these [long-range breech-
> loading] arms so formidable in the hands of trained marksmen,

simply results in a waste of ammunition with those unfamiliar with
their use, which leaves an army helpless at the decisive moment
of battle. Other nations, recognizing these facts, have long since
instituted a thorough system of instruction of rifle practice. . . .
In this country, on the other hand, the matter has been entirely
neglected.

Or, as Wingate would later write, "[T]he Civil War had demonstrated with bloody clarity that soldiers who could not shoot straight were of little value." He went on: "I believed that if I could help to dispel the prevalent ignorance about rifle shooting I might bring our American rifleman nearer in authority to his legendary stature."

He and Church promptly set about doing just that.

Two

THE "ROYAL" NRA

If the goal of Wingate and Church was promoting rifle practice, they would need a shooting range. For inspiration in this endeavor, they looked across the Atlantic to a British rifle association, and ended up following their example to the letter. In fact, the very name of the NRA itself was copied verbatim from Great Britain. Established in 1859, the National Rifle Association of the United Kingdom organized rifle practice for the Home Guard civilian defense force, established the same year. Alfred Tennyson encouraged the effort through his poem "Rifleman Form!" The inciting factor was the prospect of another war with France, this time led by the adventurer Napoleon III. Queen Victoria herself—by pulling on a cord tied to the trigger of a newly designed Whitworth rifle, itself affixed to a machine rest—fired the first shot at the inaugural ceremony of Wimbledon Common, the range built by the British NRA. As its ingenious riflemen had intended, the Queen of course hit the bull's-eye.

Her Majesty's rifle association and range were by any measure second to none, and Wingate and Church were determined to make theirs in America just as good if not better. On a business trip to London, Wingate studied how the British had designed their system of competitive shooting, and then got the American NRA to follow their lead. So close would become their mutual association that by 1876, on the centennial of America's Declaration of Independence from the British crown, the American iteration of the National Rifle Association amended its charter to add two words to its name, becoming the National Rifle Association of America, to prevent "any international confusion" between the two associations.

Wingate and Church lobbied elected New York State officials for support. "Fortunately, David W. Judd, whom I had known from boyhood, and who was also a friend of Colonel Church, was elected to the New York Assembly," Wingate later recalled. "We succeeded in inducing him to take an interest in the National Rifle Association and to introduce the Judd bill," which provided New York State funds "to purchase and construct" the group's first range.

They found a property on Long Island, in Queens County, which was not yet part of New York City. Called Creed Farm, the property was partly a bushy swamp. Upon seeing the marshland, "Colonel Henry G. Shaw, a member of the Board of Directors, editor of the New York *Sun*, and a much-traveled man with a gift for words," suggested a name. As with so many things in these early days, a British influence was apparent. "'Just like the moors of southern England,' Shaw observed. 'Perhaps we should call it Creed's Moor, rather than the Creed Farm.' And so Creedmoor, one of the most famous names in shooting history, became the official name of the range before the first spade of earth had been moved to develop it."

George Wingate was the first to fire at a target, "while Gen. John B. Woodward, the treasurer, marked the shots with his hat."

Wingate designed Creedmoor to be the spitting image of Wimbledon. The NRA adopted the range distances, target designs and marking, and scoring systems that Wingate had seen on his trips to Britain as well as Canada. This effort represented a major investment for the new nonprofit group, who shipped materials across the Atlantic, including over a dozen iron slabs weighing up to 400 pounds each, at a total cost equivalent to over $89,000 today. Wrote Secretary Wingate in his report to the NRA board on January 14, 1873:

> Finding that there were no American establishments which were familiar with the making of the targets and appurtenances required upon the range, and also finding that they could be purchased . . . at a much lower price in England than here, the Association, in August last, purchased fifty target slabs, one double and one single mantlet (the fourteen slabs comprising which being also available for targets), seventeen ringing centers, eighteen trigger testers, together with a number of articles. They cost $4,153.47, iron having greatly increased in price during the summer. They are all first-class articles, however, and could not be replaced for the money.

The NRA continued to follow the British, replacing their own rectangular targets with round ones after the British did so. But the American NRA finally went their own way after the British replaced Wimbledon's iron slabs with canvas targets. "The fact is that the shooters, accustomed to hearing the soul-satisfying 'splat' or 'ping' of a bullet hitting iron, felt that shooting had lost some of its thrill when they had to punch silent holes in cloth," noted the NRA in its first official history. The American NRA decided to stick with iron after they found a reliable domestic source of slabs for much less than what they had paid to import them from London.

It is interesting to note that the NRA's second official history, *NRA: An American Legend*—compiled with the help of six NRA officials, according to its acknowledgments, including the NRA secretary, operations research analyst, archivist, chief photographer, and *American Rifleman* editor—makes no mention of the debts owed to the example of the National Rifle Association of the United Kingdom. It was written by Jeffrey L. Rodengen, who is known for "his leadership in corporate history publishing" and is chairman and CEO of Write Stuff Enterprises, which specializes in such histories.

In a report to the board in 2001 signed by NRA secretary Edward L. Land Jr., it can be gleaned that the NRA leadership is both preserving and keeping secret the Association's own historical materials in a state-of-the-art, secure, and previously undisclosed archive, perhaps beneath a nonpublic section of their own National Firearms Museum within their headquarters seven miles outside the D.C. beltway: "The NRA Archives, which was officially started in 1995, has now gone through the process of collecting available materials, doing a loose sort followed by a more precise culling and cataloging everything into a central computer system. The Archives is located in a special climate-controlled room with restricted access. There are currently three hundred and thirty two (332) file boxes that contain over twenty thousand (20,000) pieces of material" along with 280 movie reels of NRA matches and activities dating back to the 1930s. "All items are keyed to both the central computer located in the NRA National Firearms Museum and the Master Control Book in the Archives."

The existence of the archives is something the NRA has never made public. Nor has it ever revealed what historical treasures it contains.

* * *

One result of the NRA's sidestepping of its own history is that it invites fabulists to conjure their own peculiar tales about the genesis of the American NRA and its mission. Michael Moore, in his documentary film *Bowling for Columbine*, pointed out that the NRA and Ku Klux Klan were both founded after the Civil War, insinuating there might be a link between the two groups. Allen West, a retired Army lieutenant colonel, later claimed the complete opposite. A veteran of both the Gulf and Iraq wars, Lieutenant Colonel West was fined during the latter campaign over what he admitted was the mock execution of an Iraqi policeman under interrogation. Still allowed to retire with his rank, he later became a Florida congressman, and today is one of a handful of African Americans on the NRA's governing Board of Directors. Right before he publicly sided with Oliver North against Wayne LaPierre in the 2019 public feud, West told members meeting in Indianapolis that the early NRA, back during Reconstruction, had "stood with freed blacks to make sure they had their Second Amendment rights." These completely opposite claims—Moore's and West's—are equally unfounded.

In reality, the men who gathered in New York City to establish the NRA had emerged from the victorious, Union side. The Klan was anathema to them; neither could they be said to be particularly progressive on race. Church was a staunch Unionist who during the Civil War had derided abolitionists as "noisy" pests.

Church also never showed any sympathy for the Native Americans the U.S. Army increasingly fought with and repressed in the years after the Civil War. His *Army and Navy Journal* "expressed nothing but scorn," too, for groups trying to improve their condition, such as the Quakers. As the "Indian Wars" were just beginning to escalate once more, Church wrote, "From this time forth . . . let the word be to whip the Indians—and one good sound thrashing . . . will do more to hold the Indians in check . . . than anything else."

The other NRA cofounder always chose more measured words and rarely opined about matters outside his own areas of expertise. But Wingate hardly sympathized with the continent's indigenous people, either. "We should never forget that the existence of this republic was maintained and its liberties won by the skill in shooting shown by our ancestors against the Indians and the British," he said in a speech to New York City public high school boys in 1907.

Notwithstanding either man's other views, Church still stands out today as the first individual on record to speak out against the use of racial epithets within the military, doing so more than a half century before the military ended segregation. According to his biographer: "He asked that 'nigger' and 'dago' be banned from the army's vocabulary. As for the delicate question of observance of the Sabbath, Church always maintained that each man should have the largest liberty as to the use he made of his time on Sunday."

The attitudes of both men certainly reflected the militaristic, if not imperial, attitudes of the day. Both seemed to see America's expansion west as part of the nation's Manifest Destiny. "We cannot have 20,000 or 30,000 miles of seacoast and gulfcoast, and leave it without garrisons; we cannot unite Esquimaux and Indian, Canadian, Chinese, Mexican, Spaniard, and Dane, fusing these and all the other nationalities of the globe into the crucible of our Republic, without being prepared to guard against an occasional detonation or explosion," editorialized the *Army and Navy Journal* in 1869 in support of President Grant's plan to annex Santo Domingo, now known as the Dominican Republic. The *Journal* would also later become "an early advocate of imperialist designs on Cuba."

Like many others both then and now, Church saw the world like a "classical realist," perceiving it as a zero-sum game. "To devour or to be devoured seems to be the only choice for the carnivorous races," he said in a speech in Albany, "or at best they must content themselves with the peace which is born of respect for prowess." He told his readers not to be deluded "into inaction by unwise reliance upon the continuance of peace," and told them that maintaining a standing army, even in peacetime, was "as necessary an 'institution' of America as the Town-meeting, the Legislature or the Judiciary."

Fundamentally the NRA had been founded to support the armed

forces of the United States, and that would remain the principal goal of the organization over the next hundred years. But Church and Wingate slowly drifted apart over labor unrest at home. In 1895, during the Great Trolley Strike in Brooklyn, Wingate wrote that many Guardsmen sympathized with the striking workers and did not feel "kindly toward the trolley companies." Church, on the other hand, was far more critical of strikes led by organized labor during the same period across the country, seeing their "contempt for authority" as showing "the necessity for a larger Army."

* * *

In 1873, the same year that Creedmoor Range opened, the Irish rifle team unexpectedly beat both the English and Scottish teams at Wimbledon in London. Looking to establish themselves as global champions, the Irish group placed an open letter in *The New York Herald* challenging any American rifle team to a match in the United States.

Wingate, by now promoted to colonel in the New York National Guard, was also president of the local amateur rifle club, which accepted the challenge. The NRA hosted the match at Creedmoor after opening the range to the local club for practice. *The New York Herald*'s publisher happened to be one of the NRA's first life members, and he made sure the paper gave the match extensive publicity.

The betting odds on both sides of the Atlantic favored the Irish through the summer of 1874. The day of the contest, in late September, was unseasonably hot, giving an edge to the Americans, as "the cool climate of the Emerald Isle never produced heat waves that set the target to dancing," as recounted in full in the NRA's 1967 authorized history *Americans and Their Guns*.

The match brought out nearly eight thousand spectators. "The regular and special trains of the Central Railroad were filled to capacity with the cream of New York society mingling with denim-clad Irish laborers who had come to watch the lads from the Old Country clobber the Yankees."

"A roar of applause swelled from the crowd" as the umpire and the two team captains—an Irish major and Colonel Wingate—"strode to the center of the line. The two heavily whiskered captains shook hands and tossed a coin for the choice of targets while the respective teams grouped on either side. To the spectators, the Irish, in smart tweed shooting outfits and pith helmets or deerstalker caps, looked more like shooters than the Americans. In their ordinary business suits and slouch hats or toppers, the Americans might have been a delegation of hardware salesmen."

The Irish won the coin toss, and an Irish captain with a muzzle-loading rifle in hand, the weapon of choice of all the Irish, stepped to the line. But he, "[l]ike all of the Irish," was "bothered greatly by the heat." His first shot was a clean miss. "The American rooters cheered, but Colonel Wingate quickly reprimanded them for their poor manners." The *Herald* and other newspapers telegraphed shot-by-shot scores to New York, where they were quickly posted on bulletin boards and relayed by cable to London and Dublin.

Next up for the Irish was a British military doctor. "Only Dr. J. B. Hamilton, who had been an Army surgeon in India, where he had won the colonial rifle championship, had experienced such temperatures." A "handsome man with blond muttonchop whiskers," he "made a bullseye on his first try."

After a long day of close competition, the Irish were ahead by just one point, 931 to 930, when Colonel John Bodine stepped up as the very last man to shoot. "Wingate had arranged the order of his shooters to be certain that the tall gray-haired infantryman would be the last to fire." Before taking his turn, Bodine, after a long, hot day, went to take a swig of ginger beer, handed to him by a friend. The colonel pulled the cork out of the bottle.

"Suddenly there was a report like a pistol shot, followed by a tinkle of glass. The sun-heated beverage, innocent of ice, had exploded. Broken glass had sliced deeply in the tall colonel's right hand, and he stood in momentary shock watching the blood drip from his fingers."

Dr. Hamilton approached, offering to help. But Bodine waved him off, and instead wrapped a handkerchief around his hand to field-dress the wound himself. He raised his breech-loading rifle, the weapon the Americans preferred, and steadied to fire.

"Every one of the thousands of pairs of eyes present at once shifted from the man to the target, a little point a half mile off. When the spat of the bullet on the iron target was heard, it was followed by a roar from the crowd. 'He's on,' and then came slowly into sight a large white disk which showed that a bullseye had been made, and the match won by the American team," Wingate himself wrote later. "Pandemonium broke loose, and the sky was darkened with hats that were thrown into the air."

The victory over the Irish, the reigning Wimbledon champions, put Creedmoor on the map and marked the real emergence of the American NRA.

* * *

In other ways, the NRA had gotten off to a slow start. The first man to serve as the Association's president, the famous Union general Ambrose Burnside, proved to be a disappointment, never coming to a single meeting. Church—who had already presided over every meeting in Burnside's absence—replaced Burnside in 1872, becoming the NRA's second president.

However brief his leadership, Burnside's presence as a figurehead still shows the kind of influence the NRA enjoyed from the start. Burnside was a former Union commander with a storied but imperfect Civil War record, who became a railroad executive after the war and who had more recently served as governor of Rhode Island. Burnside is popularly known for inspiring the term "sideburns" due to his thick side facial hair, which gave him a signature look. He also lent his name to the Burnside carbine, a breech-loading rifle among those favored during the war by the Union. Years after resigning as NRA president, Burnside was elected to represent the state of Rhode Island in Washington. Senator Burnside became an ally of the Association on Capitol Hill.

* * *

After their 1874 victory over the Irish, the Americans won again in a rematch a year later in Ireland at the Dollymount Range on the island of North Bull in Dublin Bay. But they still needed to defeat the British to claim their place as world champions, and they applied to the National Rifle Association of the United Kingdom for permission to participate in the next international match at Wimbledon. Traditionally, it was open only to English and Scottish teams; even the Irish had been permitted to compete only under a special dispensation. The British NRA's governing council ruled that no exception would be made for the Americans.

The American NRA soon sent a "very diplomatically worded" letter to the British NRA, inviting them to join in a match at Creedmoor Range. The British agreed, but instead of sending an English team, they decided to send a geographically broader one drawing from the best riflemen from England, Scotland, and Ireland.

In the spring of 1877, the "Imperial team was received in New York with great courtesy and hospitality. But it was all serious business on the Creedmoor firing line." It was a tough match between what were by then no doubt the two best rifle teams in the world. By the end of the day, the Americans had beaten Her Majesty's riflemen by "a very decisive" score of 3,334 to 3,242 to finally establish themselves as champions of the English-speaking world.

By then the NRA had already commissioned the Grand Centennial Trophy from the famed jewelry retailer Tiffany's at a cost of $1,500—about $35,000 today:

> It was a full-size replica of an ancient Roman legionary standard executed in silver, gold, and bronze, bearing on its silver banner the legend: "In the name of the United States of America to the Riflemen of the World." Below the beautifully sculptured crowning eagle, which clutches in its claws a wreath of palm leaves, was a plaque bearing the single word PALMA, the Latin word for palm tree, which was used in the days of the Romans to signify victory or the ultimate in excellence.

This piece, known as the Palma Trophy, became the Association's most coveted, legendary prize—until it was discovered missing from the NRA's own archives in 1954.

Both Church and Wingate were pleased by the victory over the Imperial team, but soon after his term as president ended, Church began complaining in person and through unsigned editorials (which no one doubted were by him) that the NRA was still too provincial, too much a New York institution. Read one editorial in 1877:

> The National Rifle Association of Creedmoor has two paths now open before it. One leads to its recognition as a real National Institution: by following the other it must end in sinking into a local club. . . . To gain a national position is still easy if the directors will remember for a while that New York city and Creedmoor Range are only a part of the great rifle movement in America.

To further drive home the point, the *Journal* restated in 1878 (the first year after Reconstruction ended) Church and Wingate's long-shared goal:

> *The National Rifle Association was formed to promote military*
> *shooting, and to raise the standard of marksmanship among*
> *American troops, and if it does not perform that duty it loses more*
> *than half of its usefulness.*

Such frank, loyal dissent is unusual for any group or institution. The public airing of internal criticism suggests early in the NRA's history a basic transparency within the Association, one that would not last forever.

The NRA responded to Church's prodding by inviting local rifle groups from across the Northeast, from Massachusetts to Maryland, to a "Convention of Riflemen" at Creedmoor. The NRA also organized the first International Military Match, featuring domestic state guard and U.S. Army teams from across the country. Each guardsman or soldier shot in uniform and with his standard-issue military rifle. The winner was awarded the Hilton Trophy, a massive silver shield named for a New York judge and benefactor, Henry Hilton. The New York National Guard, which Wingate had personally trained, "won easily" with a score of 1,044. The runner-up team consisted of army shooters from Missouri, with 803 points. This 1878 military match was the first instance of a public-private collaboration that would last well into the next century before being severed completely.

* * *

The pace of competition at Creedmoor was soon furious, with the NRA range hosting up to 138 matches of one kind or another a year.

The rifle practice program developed by Wingate, meanwhile, soon became the standard. His "scientific" system, as Church dubbed it, was detailed in seven editions of the *Manual of Rifle Practice*, with all revisions done by Wingate. The shortest editions were over 170 pages long (including advertisements) and covered every conceivable matter, from the duties of commanding officers and sergeants to the handling and cleaning of rifles, from the steady pull of the trigger, which Wingate marked as among the most important skills to master, to the distances of targets and the size of the charge in the rifle.

Wingate focused on safety at every turn. Lookouts should be placed on the range, he wrote, so "that the firing may be easily stopped when necessary." Embankments or hills behind targets should be built "at an angle of 45° at least" to avoid "the chance of a ricochet." Precautions should be taken against a firearm's "premature discharge."

Wingate's system was adopted first by the New York National Guard and later by most other guard and military forces around the country. The NRA's efforts led to "systematic instruction in rifle practice" in both the National Guard and the regular army.

Despite Church and his exhortations in the *Journal*, the NRA was still a New York group dependent on the state for its funding. And in 1880, after a gubernatorial election, the NRA got cut off. Governor Alonzo B. Cornell, a Republican (and the eldest son of the founder of Cornell University), had run on a pledge to shrink government. Wingate went to meet with him, but the governor was unmoved. "There will be no war in my time or in the time of my children," he told Wingate. He reduced funding for the New York National Guard and cut off all state funding for the rifle practice the NRA had been providing at Creedmoor Range.

The group was in trouble, and they thought bringing in a man like their personal hero and the Union's former commanding general might help. In 1883, a committee chaired by Wingate and supported by Church recruited former president Ulysses S. Grant to serve as NRA president. In poor health, Grant lent little more than his name and assumed no duties. He was succeeded in 1885 by General Philip H. Sheridan, the commanding general of the United States Army and the first regular army officer still on active duty to serve as NRA president.

Yet the NRA was still insolvent. The collapse of banks and businesses in the Panic of 1884 did not help. By then the NRA, expecting better times, had moved from 192 Broadway to more expensive offices five blocks away in one of New York City's first skyscrapers, Temple Court, at 5 Beekman Street in lower Manhattan. By 1892 the organization ran out of money and essentially collapsed. The board placed the organization's records in storage and reached out to the New Jersey State Rifle Association, a local group operating in the NRA's shadow, to try to hold future competitions at the New Jersey group's new Sea Girt Range instead of Creedmoor, which the NRA could no longer afford to maintain. Wingate, now NRA president, wrote a letter to the editor of the magazine *Shooting and Fishing*, which by then was acting as the NRA's first unofficial publication. Wingate's letter began: "I enclose a formal obituary of the NRA."

* * *

The NRA lay dormant for nearly a decade, making Wingate's words seem prophetic. Competitions such as the President's Match for the Military Rifle Championship of the United States were reorganized to take place at Sea Girt, with the New Jersey Rifle Association graciously opening its club and range to members of the New York–based NRA.

Finally, in 1900, the NRA board reconvened for the first time in eight years. Church had spent the time still writing and editing the *Army and Navy Journal*, starting research for a number of books (including one on the role of Ulysses S. Grant in both the Civil War and Reconstruction), and serving as an inspector for the Northern Pacific Railroad. Wingate had continued rifle practice with the New York National Guard and local gun groups, and journeyed west with his wife and daughter to write the book *Through the Yellowstone Park on Horseback*. In an attempt to further ingratiate the Association to the military, the Board of Directors expanded the NRA's ex officio membership "to include the Secretary of War and all general officers of the United States Army, including the Chief of Ordnance and the Adjutant General of the United States."

In the end it was President Theodore Roosevelt and the statesman Elihu Root—who served in the cabinets of two presidents as either secretary of state or secretary of war—who saved the NRA. President Roosevelt, a rifleman and big-game hunter himself, and Root, whose diplomacy would later earn him a Nobel Peace Prize, were both enthusiastic supporters of better riflery.

At President Roosevelt's instigation, Congress in 1903 established the National Board for the Promotion of Rifle Practice, a federal government agency that allocated funds to bring teams of competitors from state national guards and every branch of military service to compete in matches. These matches were to be organized by a rejuvenated NRA. The National Board matches restored a line of dependence by the NRA on government funds, only now the source would be Washington, not Albany.

* * *

Both Wingate and Church lived long enough to see their initial aims vindicated. As World War I neared and President Woodrow Wilson, after initial hesitation, "finally issued his call to arms," the need for capable soldiers including trained riflemen was now clear. Wingate would live till 1928, but Church died a month after the United

States' entry into the European war he had foreseen and which he had helped ensure the nation was prepared for. After Church's death, a member of his staff wrote a poem published in 1917 in the *Army and Navy Journal*:

> *Prophet and patriot, he lived to know*
> *The flag he loved waves where the war-winds blow*
> *Above the hosts that hold the Huns at bay;*
> *In joy he smiled, and hopeful went his way.*

The same monikers of prophet and patriot are worthy of Wingate too.

Three

THE PROMISCUOUS TOTING OF GUNS

The second generation of NRA leaders was in many ways as impressive as the first. Take James A. Drain. Born in 1870, Drain lost his right hand in a hunting accident as a young man. He still managed to become an expert marksman (and was also able to play golf). A decorated World War I veteran awarded the Army Distinguished Service Medal, Drain served as a lieutenant colonel in the Ordnance Corps in France before representing the United States in a joint commission with Great Britain that designed and deployed the tanks credited with having helped defeat the Central Powers.

Drain had become involved in the NRA before the war, when he served as the youngest commander of the Washington State National Guard. He "was a youthful, bustling, handsome figure of a man who, at the age of thirty-four had been appointed Adjutant General of the State of Washington, the youngest man in history to attain that post." After moving east, Drain played an increasingly instrumental role within the NRA.

The Association did not have its own publication back then. For years a magazine initially called *The Rifle* and later renamed *Shooting and Fishing* had covered many NRA matches. But in 1906 Drain, then an NRA board member who had just moved east, bought *Shooting and Fishing* outright. He renamed it *Arms and the Man* and made it the NRA's unofficial press outlet.

Drain was elected NRA president in 1907. He moved the group back to New York City—during its wilderness years the penniless organization had occupied a borrowed one-room office in Passaic, New Jersey—to 299 Broadway, near Duane Street, on what was then known as "Sporting Goods Row." But only a year later, in 1908, the NRA board made the decision to move to Washington, D.C., into the prestigious Beaux Arts Woodward Building, two blocks from the White House. Drain established the office for *Arms and the Man* nearby.

Although there is no record of what prompted Drain to rename the magazine *Arms and the Man*, he was most certainly at least aware of the play by the same name written by George Bernard Shaw and released in London in 1894, twelve years before he purchased the magazine. The title of Shaw's play in turn is derived from the opening words of Virgil's *Aeneid*: "Of arms and the man I sing."

It was under Drain's leadership that the NRA and the gun industry became fully intertwined. In 1907 the NRA held the first of its National Matches at Camp Perry, a National Guard training facility on Lake Erie, at which gun manufacturers displayed their wares in what was initially called "Commercial Row." This display became a familiar feature at all NRA matches in the following years. "The hit of the commercial show that year was Tom Keller of the Peters Cartridge Company, who toured the establishment in a rented buckboard behind an ancient white nag named Alice. With his battered buckboard emblazoned with the Peters banner, Keller and Alice were everywhere, providing transportation for everyone from General Drain and [another executive officer] of the National Matches, down to individual team members hitchhiking from one point to another over the muddy range!" Today the vendors displaying guns and accessories indoors at NRA annual meetings occupy up to fifteen acres.

Meanwhile, the Winchester Repeating Arms Company in 1909 "commissioned Frederic Remington, the noted western artist, to execute an original bronze of a cowboy on a bucking horse. The Winchester Bronco Buster Trophy was offered as first prize in a regular NRA match in which the shooter tried to score as many hits as possible in one minute on a disappearing target at 200 yards."

Gun legislation was not a concern of the early NRA, but that would change starting in the 1920s, albeit in a way that would take years to unspool. Until the state of New York passed the nation's first major gun control law in 1911, "there were few other restrictions on the gunowner" at the time besides prohibitions against the carrying of concealed firearms, reported the NRA itself in its first authorized history, *Americans and Their Guns*. "The right of the citizen to carry firearms openly or to keep them in his home or place of business without restriction was accepted almost universally by state law, and the federal government found no reason to enter the regulatory picture."

The New York law required anyone besides police to obtain a court-issued license to possess a firearm. This law is still on the books in the state of New York. (Its sponsor, Timothy D. Sullivan, was a politician and kingmaker of the city's notoriously corrupt Tammany Hall, who at the same time supported women's suffrage. He also suffered from mental illness, and was later killed by a railroad train.) The NRA took no position one way or another about this law at the time of its passage. But it would begin warning about its impact within a decade.

In 1910, a year before the passage of the New York law, the NRA had elected another army veteran to serve as the organization's president after Drain. The new NRA president was Lieutenant General John Coalter Bates of St. Louis, Missouri. At sixty-eight, Bates was a veteran of three conflicts—the Civil War, the Spanish-American War, and the campaign in the Philippines.

The NRA was struggling at the time to keep up with the pace of domestic and international matches launched by Drain. So Bates appointed a committee to reach out to Congress to request funds. They paid a visit to Senator Henry du Pont, chairman of the Senate Military Affairs Committee. Du Pont drafted a rider to the army appropriations bill that earmarked $25,000 (more than half a million dollars today) "to help the National Rifle Association meet the cost of proposed matches."

Du Pont's rider, which became law, authorized the War and State departments and their respective military and diplomatic officials to further assist and represent the nonprofit NRA. "In addition to providing the needed funds, the du Pont rider authorized the War Department to cooperate with the NRA in managing the matches and requested the State Department to lend its offices in extending invitations to national shooting organizations throughout the world."

As Church had urged earlier, the NRA was finally moving beyond the mid-Atlantic region. The matches it hosted at Camp Perry, on the shores of Lake Erie in Ohio, grew and became a source of pride. "The great matches of 1913 exceeded in scope, size and worldwide interest any that had been held in America. France, Switzerland, Sweden, Argentina, Peru and Canada sent their best marksmen to pit their skill against the Yankees."

As the war in Europe neared, the NRA began expanding training for males ages eighteen to forty-five through local affiliated clubs in collaboration with the War Department, which provided funds along with trophies and medals. "Under the increasingly tense international situation, a close relationship sprang up between the military and the civilian rifle clubs" organized by the NRA, as their joint civilian readiness program began to accelerate. By then, too, the federal National Board for the Promotion of Rifle Practice and the nonprofit NRA had become more entwined. Nearly half of the sitting members of the recently expanded U.S. agency were current or former active-duty military officers who were also senior NRA officials. Among them were three past NRA presidents, including Drain and a septuagenarian George Wingate.

Meanwhile, in New York in 1916, Drain was preparing for deployment to Europe, and he ended up selling *Arms and the Man* to the NRA for one dollar, converting the magazine into the Association's first official publication. As the American role in Europe grew, commanders recognized the renewed need—long preached by the NRA—for better marksmanship. "Long experience with conditions in France confirms my opinion that it is highly important that infantry soldiers should be excellent shots," noted General John J. Pershing in a communiqué to the secretary of war six months after America entered World War I.

Finally, during the war's last year, the military established the Small Arms Firing School for the Instruction of Officers and Enlisted Men in Rifle and Pistol Shooting at the NRA's range at Camp Perry, and it made the NRA match master, Morton C. Mumma, who was by now an Army lieutenant colonel, its commander. He was the first in an NRA family legacy that would span three generations.

* * *

The 1920s saw a National Rifle Association of America whose aims had been validated by the U.S. victory in the Great War. The victory had been costly: the United States suffered 2 percent of the war's total military fatalities, with more than 116,000 men killed. Unlike after the Civil War, however, federal support for the NRA and its aims was now enshrined. Starting in 1903, the government contributed $2,500 a year (worth about $72,000 today) "for a national trophy and medals and other prizes." The support climbed to $7,500 annually (about $112,000 today) by 1924, in addition to another $10,000 (equivalent to roughly $150,000 today) "for arms, ammunition, targets and other accessories." Congress the same year allocated an additional $89,900 (around $1.3 million in today's dollars) in order

> to establish and maintain indoor and outdoor rifle ranges for the use
> of all able-bodied males capable of bearing arms . . . [and for] labor in
> operating targets; for the employment of instructors; for clerical services;
> for badges and other insignia; for the transportation of employees,
> instructors, and civilians to engage in practice; for the purchase of
> materials, supplies, and services, and for expenses incidental to
> instruction of citizens of the United States in marksmanship, and
> their participation in national and international matches.

In addition to having the NRA administer nearly every aspect of these matches in cooperation with the federal government's National Board for the Promotion of Rifle Practice, in 1924 Congress would give the NRA another perk that would last for over a half century: the "sale to members of the National Rifle Association" and affiliated gun clubs of surplus military rifles "at cost to the Government."

The 1920 Olympic Games, which were held in Antwerp in recognition of the suffering endured by the Kingdom of Belgium and its people in World War I, "placed the United States solidly on the top of the shooting world in [nearly] every team event involving rifle, shotgun and pistol." Meanwhile, back at home, target shooting was more and more popular, extending the Association's reach. By 1920, "the Association had 766 affiliated organizations distributed through every state and territory," many of which fielded teams at Camp Perry. The NRA started inviting more police from across the country to compete at Camp Perry, too, accelerating an effort begun before the war. The NRA even developed a shooting course for railroad mail clerks: "After a major outbreak of mail train robberies, Colonel

Mumma, of his own initiative, had developed a course in shooting for railroad mail clerks. Practically all of the country's 10,000 mail clerks were armed but few had any training in the use of their weapons." By then Mumma's son, Navy midshipman Morton C. Mumma Jr., was also a frequent competitive shooter at Camp Perry.

It was only after the war that the NRA began inveighing against what it perceived as the dangers of excessive firearm regulation. The truth is that the NRA—despite modern NRA leaders' claims to the contrary—took no position on gun control whatsoever through the first fifty years of its existence. By now other states besides New York had begun considering legislation modeled on the 1911 Sullivan law. An unsigned editorial in the *Arms and the Man* issue dated October 1, 1922, comments, "Our readers are the kind of men who can, by working in their own communities, do much to combat the passage of Sullivan laws." The editorial went on: "Have you, who realize the danger of the Sullivan law, ever thought that Bolsheviki Russia is a disarmed people?" Four years before, *Arms and the Man* had profiled "The Bolshevik Fusee," or rifle, just eight months after the 1917 Russian Revolution. These articles mark a strand of thinking within the NRA that—more than fifty years later—would grow to define it.

At the same time, however, the specter of gun control as a perceived threat played little role in the NRA's increasingly close ties with government. By 1925 a sitting United States senator, Francis W. Warren, Republican of Wyoming, was elected NRA president. That same year an embezzlement scandal on the board led the NRA to undergo a reorganization of its board. From that point on, the organization would be led by a paid executive vice president. The first executive vice president was General Milton A. Reckord, who would end up holding that position until well after World War II.

* * *

Born in 1879, Reckord was a Maryland National Guard officer who by then had served in two conflicts. As a major, he was deployed in the border area for the Mexican Expedition against Pancho Villa. He was promoted to lieutenant colonel as an infantry commander leading troops in the Battle of Meuse-Argonne in the final Allied offensive of World War I, for which France bestowed upon him the Croix de Guerre with Palm and his own nation awarded him the Distinguished Service Medal. A year after that war was over, Reckord was appointed Maryland's adjutant general, in which post he would command the state's national guard, and was promoted to the rank of brigadier general.

He took over the NRA as more gun regulations were coming under consideration. By 1925, a federal bill had been proposed to restrict pistols and revolvers in the District of Columbia. The NRA's new acting secretary, Charles Baynard Lister, born in 1899, was also an *American Rifleman* writer whose preferred byline was either C. B. Lister or simply C.B.L. In his annual report to the board, he flagged the D.C. bill in language that would anticipate the NRA's stance many years later:

> It is felt that the N.R.A. has a vital interest in the matter of anti-pistol
> legislation, first, because the pistol has become a most important
> arm in modern warfare; second, because most of our members are
> interested in pistol shooting as an adjunct to their work with the rifle;
> and third, because signs are already seen that, following the elimination
> of the pistol, a similar campaign against the rifle will be waged.

However, Lister and the NRA in general had a much more nuanced attitude toward gun control than that passage would suggest. Both Reckord and Lister were willing to consider some forms of gun control to curb the rise of organized crime in America, to the point—stunning today—that the NRA's first authorized history itself said that gun control was unavoidable. "Under the conditions that prevailed in the 1920s and early 1930s," reported *Americans and Their Guns* in 1967, "tighter regulations of the sale and use of firearms soon became inevitable."

Even before Prohibition began in 1920, the nation was already feeling the effects of organized crime. In 1919, eight players of the Chicago White Sox were accused of throwing the World Series, allegedly at the behest of a New York gangster named Arnold "The Brain" Rothstein.

For decades, the spread of railroads through rural parts of the United States had drawn gangs of train robbers on horseback. But by the 1920s, the federal expansion of the road network facilitated a new generation of criminals who fled in cars across state lines— iconic names such as John Dillinger, Pretty Boy Floyd, and Bonnie and Clyde. Prohibition, meanwhile, was fueling bootlegging and was responsible for the mushrooming of criminal syndicates in major cities. The New York Commission on Uniform Laws, a body that met annually with representatives of other states, chose to examine the intersection of firearms and crime, and in 1926 made recommendations for states and the federal government. One of the members of this commission was the New York lawyer and three-time Olympic team and individual pistol gold medalist, Karl Frederick.

The commission recommended outlawing anyone feloniously charged or convicted from moving weapons across states, adding criminal penalties for the handling of either stolen guns or any weapons with missing or altered serial numbers. The NRA under Reckord and Lister favored the recommendations and was so impressed with Frederick that they made him—one of the nation's leading gun control advocates—a board director the following year.

As lawmakers continued deliberating over options, gangland violence continued to take a toll. In 1929's St. Valentine's Day Massacre, four armed men wearing police uniforms, two of them firing Thompson submachine guns, killed seven rival gangsters in Chicago. "A postmortem of the bodies revealed that each one bore from twenty-five to thirty bullet wounds."

Later that year, an editorial in the *American Rifleman* laid out a list of measures the NRA supported, including requiring firearms dealers to keep records of sales, "so that police in recovering a weapon may trace it to its original purchaser," and requiring permits for the concealed carry of handguns. It is worth noting, however, that the same editorial reported the NRA remained "unalterably opposed to any law requiring a man to obtain a permit in order to *purchase* a gun or keep it in his home or place of business." Here can be seen the seeds of an attitude that would blossom in unexpected directions decades later.

Karl Frederick would eventually be elected NRA president by the organization's Board of Directors. In 1934 the Association's top two leaders, NRA executive vice president Reckord and NRA president Frederick, testified in Congress about a bill called the National Firearms Act. This bill—which was *endorsed* by the NRA—aimed to restrict machine guns by adding a tax and registration regime that would all but block new sales, and to ban sawed-off shotguns or any gun with a barrel under eighteen inches. It also banned silencers.

Appearing before the House Ways and Means Committee, Frederick ended up fielding a number of questions. The impromptu exchanges before the House committee and the NRA president mark the beginning of a national dialogue about gun control, and they are instructive. Frederick's replies show how the NRA of the 1930s had barely even begun to consider, let alone adopt, the views that would end up driving the modern NRA.

To be sure, Frederick defended the rights of gun owners: "I do object to being singled out with the criminal element and having my fingerprints taken and put in the Bureau of Criminal Identification because I like to use a pistol or because I may need one for self-defense." He went on, "I think we should be careful in considering the actual operation of regulatory measures to make sure that they do not hamstring the law-abiding citizen in his opposition to the crook." These comments show that the fear of a registry could already be seen in an earlier generation of NRA leadership.

He made remarks in another vein, however, that still stand out. A Democratic congressman from Missouri asked Frederick whether he believes "this bill is unconstitutional or . . . violates any constitutional provision." The NRA president replied: "I have not given it any study from that point of view. I will be glad to submit in writing my views on that subject, but I do think it is a subject which deserves serious thought." There is no record of Frederick later submitting his views to Congress. Nor did the matter appear or even come up in any form in the *American Rifleman* for a few more decades.

When another congressman asked how many men carried revolvers, the former Olympic champion began his answer with his own case: "I have never believed in the general practice of carrying weapons. I seldom carry one." He went on in his answer, "I do not believe in the general promiscuous toting of guns. I think it should be sharply restricted and only under licenses." As reasonable as his words may seem, they would be anathema to the leadership and activists in today's NRA.

The National Rifle Association hailed the National Firearms Act of 1934, passed with the NRA's support, as "an excellent law, sane, reasonable and effective," as General Reckord later recounted in the NRA's oral history. He did point out that he and Frederick together negotiated with Congress to ensure that "everything pertaining to registration was eliminated from the bill" so as not to burden law-abiding gun owners.

The NRA-backed 1934 law remains on the books today, although parts of it were weakened during the Reagan administration as a result of lobbying by the modern NRA. The act established a national tax and regulatory regime to limit access to certain weapons, such as machine guns and short-barreled shotguns and rifles, favored by gangsters. It still effectively bans fully automatic firearms—which spray bullets for as long as one holds down the trigger—from general use in the United States. However, semiautomatic weapons, which reload automatically to allow repeated fire with each trigger pull, would prove to be another story.

Four

A HIGH PLANE OF HONEST, FRANK DISCUSSION

During the presidential election of 1936, which would end in an overwhelming victory for the incumbent, Franklin D. Roosevelt, an unsigned editorial appeared in the NRA organ, the *American Rifleman,* that is worth quoting at length:

> This is a political year. Before many moons, life-long friends will have "fallen out" over the relative merits of one party and another or the relative value of this candidate as compared with that candidate. Just why men who can intelligently discuss every other problem in the world become such unreasonable, unreasoning "die-hards" about politics is one of the unexplained mysteries of mankind. . . . Take an active interest in politics this year, Mr. Shooter. The Nation needs your intelligence, your patriotism, and your sportsmanship. In many local elections you can wield an amazing influence for good. But keep your political interest and activity on a high plane of honest, frank discussion; and remember that there is neither rhyme nor reason in splitting open a good rifle club over a bum political argument.

* * *

During Roosevelt's second term, a new bill, the Federal Firearms Act, was introduced by Senator Royal Copeland, Democrat from New York. The bill proposed extending the 1934 law to establish a federal licensing regime for firearms dealers and to record their sales while barring sales to "prohibited" individuals including convicted felons. The NRA supported the legislation, noting that it would "not in any way impinge upon" owners of pistols or revolvers. Additionally, the organization supported legislation to restrict a new, "'freak' class of weapon" called the Magnum revolver.

The NRA's position was articulated in 1937 by C. B. Lister in the *American Rifleman*. (The NRA still awards a trophy in his name, honoring him for his leadership in "building the NRA to an organization of national stature.") In his article about the "freak" Magnum revolver, Lister seems to foreshadow the views of many gun reform advocates today:

> In view of the fact that the Magnum is, from the standpoint of the sportsman, definitely in the "freak" class of weapon, and inasmuch as the hunting of big game with a one-hand gun is definitely not within the capabilities of the average shooter, who has difficulty enough aligning his sights and securing hits with the rifle, it seems most probable that Congress will feel that legislation is desirable which will have the practical effect of restricting sale of the Magnum to Police Departments.

The Magnum, in Lister's opinion, was a "freak" weapon because the charge in the round was more powerful than that used in other handguns. Making an argument that would cause today's NRA leaders to cringe, Lister concluded that such weapons should be restricted not just to the police, but only to those police "especially trained *in the use of these weapons.*"

The *American Rifleman* ran an unsigned editorial on the page next to Lister's signed article that made the same point: "Inasmuch as the gun performs no practical function for the sportsman which cannot be [performed] as well or better by arms of standard type, it is impossible to defend the Magnum against legislation which would have the practical effect of limiting its sale to agents of the Federal, State, and local police."

These signed and unsigned editorials represent a part of the NRA's history that its modern leaders would prefer to forget, besides also marking a time when the NRA was willing to stand up to the gun industry. The *American Rifleman* pieces about the "freak" Magnum apparently prompted swift pushback from the legendary gun manufacturer Smith & Wesson, which pioneered the Magnum revolver. An unsigned editorial in a subsequent issue of the magazine noted that "one of the 'daddies' of the S. & W. Magnum, and some of the other members of the clan," protested the earlier editorial. But the NRA under Reckord and even Lister held its ground despite Smith & Wesson's efforts to compel them to see the company's Magnum as just another firearm that should be available to not only law enforcement but also civilians.

At the same time, Reckord and Lister remained adamantly opposed to any federal registration of firearms as a condition of purchasing a gun, saying that it would be both impractical and ineffective, in addition to imposing a burden on law-abiding gun owners. "We believe a murderer should be tried and convicted for murder, and sent to the electric chair. We think it is folly to provide legal machinery whereby a murderer may be tried for possessing an unregistered gun, given a light sentence, and a little later returned to society," noted Lister in the *American Rifleman* in January 1938. Yet in this same piece Lister wrote, "In opposing such a law we do not, however, say that nothing can be done about the use of firearms by criminals," arguing that the

Copeland Bill, instead of requiring individuals to register their fire-arms, "strikes directly at the *criminal* use of firearms" instead of "the honest citizen's possession of a gun."

The NRA led by Reckord and Lister had used this same logic to help pass the nation's first major federal gun law in 1934, and continued the same logic to pass the second, the Federal Firearms Act of 1938. This act required licensing all manufacturers and dealers involved in the interstate commerce of firearms. But unlike the 1934 law, this second law was "deficient in a number of respects" and was "further crippled" by weak law enforcement. The 1938 law prohibited licensed firearms dealers from transferring a weapon if they had "reasonable cause to believe" that the buyer was a convicted felon or a fugitive, but it did not require dealers to verify the person was neither convicted nor under indictment. It marked the first of what both proponents and opponents of gun control would claim were a series of ineffective gun laws.

* * *

In 1940 Nazi Germany ended the "phony war" that had broken out the previous year by launching simultaneous blitzkrieg raids across Belgium, the Netherlands, and France. In France, Allied forces retreated to the beaches around the city of Dunkirk, on the North Sea near the mouth of the English Channel. Surrounded by German forces on land, including panzers, the troops were rescued by sea on a quickly assembled, motley fleet including hundreds of small fishing and pleasure boats of all kinds.

The Dunkirk evacuation was hailed by British prime minister Winston Churchill as a "miracle of deliverance." The publicity surrounding the effort spurred Americans of all kinds to collect and ship weapons to the United Kingdom's police and domestic Home Guard. The NRA bundled packages gathered by hundreds of affiliated local gun clubs, sending more than seven thousand small arms along with working binoculars, stopwatches, and vintage military helmets. Their goal was "to rearm the police and Home Guard." Churchill later praised the volunteer American arms effort. The National Rifle Association of America, following principles established at its beginning and articulated by cofounder Church, had come to the aid of a civilian militia force, beginning to collect and ship arms across the Atlantic eighteen months before the Japanese attack in the Pacific brought America into World War II. In a history with many honorable hours, this was one of the NRA's finest.

After Pearl Harbor, Reckord took a leave of absence from his post as executive vice president to organize the training of new recruits at home, and then, at the ripe age of sixty-four, he headed overseas to become the provost marshal general for Europe. Back at NRA headquarters in Washington, in an old mansion near Embassy Row that the NRA had purchased in 1939 after renting a series of offices, C. B. Lister "worked unceasingly to carry out" NRA programs in support of the war effort. These included development of pistol and shotgun training manuals for armed guards protecting industrial plants vital to military production.

After V-J Day, officers, board directors, staff, and local members of the NRA who had served overseas slowly filtered back. "At least three prominent members—Brig. Gen. Merritt A. Edson and Col. D. M. Shoup of the United States Marine Corps and Comdr. John D. Bulkeley of the Navy—wore the star-studded, pale-blue ribbon of the Congressional Medal of Honor," the nation's highest military decoration. General Reckord was awarded the Distinguished Service Medal with a bronze oak leaf cluster for the "operating efficiency" he brought to training enlisted men and the Bronze Star Medal for his "effective supervision" of enemy prisoners. Among his duties as the U.S. military police commander for Europe, he personally led an investigation that broke up a cigarette-smuggling ring and indicted two hundred men, including two officers.

Upon his return to Washington, Reckord, whose personal integrity was well known within the NRA, resumed his duties as the NRA's chief executive. Lister remained editor of the *American Rifleman*. The NRA received a congratulatory letter from President Harry S Truman:

> *The tradition of the citizen soldiery is firmly, and properly, imbedded in our national ideals. Initiative, discipline, and skill in the use of small arms are essentials for the development of the finished citizen soldier . . . I hope that the splendid program which the National Rifle Association has followed during the past three-quarters of a century will be continued. It is a program that is good for a free America.*

* * *

Over time the focus of C. B. Lister's column shifted. He penned one piece after another warning of the dangers of communism. These columns often contained a further warning that a disarmed population was the key step in the ascent of a totalitarian regime.

"Listen, America!" wrote Lister in a column in March 1944, even before the war ended. "Think! *Decide* whether a Nation disarmed by its politicians can hope to maintain that democracy for which its sons die!" Two years later, in another column, Lister wrote: "Whenever objections are raised to the Gestapo idea of police registration or privately-owned firearms the proponents of registration have a stock reply which runs like this—Why should an honest citizen object to registering his guns? . . . Confiscation of arms owned by individuals of the opposing parties is *always* the essential step in the imposition of the will and government of the minority by the majority."

Lister was challenged in a letter to the editor by a reader, a lawyer, who said, "There is nothing in the history of our country to indicate that registration would lead to confiscation." Lister replied not with evidence but with a series of rhetorical questions: Who had expected that "a toothbrush mustached Austrian corporal would one day become master of Germany and near master of Europe?" Who among those wearing "rosy-tinted spectacles" had expected to be "smashed to bits by Jap bombs at Pearl Harbor!"?

By 1947 Lister was escalating his warnings about communists. Until they were strong enough to take power, he said, "they [would] resort to every form of trickery, subterfuge, and lying that will enable them to advance the cause. All this is in the record. It is widely known." A year later he became the first in the NRA since the 1922 unsigned editorial in *Arms and the Man* to tie proposals for firearms registration with totalitarianism, reminding *American Rifleman* readers that "it was the *police* state which set Mussolini and Hitler into power" and concluding, "General firearms registration fits perfectly into the established pattern of Communist action and is at the same time the typical example of *police* state psychology."

The board elected Lister to take over as executive vice president from Milton Reckord in 1949. Over the next seventeen months, he ran both the NRA and the *American Rifleman*. But by then, Lister may have already been suffering the effects of the brain cancer that would take his life in 1951. Certainly what he wrote is congruent with the paranoid backdrop of the McCarthy era. Lister's editorials took on an ever more alarmist tone. He connected "the Communist and the criminal," saying that both "prefer dealing with a disarmed citizenry"—presaging another cardinal star in the worldview of today's NRA. In March 1951, three months before he died, Lister complained that "carefully planted and skillfully nurtured communist propaganda" had "resulted in the complete disbanding of the world's greatest armed force." But with Lister's death, the alarmist tone of the editorials ceased, and his apocalyptic language would not be revived in *The Rifleman* till many years later.

Also in 1949, the National Rifle Association of America elected the first woman to its Board of Directors—twenty-three years before the National Press Club in Washington, D.C., would do so, and thirty-six years before most Fortune 500 companies. Alice H. Bull, from Washington State, was "a tough athlete, with lots of broken bones and screws in her body not related to shooting sports." Born in 1910, she got her first gun, a .22-caliber rifle, not long after her seventh birthday. She was captain of the women's rifle team at the University of Washington, where she earned a business degree. Bull first competed in the NRA's National Rifle Matches at Camp Perry in 1935.

For decades, Alice Bull was the sole female competitor at these events. "She often said her greatest pre-war distinction was to place 33rd out of 1,400 of the nation's best competitors in the President's Hundred-Rifle Match in which the top 100 finishers were honored with a parade through the camp," her son later recalled. "She was the only woman in that parade until the mid-1960s."

Bull appreciated the workings of firearms. "I like mechanical things. A finely made gun is like a well-made micrometer. It is a very fine piece of machinery and beautiful to look at. I don't love it because it goes boom."

Beginning in the postwar period, too, the NRA worked closely with the Boy Scouts and also established junior clubs in association with the Future Farmers of America, 4-H Clubs, the Veterans of Foreign Wars, the American Legion, and at high schools and colleges. More than a decade before the establishment of Earth Day, the NRA was also a pioneer in the promotion of wildlife conservation as part of its effort to preserve lands for hunting and recreational shooting. The Association worked closely with local affiliate gun clubs to advocate for access to lands with fowl and game. The NRA developed guidelines on how to approach landowners as well as on the responsibilities of "the hunter." On private land, the hunter should first ask permission. Once given access, "[t]he sportsman-hunter will always take great care not to break down fences, trample crops or injure stock. He will be careful to *leave all gates as he found them* and refrain from shooting near any houses or other buildings." He "leaves his hunting and camping grounds, if possible, in better condition than he found them."

As always, the NRA excelled in advocating for firearm safety. "Not a day passes but that more and more State Conservation and Education Departments, National institutions and organizations look toward the National Rifle Association for adequate instruction in safety education with firearms," noted the NRA's new executive director, a war hero recently retired from the Marine Corps, Major General Merritt A. Edson.

Born in 1897, Edson joined the Vermont National Guard and was deployed, like General Reckord, in Texas along the border during the Mexican Expedition. He later enlisted in the Marines and by the late 1920s was a captain deployed on a Navy cruiser docked in Nicaragua. It was there that Edson—nicknamed "Red Mike" for his red beard—led a detachment of fifty-six of his own hand-picked, specially trained Marines in expeditionary duty ashore. Captain Edson received the Navy Cross for "his exhibition of coolness, intrepidity, and dash," which "so inspired his men."

After being promoted to colonel, Edson commanded Marine combat battalions in World War II. He led one of two Marine Raider battalions that took the Pacific island of Tulagi from dug-in Japanese troops, and he was awarded his second Navy Cross for his leadership of the assault. And in the Battle of Guadalcanal, Edson, who was by then forty-five, helped give the United States its first major victory against imperial Japan. Ordered to defend an airfield from a position later dubbed "Edson's Ridge," Colonel Edson led about eight hundred Marines over two days as they repelled repeated assaults by more than twenty-five hundred Japanese troops. A Marine citation would later describe Edson as being "all over the place, encouraging, cajoling, and correcting as he continually exposed himself to enemy fire."

For his actions on Guadalcanal, Red Mike received the Medal of Honor, the nation's highest decoration for valor. Stoic in battle, Edson "was not readily given to a show of emotion," according to his citation for Guadalcanal, which went on to describe his reaction to the loss there of his aide-de-camp. "Nevertheless, when his personal runner of several months service was killed at the second battle of the Matanikau River on Guadalcanal, witnesses said he 'cried like a baby,' and later stated that the man could never be replaced."

Edson's other decorations included two Legion of Merit decorations, a Presidential Unit Citation with two bronze stars, and, from the United Kingdom, the Distinguished Service Order. Later promoted to major general, Merritt Edson served as the chief of the Vermont State Police before moving to Washington six years after the war to lead the NRA beginning in 1951.

Edson, although capable of worrying like his predecessor Lister about "the seemingly eternal struggle between Communism and Democracy," more often complained about Congress's lack of support for national rifle practice. The requested budget for the National Board for the Promotion of Rifle Practice, whose civilian implementing agency was the nonprofit NRA, was cut in half by 1952, as part of an ongoing waning of funds.

General Edson wrote in a column in the *American Rifleman* in 1952: "If that small group of men who had banded together to form the National Rifle Association a little more than eighty years ago had chosen a motto for their newly formed organization, without doubt they would have selected the Second Article of the Bill of Rights." This is the first known such reference to the Second Amendment in the *American Rifleman*. Back then Edson plucked a few chords that would swell to a crescendo by the 1970s, and which still resound loudly today.

Yet he also maintained that gun control and gun rights could coexist. Take his point of view on the regulation of the carrying of concealed weapons: "Certain controls such as those which exist over the 'wearing' of concealed weapons are clearly constitutional and their being so does not affect the basic *right* to bear arms," he once wrote. It is not an attitude that his eventual successors would share.

General Edson committed suicide in late 1955 at the age of fifty-eight. At the time of his death, besides his NRA duties, he was the Navy's representative to a Defense Advisory Committee on Prisoners of War, some of whom, after their release from Korea, were accused or suspected of having collaborated with the enemy under torture. His son Merritt A. Edson Jr., a Marine captain, said his father had been "very tired" and feeling "very badly about the American prisoner of war question." A UPI article reported that "his wife found the body of the Marine hero fully clothed in the front seat of his car in the garage of their home" with the engine running and both garage doors closed. He was buried at Arlington.

In 1951, the same year Edson was appointed to the NRA's top position, the Association changed the bylaws governing elections to its Board of Directors. Now only five eligible members were needed to nominate a candidate for the board. But this attempt toward more openness and democracy within the NRA would not last, and the number of eligible NRA members required to nominate a potential board member would later be raised. This is important because power within the NRA has long stemmed from the very controlled process by which the board appoints a Nominating Committee, which in turn chooses nearly every candidate to appear on the ballot that eligible voting members get in the mail. Not just observers but NRA board members themselves have compared the intrigue often surrounding the nomination process to a communist politburo. And, decades later, the Association's own bylaws would wind up being used against its old guard.

Five

PUBLIC OPINION DEMANDS SOME CONTROL

The National Rifle Association of America grew twelvefold in little more than a generation after World War II, over eight times faster than the growth of the nation's population. The NRA went from 84,000 members in 1945 to 250,000 in 1952, and to over 1 million by 1968. By the late sixties the NRA had evolved from a "small, exclusive group of dyed-in-the-wool, high powered-rifle competitive shooters" to a national organization where hunters accounted for three-fourths of the membership. The increase in dues from members and advertising revenues from NRA magazines fueled the Association's growth at a time when financial support from the federal government through the National Board for the Promotion of Rifle Practice was still in existence but had begun to wane.

* * *

By the fifties the *American Rifleman* was the nation's most coveted gun magazine, and it was only available through NRA membership. Articles regularly covered matters from hand-loading ammunition to profiles of both new and vintage firearms. Most years, in the months before Christmas, the *American Rifleman* of this era would expound about choosing a first rifle for one's son. Occasionally a writer would describe a trip few NRA members could afford, like an expedition to hunt elephants in the Himalayas, or a safari to hunt lions in Africa. Every now and then a piece concentrated on potential matters of national security, such as the small arms used by the army of the People's Republic of China, or the consistently excellent marksmanship shown by Soviet competitors at international shooting matches around the world. Yet, despite ongoing concerns about communism, gone was the strident hyperbole of Lister's day.

The importance of wildlife conservation to preserve hunting habitats was another frequent topic in the magazine. "Unless indiscriminate shooting is stopped, our hawks may disappear," read one conservation piece. As early as 1966, the NRA stopped listing the polar bear as eligible for big-game hunting awards, since the species was "in danger of extinction"—forty-two years before polar bears were categorized as "endangered." *American Rifleman* editorials in the early 1960s even favored the idea of a government tax on arms and ammunition to fund government efforts to support wildlife habitat preservation.

In 1956, an all-women team first competed in the national high-power rifle matches. NRA board member and champion shooter Alice Bull led the team, which "gave an excellent account of itself in a predominately male sport," reported *Americans and Their Guns*.

In 1957, in the President's Match at Camp Perry, the highest-scoring shooter for the Air Force was Captain Morton C. Mumma III, representing the third generation in what would be the storied Mumma family legacy. A year later, in the handgun matches, a Marine technical sergeant won the National Service Rifle Championship. Gertrude Backstrom won her third National Women's Championship along with the Civilian Pistol Championship—the first woman to ever defeat a field of male competitors for that award.

In 1959, the board elected Irvine C. Porter from Alabama—the first in what would become another prominent NRA family line—as president of the NRA. Born in 1910, Porter also perhaps represented the first generation of shooters from the Deep South who no longer dismissed the NRA as a New York "Yankee" project of former Union Army officers, but who saw the Association instead as promoting state-of-the-art shooting, safety, and competitions.

The same board chose a Wisconsin lawyer and World War II veteran named Franklin L. Orth to lead the NRA as its paid executive vice president. To assume the post, he resigned from the Eisenhower administration, where he had been deputy assistant secretary of the army. Later, while he was still running the NRA, he would become president of the U.S. Olympic Committee. Orth is yet another past NRA leader whose memory the NRA seems to have erased. Orth "had graduated from the School of Economics and the Law School of the University of Wisconsin," reported the 1967 authorized history. "He entered World War II as a captain in the Infantry, and, as a member of Merrill's Marauders"—a special operations jungle warfare unit led by a general named Frank Merrill—"served on extra-hazardous duty in long-range penetrations behind the Japanese lines in Burma. As the commander of a regimental combat team, he led guerrilla-type operations against the enemy." He left the army as a colonel.

NRA president Irvine Porter was succeeded in 1961, after serving two consecutive one-year terms, by a man named John M. Schooley. Schooley was "one of America's leading pistol shots," according to *Americans and Their Guns*, and his name is still on the administrative building holding the visitor center and pro shop at the NRA recreational shooting facility near Raton, New Mexico.

However, Schooley is another figure whom today's Association would likely prefer to forget. His background was as a special investigator in the Alcohol and Tobacco Tax Division of the Internal

Revenue Service, the predecessor to the Bureau of Alcohol, Tobacco, Firearms and Explosives—the government bureau most despised by today's NRA.

* * *

The late 1950s were a time of tailfins, hula hoops, and carhops, early rock and roll on the radio, and Westerns on the big and little screens. The Westerns roiled the public imagination, so much so that these glamorized stories playing out on the screen were soon inspiring not just gun sales but sales of Western-style six-shot revolvers.

"Hotter than a pistol these days is the handgun business," reported the magazine *Popular Science* in 1959. "An estimated half-million Americans have taken up the quick-draw as a hobby, most of them using new .22 caliber revolvers artfully made to resemble the weapons carried by Wyatt Earp" and others. "Today Western-style sixguns are selling at the rate of 150,000 a year—nearly 3,000 a week." Many wannabe gunslingers shot themselves accidentally while practicing the quick draw. By then the NRA itself was lamenting the rise of self-inflicted wounds by imitation gunslingers, fearing it could lead to overbearing legislation.

Another trend at work was the emerging notion that America's unchecked access to guns was responsible for too many needless deaths. Just months before *Popular Science* documented the handgun boom, the women's magazine *McCall's* ran an article called "This Very Day a Gun May Kill You!" In it, the author, Carl Bakal, a New York writer, editor, and public relations consultant, asserted that firearms were responsible for fourteen thousand deaths per year, a combination of accidents, suicides, and homicides.

The NRA responded in the *American Rifleman*'s very next issue in an editorial mockingly titled "This Very Day." "The author's proposed solution to the biased situation that he fabricates is a national system of registration and permits, with all weapons in firing condition to be kept in common storage places such as armories or in local departments," commented the magazine. The editorial went on to make another of the magazine's early references to "the right to keep and bear arms" as part of the broader "basic liberties guaranteed" by "the Bill of Rights," before calling for a strong response to "such vicious propaganda aimed at disarming the American citizens."

Three out of four Americans at the time supported strict gun control measures. In the summer of 1959, the American Institute of Public Opinion (later known as the Gallup Poll) reported that 75 percent of adults answered affirmatively to the question "Would you favor or oppose a law which would require a person to obtain a police permit before he or she could buy a gun?"

The *American Rifleman* stepped up the pace of editorials on the subject, and as early as 1959 it was beginning to defend at length what its writers were soon calling the right to keep and bear arms, a "foundation stone of American liberty." In fact, the *American Rifleman* changed its masthead in its March 1963 issue to read: "The NRA stands squarely behind the premise that the ownership of firearms must not be denied American citizens of good repute so long as they use them for lawful purposes. The strength of the NRA, and therefore the ability to accomplish its objects and purposes, depends entirely upon the support of loyal Americans who believe in the right to 'Keep and Bear Arms.'"

Yet the NRA back then was still willing to compromise, as long as the rights of gun owners were respected. The "Certainly law-abiding, God-fearing men and women have a right to protect their loved ones, their homes, and their places of business against the criminal element of our society," wrote the NRA itself in 1967 in *Americans and Their Guns*. "And it is the criminal element at which our legislative guns should be aimed, not a scatter-gun shot at every citizen."

As the Association neared its centennial, the NRA reaffirmed its support for existing gun laws, while establishing a set of criteria that would balance the effort to curb crime with the protection of gun owners' rights in order to determine whether new proposed restrictions would go too far. In its first authorized history, *Americans and Their Guns*, the NRA identified four red lines that no gun regulation should cross: "discriminatory or punitive taxes or fees" on firearms, "licens[ing] the possession or purchase" of firearms, laws restricting transport of firearms by sports shooters and collectors, and firearms "registration on any level of government." At the same time, the NRA said it could live with laws to "prohibit . . . possession of firearms" by convicts, fugitives, "mental incompetents, drug addicts, and persons while adjudicated an habitual drunkard," to impose "severe additional penalties for the use of a dangerous weapon in the commission of a crime," and to prohibit the "sale of firearms to juveniles." It would also accept a law mandating the issuance of permits for citizens to legally carry concealed handguns—as long as this was done in a "reasonable" manner, where "requirements for such carrying should be clearly set forth in the law," and where the authorized government agency was obliged to issue the license once those conditions had been met. Some of these points sound like today's NRA.

* * *

By this time, pressure was already mounting over civil rights. When Martin Luther King Jr. was organizing the March on Washington, he turned to his longtime confidant, Harry Belafonte, the calypso singer and actor, to recruit Hollywood celebrities to join them. Belafonte first turned to his actor friends Paul Newman, Joanne Woodward, and Marlon Brando. "I called Tony Bennett," wrote Belafonte. "I called Shelley Winters, Diahann Carroll, Lena Horne, Billy Eckstine, Burt Lancaster, James Garner, James Baldwin, Sidney Poitier, Tony Curtis, Ossie Davis and Ruby Dee, Jackie Robinson, Josephine

Baker, Robert Ryan, Leonard Bernstein, Sammy Davis, Jr., Joseph Mankiewicz and more."

As Belafonte recalled, King replied, "That's a lot of friends. . . . All quite liberal." King went on to ask, "Have you reached out to anyone across the divide?" Belafonte had not, later writing: "I told him I didn't see how I could reach out to Ronald Reagan, or George Murphy, two of Hollywood's best-known Republican actors. I really didn't know them at all. I did know Charlton Heston: he was on the other side of the divide."

Charlton Heston, best known at that time for his film roles as Moses and Ben-Hur, was indeed more conservative than most of his Hollywood peers, even though he had supported Democratic candidates in recent presidential elections. Belafonte came up with an idea to ask Heston and Brando to co-chair what he called "the Hollywood delegation" for the march. Heston, already a national icon, back then called himself a "Kennedy Democrat," but he would have a very different take, albeit one also promoting gun rights, decades later, when he would once again play a political role on the national stage.

President Kennedy's assassination in November 1963 was one of the watershed moments in American life. Among the changes it ushered in was a movement to further restrict firearms—especially those purchased through the mail. Earlier in the year, Lee Harvey Oswald had ordered a cheap surplus foreign military rifle advertised in the back pages of the *American Rifleman*. The fact that he obtained the weapon through an ad in the NRA's own magazine put the Association itself against the wall and fueled the call for reform in Washington.

Even before the assassination, in the summer of 1963, Senator Thomas J. Dodd, a Democrat from Connecticut, introduced a "Bill to Regulate the Interstate Shipment of Firearms," which also prescribed penalties for selling firearms to juveniles and barred criminals and those legally deemed to be mentally ill from acquiring arms. Even though the bill attracted more support after the assassination, it still failed in committee. Senator Dodd submitted a second bill in 1965 at the urging of President Lyndon B. Johnson, which also died. But Dodd persisted and introduced a third bill in 1967.

Those in favor of gun control were assisted, in an atmosphere of extraordinary racial tension, by a growing fear of armed racially defined groups, both black and white. In 1964, California prosecutors investigated claims that "the United States Army may be helping to arm Malcolm X and his fanatical Negro followers" with weapons given by the U.S. National Board for the Promotion of Rifle Practice for use in NRA shooting matches. There were also fears that arms were being diverted to private armies of white supremacists. California later dropped the investigation, as there was little or no evidence that government weapons were being diverted to such groups.

In the face of the nation's ongoing racial unrest, armed white supremacist groups with names like the Minutemen and the Rangers were appearing in a number of states. Three men who belonged to such a group were found guilty in Kansas of possessing unregistered automatic weapons and silencers. New York police later seized twenty members of another group who were preparing to launch "assaults on three 'left wing' camps" with "pistols, rifles, shotguns, mortars, bazookas, machine guns and rocket-launchers." One nationally syndicated columnist, Inez Robb, called such groups "private armies of the extreme right," saying new laws were needed "to bring under control the pistol-packing morons."

Concerned that accusations of arming or supporting such groups could tip the balance of public opinion against them, no fewer than thirty-seven NRA senior officials, including top executive officers such as Franklin L. Orth and former Texas Border Patrol officer Harlon B. Carter, board members including Alice Bull, and Executive Council members such as Milton Reckord and Irvine Porter, all signed a statement published in the *American Rifleman* in 1964 denying the charges of either diverting arms or supporting extremist groups. "The NRA vehemently disavows" any link to any "private armies or group violence," the statement said, and "does not approve or support any group activities that properly belong to the national defense or the police," or which advocate "the overthrow of duly constituted government authority" or "subversive activities" against any government.

The same joint NRA leadership statement reaffirmed an "NRA MEMBERSHIP PLEDGE" requiring prospective members to avow that they do not belong to any group seeking "the overthrow by force and violence of the Government of the United States or any of its political subdivisions." The same joint NRA leadership statement made no mention of gun rights, even as it said the Association's purposes included education, training, safety, and national defense. The NRA's 1964 statement remains completely unlike anything articulated by modern NRA leaders today.

* * *

What could be called the first modern mass shooting took place at the University of Texas in 1966. A former Marine, after stabbing his mother and wife to death the night before, carried an arsenal of weapons, including a bolt-action Remington 700 ADL rifle (popular among hunters as well as military and law enforcement snipers) equipped with a vintage Leupold scope, up to the top of the clock tower on the University of Texas campus in Austin. From that tower, over a period of ninety-six minutes, he fired at students, other pedestrians, and police at ranges of more than four hundred yards, ultimately killing thirteen people, including a pregnant woman whose unborn child also did not survive, and wounding more than thirty others before being killed by police. Before then there was no mass movement for gun control to speak of, apart from a few magazine articles that had begun to make the same case.

* * *

In California in the spring of 1967, a group of Black Panthers decided to make a statement. Aware that the state's permissive gun laws would be on their side, they entered the state house in Sacramento with holstered revolvers and pistols and holding shotguns openly in their hands, in an incident that went long forgotten until its memory was revived in 2011 by the legal scholar Adam Winkler. The Black Panthers—inspired by Huey Newton and led by Bobby Seale—were taking advantage of a California law that permitted the open carrying of loaded firearms in public.

"It was a noon-hour session of the assembly that a dozen of the armed youths—members of the 'Black Panther Party'—succeeded in penetrating briefly before they were ushered out," reported The Associated Press at the time. "They remained silent except for a spokesman, Bobby Seale, 25, of Oakland," who said they were there "to defend their constitutional right to bear arms."

The same month the *American Rifleman* ran a piece titled "Who Guards America's Homes?" in response to race riots, such as those that took place in the Watts neighborhood of Los Angeles, advocating the keeping of firearms in the home. More riots broke out that summer, first in Newark and then Detroit.

The "dramatic incident" inside the Sacramento statehouse led Governor Ronald Reagan to sign into law an act banning the open carrying of firearms in California. The NRA supported the new California restriction, monitoring its progress in the *American Rifleman* without any critical comments or reaction.

The Association and the *American Rifleman* were preoccupied instead with the latest gun control bill introduced by Senator Dodd. By then the organization's official history, *Americans and Their Guns*, had been in print nearly a year. It eloquently puts down on paper the NRA of that era's thinking at the time about gun rights.

> *Actually, we have a very imposing and effective array of firearms laws, a demonstrable fact that must be recognized in any fair appraisal. But this does not mean that our laws are perfect, and new proposals which are sensibly designed to cope with crime should be accorded open-minded consideration.*

Open-minded consideration was what NRA executive vice president Franklin L. Orth, the Association's chief executive, brought to Senator Dodd's gun legislation. Orth was at times critical of Dodd's first two bills, testifying in the Senate that it was "an attempt to convict the 'firearm' as a causal factor in the alarming crime rate in this country." Yet Orth still concluded that some measure of gun control was necessary. He wrote an open letter to NRA members:

> *It is a fact that known felons, juveniles, and other unfit persons have been able, with relative ease, to purchase concealable firearms by the mail-order route in circumvention of state laws. . . . Public opinion demands that some control be applied to this traffic and public opinion will be served.*

When Senator Robert F. Kennedy accused the NRA of being unwilling to support any gun legislation, Orth fired back: "The National Rifle Association has been in support of workable, enforceable gun control legislation since its very inception in 1871." (A more accurate statement would have been: The NRA has been in support of effective gun control since the 1930s when rising crime made it a national issue for the first time.)

Orth was responding to an accusation by Senator Kennedy, who had said, "I think it is a terrible indictment of the National Rifle Association that they haven't supported any legislation to try and control the misuse of rifles and pistols in this country." Orth called this "a smear of a great American organization." A few days later Orth himself urged Congress to pass a new gun control law proposed by President Lyndon Johnson to curb mail-order sales:

> *The duty of Congress is clear . . . it should act now to pass legislation that will keep undesirables, including criminals, drug addicts and persons adjudged mentally irresponsible or alcoholic, or juveniles from obtaining firearms through the mail.*

It would be Senator Kennedy's own assassination, along with that of Martin Luther King Jr., that pushed Dodd's third bill through with the NRA's support. Three months before he left office, President Johnson signed the Gun Control Act of 1968. The law banned the interstate retail sale of guns, prohibited all sales to juveniles, convicted felons, and individuals adjudicated as being mentally unsound, and stopped the import of surplus military firearms and other guns not "particularly suitable for sporting purposes."

The NRA's support for the Gun Control Act of 1968 was a watershed moment for the ninety-seven-year-old Association. Orth and his supporters within the NRA leadership and the group's rank and file believed the law sensibly balanced the rights of gun owners with the need to curb gun violence. In 1967, during the debate over the act, the NRA released a statement attributed to Executive Vice President Franklin L. Orth that still stands out as being not only remarkable, but completely the opposite of what NRA leaders have said consistently since the shift in 1977.

"The NRA does not advocate an 'ostrich' attitude toward firearms legislation. We recognize that the dynamism and complexities of modern society create new problems which demand new solutions. Accordingly, the National Rifle Association has come forth with a positive, specific and practical program for reasonable and proper firearms controls," Orth is quoted as saying in an NRA press release.

To some, Orth was a reasonable gun control advocate. He took on the press and defended the rights of gun owners when he felt they had been unfairly maligned. But he also made it clear that the NRA was willing to compromise to help curb the kind of gun violence that had led to devastating assassinations in recent years.

Others within and outside the NRA immediately lashed out, seeing the NRA's and Orth's support for the act as a betrayal. Some NRA life members resigned. An editorial from the outdoor magazine *Fishing and Hunting News* accused Orth and the NRA of betraying "every sportsman who ever belonged or believed in that organization." Others demanded that Orth resign. He even received some death threats.

At the same time, President Johnson, as he was signing the legislation, blamed the NRA and Orth for blocking even stricter legislation that would have mandated registration of firearms. His White House had proposed such a bill, but neither Congress nor the NRA would accept it.

Yet the same battle left the NRA leadership feeling wounded by the press. The *Washington Post* cartoonist known as Herblock had satirized the Association over Dodd's gun bills. The *American Rifleman* saw his cartoons as the embodiment of "the ruthless spirit of the editorial lynch mob which, in recent years, has rioted on occasion through the pages of newspapers like *The Washington Post* and *The New York Times*."

* * *

The NRA's first hundred years were steeped in patriotism and service to the nation. Generations of NRA leaders, dominated by decorated military officers, made better riflery a national goal in every era of the group's first century. From the start the NRA set and upheld a standard for marksmanship through training and competitions respected around the world. Both the leadership and the rank and file were interwoven with every branch of military service and the National Guard units of each state. By 1903, less than forty years after its inception, the NRA had become a quasi-government agency, subsidized by federal funds to host shooting matches at home and to compete abroad. But by 1966, during a time of shifting priorities, federal support for rifle training provided by the NRA finally came to an end.

The NRA saw no reason at all over its first fifty years to even take a position on gun regulations. But over its second half century, the Association began to warn about government overreach, and soon applied a balancing test to all gun legislation. Was the greater good or public interest worth the limits and inconvenience to gun owners? In the 1920s the NRA came out in favor of issuing permits for the concealed carrying of handguns, but in the 1930s it drew a hard line against any government registry of gun owners. Yet the NRA still supported two major national gun control laws in 1934 and 1968 in response to surges in criminal violence and political assassinations, respectively.

Throughout the same period the Association never even suggested that citizens need the same level of firepower as police. On the contrary, in 1937 the NRA said that only trained police should handle the Smith & Wesson Magnum. Moreover, it was only in 1952, more than eighty years after the NRA was established, that mention of the Second Amendment first appeared in the *American Rifleman*, where it was referred to as "the Second Article of the Bill of Rights." In 1964 the entire Executive Committee approved a statement against "private armies" and "disavow[ed] any connection with, or tacit approval of" groups advocating "the overthrow of duly constituted government authority."

The NRA leaders who backed further gun control in 1968, on the eve of the organization's centennial, underestimated the backlash to come. What would follow would soon mark the end of the Association as anything resembling an organization Wingate or Church would recognize.

* * *

On November 17, 1971, the NRA celebrated its centennial "as one of the largest and most active sportsman's organizations in the entire free world," remarked the *American Rifleman*. "The second hundred years will not be easy, but they could be the best." The leaders of the NRA in 1971 looked back on an organization that had promoted marksmanship, helped to prepare the nation for several wars and other military campaigns, and encouraged responsible gun ownership and safe handling of guns. But the times were changing, and the tension inside the NRA between principles such as hunter conservation and gun rights was coming to a head.

PART TWO

THE SHIFT

At the National Rifle Association, which was formed in 1871, we spent a hundred years basically providing technical information to shooters, working with hunters, running national and international competitions and the like. But when it came to the time when our rights in the United States were threatened, we shifted our focus to defending those rights.

**—David A. Keene, president,
National Rifle Association of America,
Moscow, 2013**

Six

THE AWAKENING

The 1970s represents the fulcrum decade in the NRA's history, culminating in an event still known in the lore of the organization as the "Cincinnati Revolt." The principal victor at the 1977 NRA meeting was a Texan named Harlon B. Carter, who is the only NRA leader over the past century and a half honored by a statue of his likeness—a bronze bust—on display at the NRA's National Firearms Museum at its headquarters in Fairfax, Virginia. No one better represents the new breed of NRA leader than Carter, although he had been a member of the organization for quite some time. Born Harlan B. Carter in Granbury, Texas, on August 10, 1913, Carter had joined the NRA when he turned eighteen in 1931—just months after he shot and killed a fellow minor and was convicted of murder. He became a life member in 1936, not long after his murder conviction was overturned on appeal and he was released from prison. Only then did he change the spelling of his first name to "Harlon," with an *o*.

Carter was the son of a U.S. Border Patrol officer in Laredo, on the Mexican border. He was seventeen years old on the day he came home to find his mother upset, as was reported in 1931 in the *Laredo Times*. Three Hispanic boys a little younger than him had been loitering near their home. Three weeks before, the Carters' family car had been stolen from their yard, and the mother wondered if these boys might be responsible. With his father away at work, Carter grabbed the family shotgun and went looking for the boys.

He found them returning from a swimming hole, and demanded they accompany him back to his home to speak to his mother. Ramón Casiano was no more than sixteen and his companions were younger. Casiano, facing Carter, who was holding the shotgun, removed his coat, pulled a knife from his belt, and challenged Carter to a fight, according to court testimony. Carter replied, "You think I won't use this?" and then fired, as one of the surviving boys later testified in Carter's murder trial. The blast opened a two-inch wound in Casiano's chest as he collapsed. Carter then warned the other two youths not to move.

Casiano was still conscious but knew he was dying. He "bade his friends goodbye and then offered his hand to Carter, saying, 'You're my friend.' Carter, the witness stated, shoved the proffered hand aside with the words, 'You're my friend nothing,'" reported the *Laredo Times* during the trial. Casiano died of his wounds.

Carter's trial on murder charges, including the above exchange between Carter and the dying boy he had just shot, was front-page hometown news in the spring of 1931. But the man who had quietly replaced one vowel in his first name to henceforth become known as Harlon B. Carter managed to keep any reference to the murder case from ever coming to light for the following fifty years.

After graduating from the University of Texas and Emory University Law School, Carter joined the Border Patrol himself in his native state. It took him only fourteen years to become chief of the U.S. Border Patrol in 1950, leading American border efforts for seven years. In 1961 he became the Southwest regional commissioner for the Immigration and Naturalization Service, serving for another decade.

Carter was a longtime champion competitive shooter, and one of the few who could compete alongside the military men who had dominated the NRA for so long. The *American Rifleman* noted that Carter "is one of a handful of civilian shooters classified as both Distinguished Rifle and Distinguished Pistol, and is a Lifetime Master in high power, outdoor smallbore prone, and indoor and outdoor pistol. He is also a big game hunter and shotgunner."

While he was running the Border Patrol, Carter started writing once in a while for the *American Rifleman*. He was able in these columns to conjure the mood of fellowship that the NRA had long provided. To take one example:

> *We were hundreds of miles deep in Mexico. There were six of us spread out wide along the edge of low brush on the east side of a low prairie. It was the only cover we had. A line of geese was coming in low, down a brisk northwest wind, headed toward Laguna de Guadalupe several miles from their feeding grounds. . . . It seemed just like being on the 1,000-yard line at Camp Perry, a long time ago.*

Carter was elected to the NRA Board of Directors in 1951, when he was running the Border Patrol, and was elected to the voluntary post of president of the NRA in 1965. Eight years later, he testified before a federal grand jury investigating allegations that he had stolen up to fifty thousand rounds of government ammunition for his own personal use in retirement. He denied the allegations, and no charges were ever filed. By then, 1967, Carter had joined other past leaders on the NRA Executive Council. He was an unlikely candidate for the role of insurgent, but an insurgent he would be.

Carter's principal lieutenant in the Cincinnati Revolt would be a younger man, twenty-two years his junior. Although they were generations apart, one with a background in law enforcement and the other in journalism, they shared an unyielding vision of gun rights along with the fear that the NRA over time was being led down the wrong track.

Born in Oklahoma, Neal Knox grew up amid the wheat and cotton fields of the Red River Valley in North Texas. "When he was 5 years old, he split open his piggy bank, counted out $1.04 and went with his grandmother to buy his first BB rifle," wrote a journalist years later. He attended Abilene Christian College, where he met his wife, Jay, "the only girl on . . . campus who kept a rifle in her dormitory closet."

Both Knox and his wife "came from divorced families—an unusual circumstance in 1950's Texas," wrote their oldest child, Chris, and "they understood each other like no one else from the start." One of their more endearing photos is a color picture of Neal and Jay in the twilight of their lives standing in front of a large black-and-white portrait of their younger selves on the Red River after they got engaged, with Neal holding a rifle and Jay with her hand on his arm.

After leaving college, Knox joined the Texas National Guard. He worked briefly in the insurance and oil businesses before getting a job with a small-town paper, *The Vernon Daily Record*. He later moved to the *Wichita Falls Times* before ending up at the *Times Record News*. Later he started freelancing for gun magazines. Knox was "a gun buff" above all else. "A modified choke is about right," he wrote about hunting chukar partridges along the Snake River in Idaho in *Handloader Magazine*, "since most shots are fairly long, and the load should be all No. 6 shot the shell will handle, wrapped in a pellet protector sleeve for uniform patterns."

He wrote for *Guns and Ammo* and *Guns*, too, before becoming the founding editor of *Gun Week* in 1966, on the eve of Senator Dodd's introduction of his third gun control bill. *Gun Week* was the "only source of real information" about gun legislation, wrote Knox's protégé, Tanya K. Metaksa, years later. In 1972, Knox and a partner won a 1,000-yard two-man team rifle championship. "At the time he was shooting a lot of bench rest and was a fair hand at reading mirage, the 'visible wind' that boils in the scope before a far-off target."

But it was Neal Knox's uncompromising advocacy for gun rights that made his name. "The anti-gun clan has based its arguments on numerous subjects over the years—crime, fifth columnists, gangsterism, firearms accidents, extreme armies, even world peace and disarmament—but the movement has always relied most on 'waving the bloody shirt' of emotionalism," he wrote in 1966, borrowing a phrase coined back during Reconstruction for "Radical Republicans" calling out Klan and other southern white resistance violence. Knox was at the time perhaps the loudest voice in the nation for gun rights, writing in his own newsletter and other gun magazines—not the *American Rifleman* and other NRA monthly magazines (yet), notably—and independently lobbying elected officials, too.

These two men, Carter and Knox, were the primary orchestrators of the NRA's gun rights revolt. In a sense they are every bit as much foundational to the NRA as Church and Wingate. Yet aside from Carter's bust in the firearms museum, his name rarely comes up much anymore. However, Knox's name can still evoke memories of his repeated attempts to take power after Carter had retired.

* * *

In 1967, at the height of debate over Dodd's third gun bill, the NRA leadership, still consisting of the old guard, agreed to cooperate on a documentary being produced by NBC News. The NRA executive vice president, Franklin L. Orth, went on camera for the program, expecting to field questions that had been determined in advance. "Suddenly one of the interviewers reached into his brief case and pulled out a surprise batch of catch questions" containing "obviously 'loaded' inquiries which we had not previously discussed.'"

The documentary's on-air correspondent was Robert MacNeil. Four years before, he had reported from the bloody motorcade in Dallas on President Kennedy's assassination, and over a decade later

he would become the co-anchor of what became PBS's *MacNeil/
Lehrer News Hour*. In his memoir, MacNeil would complain that the
NRA used its contacts on Capitol Hill to reframe the 1967 program
before it aired. "After I had finished my work on the documentary,
the NRA brought pressure through a tame congressman and the
piece was reedited without my knowledge to allow the head of the
NRA to filibuster and obscure the relevant point."

But, in fact, a point was made, and the NRA heard it. The producers used two children—in a demonstration unlikely to be repeated
now—to show how easy it can be for minors to buy guns. In New
York, they compelled a twelve-year-old boy to check a box on a mail-
order slip affirming he was old enough to order and receive a rifle.
Producers also had an underage NBC page go into a store and buy
a semiautomatic pistol. Meanwhile, an NBC journalist went into a
store in Arizona and came out with a nine-foot-long, 20 mm anti-
tank weapon capable of penetrating six inches of armor plating.
After putting the weapon in the back of a pickup truck, the journalist stopped a police officer to show him the weapon and ask him if it
was okay to transport it. The officer correctly said it was not against
the law.

The NBC documentary, titled *Whose Right to Bear Arms?*, also
drew a few conclusions that the NRA construed as evidence of bias,
if not also exaggeration. "In all the ads in hunting and gun magazines," MacNeil said on camera, "there is a strong appeal to sadism.
A gun will be advertised as having been used by 'sadistic SS killers.'"
No such ad was shown to support the point, and MacNeil's claim of
a sadistic appeal in "all the ads" is certainly hyperbolic; gun collectors
look for such military markings as signs of authenticity. But it was
the documentary's final thought that may have most irked Orth and
other NRA leaders, as NBC pointed out how tightly regulated many
activities were when compared to owning guns. "A man gets in his
car to go hunting. His car is registered, and he needs a license to

drive it. He needs a license for his hunting dog, and when he gets to the hunting grounds, he needs a license to hunt. But he has been able to buy the gun and carry it around with him without any restrictions whatsoever," said MacNeil. "The lapses in this logic are apparent."

After Orth died of a heart attack, Maxwell Rich, a retired major general, was confirmed as the NRA's new chief executive by 1971. Rich had served in the Utah National Guard as a private in a horse-drawn artillery battery, and later joined the army to become a field artillery commander in World War II. Fighting in Germany and France, including in the Battle of the Bulge, Rich was awarded the Silver Star and the Bronze Star as well as France's Croix de Guerre. He later became the youngest adjutant general of the Utah National Guard, retiring as a major general. Maxwell Rich would end up being the last guardsman to lead the NRA as part of a long line of guardsmen that had begun with the New York National Guard's George Wood Wingate. A conservationist and member of the Association's old guard, Maxwell backed a plan to move NRA headquarters to new facilities with expansive gun ranges in the Colorado Rockies and New Mexico and leave Washington, D.C., for good—a plan that would soon come to enrage other NRA figures who were more concerned about gun rights and who wanted more, not less, of a presence in Washington.

In New York City in 1971 the mayor was John Lindsay. That summer he switched his party affiliation from Republican to Democratic as a first step in a planned campaign for president. Two weeks later Lindsay appealed to the Nixon administration and Attorney General John N. Mitchell to back laws to curb the flow of handguns into American cities. With that appeal Lindsay began making a case to a national audience that the 1968 act was too loose.

NRA leaders, meanwhile, now argued that the act was too strict. The *American Rifleman* began laying out the NRA's "principal objections" to it, arguing that the tight controls on the importation as well as on interstate transfers of weapons posed an inconvenience to law-abiding gun owners: "This means that a father who lives in Virginia could not give his adult son who resides in Pennsylvania a shotgun which has been in the family for years" without going through "a licensed dealer in Pennsylvania." In addition, military firearms, like the vintage Italian rifle bought by Oswald, could no longer be imported, even though "many so-called 'surplus' firearms make, or can be converted to, good, inexpensive target or hunting guns."

Only days before he made his appeal to Washington, Lindsay had attended the funeral of patrolman Kenneth Nugent, the ninth New York City police officer killed so far that year in the line of duty. Nugent died in Queens after he surprised three men robbing a luncheonette one Friday night. Across the nation, more than 560 policemen had been slain in the line of duty in the 1960s, three-fourths of them with handguns.

By then the "Saturday night special," a small-caliber weapon made of pot metal instead of tempered steel, seemed ubiquitous. "Notoriously inaccurate, such guns can cost as little as $1 to manufacture. They sell illegally on the street for as low as $5, although they usually go for $10 or $15. By contrast, a well-made pistol will cost upwards of $50 from a dealer," a *New York Times* article explained. In New York City, where since the Sullivan law was passed in 1911 handguns could only be purchased with a license and were largely restricted to law enforcement personnel (a situation that continues today), most of these cheap handguns had been legally purchased out of state and then illegally brought across state lines.

The pressure to regulate, if not eradicate, handguns opened a fault line within the NRA, one that had the potential to cleave the Association. In response, the NRA—still led by the old guard but under the increasing influence of newer, more strident voices—began to develop a narrative around the need for unity among gun owners. Then as now, maintaining the unity of gun owners in the face of gun control efforts meant that hunters, competitive shooters, sporting shooters, and those concerned with self-defense all had to be joined together against a common enemy. To allow nonsporting weapons to be distinguished from guns designed for hunting was to allow the possibility that these constituencies might splinter. As the *American Rifleman* put it in 1971: "There is already afoot a movement which would divide firearms ownership by passing laws directed against handguns, but not rifles or shotguns. . . . [We] need unity in the ranks of American firearms owners."

* * *

In its last years at the helm, the old guard of the NRA would add to the legacy of this singular institution in a way that may be surprising, even haunting, to ponder today. "Never before has the need for conservation, long recognized by the NRA, been so imperative to us all. And never before has the preservation of American concepts and ideals been more essential," read a statement of "Staff Officers" led by Executive Vice President Maxwell Rich. The same statement referenced the monitoring of "firearms legislative information," but still made no explicit mention of gun rights.

In the pages of the *American Rifleman* was coined the term "hunter-conservationist," and certain back issues of the magazine sound as "green" as the materials of any of the nation's then-emerging environmental groups. For example: "Today, with American industry, commerce and households annually dumping 360,000,000 tons of solid wastes and 200,000,000 tons of toxic chemicals and vapors into the air, the problem of preserving life extends to humans as well as wildlife."

The NRA's magazine revived the legacy of NRA life member and American president Theodore Roosevelt, profiling him as a "trail blazer among hunter-conservationists." The magazine also returned its gaze to the polar bear, reminding readers that the Association had "questioned the hunting of polar bears and other Arctic game from aircraft," as had grown common through the 1960s, "as contrary to the sportsman's creed of 'fair chase.'"

The NRA's ideal hunter-conservationist was a forward-thinker. "What to do or not to do about hunting is to some a part of a far bigger question raised by the soaring interest in environment, pollution, ecology," read an April 1971 article in the *American Rifleman* marking Earth Day. By 1975 the old guard even added the line "to promote good sportsmanship and to foster the conservation and wise use of our renewable wildlife resources" to the NRA's mission statement.

The *American Rifleman* warned about the ecological erosion of elephant grounds in Kenya. The publication reported on cooperation between the United States and Mexico on wildlife issues: "Joint teams will be formed to determine the present status of the Mexican grizzly bear, Mexican wolf, and jaguar, and to develop appropriate conservation measures. Each of these species has been extirpated over much of its former range." (The Mexican grizzly subsequently went extinct.) The NRA's first vice president during this period was C. R. "Pink" Gutermuth of Indiana, who served simultaneously as president of the Wildlife Management Institute, an established non-profit conservation group.

The NRA encouraged hunters to help game wardens crack down on poaching. "More and more American hunters are coming to realize that those who take game illegally are no better than common thieves," scolded the *American Rifleman*. "There is a gradual increase in the number of hunters who cooperate actively with game law enforcement officials to stop such thievery."

The NRA, much as it had done for hunter safety, launched a national program to facilitate the reporting of game law violations and related offenses. The Association published the "NRA Hunter's Code of Ethics," which included a pledge to "support conservation efforts."

In 1975, the Association announced it would host a three-week summer conservation camp for young people at its Outdoor Center in Raton, New Mexico.

One is left wondering what the Association's legacy might look like were it not for the events that would soon transpire in Cincinnati.

* * *

The national debate over handguns roiled on, ever louder. As the media continued to cover gun violence, the tone of the *American Rifleman* became increasingly hectoring. "On the evening of Nov. 1, millions of television viewers sitting in their homes were solemnly warned by Walter Cronkite of CBS that people who kept protection guns in their homes were more likely to shoot themselves or relatives than prowlers," complained the publication in 1971, saying Cronkite's evidence— which was based on Senate testimony by the head of the International Association of Chiefs of Police—was thin.

In this era the NRA, rather than simply shun allegedly unfriendly media, as it tends to do today, engaged with critics of all kinds. "Ann Landers, the syndicated sexpert, took another jab at guns recently and broadly missed a chance to say something constructive," commented the *American Rifleman* scornfully. "One of her always anonymous correspondents wrote a tearjerker saying that her parents died of murder-suicide by gun, her best friend committed suicide with a gun, and then her husband had an affair with a girl who threatened him with a gun—all very sad if true."

The NRA, besides doubting whether the "much-bereaved correspondent ever existed," said about Landers, "[t]his paragon of social wisdom suggested that the 50 or 60 million guns in private hands be bought up at $10 apiece (most are worth $50 to $150) in continuing her propaganda campaign against legitimate gun ownership."

On another occasion, the Association not only engaged with but even asked for the media's help. On CBS News in the summer of 1972, Senator Edward M. Kennedy challenged the NRA "'to develop its own educational program, so buyers of guns will have some certification to show they know how to use the weapons they buy.'" The NRA responded by declaring to all three networks "that it was ready, willing and able to teach firearms safety on a national scale" if the "television networks would cooperate" by providing a forum for this programming. The offer was not accepted.

The NRA leadership encouraged members to write to the Federal Communications Commission and complain that the biased coverage of gun issues by the networks was in violation of the Fairness Doctrine, at the time still in effect. The Association discussed as well whether to boycott the products of sponsors advertising on the same networks, and later suggested that NRA members and others should perhaps simply stop watching network news.

The pages of the *American Rifleman* began revisiting fears about communism first stoked in 1922, referring to a set of "rules" allegedly confiscated by Allied intelligence officers from a small communist action group in Germany after World War I purportedly showing that disarming people was part of a global communist plan. "Yet," lamented the magazine, "some U.S. Senators, Congressmen, officials and newspapers, notably including, of course, *The New York Times* and *The Washington Post*, have examined the rules and their background and pronounced them nothing more than pro-gun or right-wing propaganda."

More and more, the *American Rifleman* took sides in the cultural wars already separating the nation. "Nearly all the clamor for more gun control or gun bans comes from those who take a soft attitude toward Communism, toward marijuana and other drugs, and to what many old-line Americans regard as moral laxity."

* * *

It is illuminating to consider that the NRA—which would one day become the most vaunted and powerful of America's lobbyists—only became a registered lobby in 1974. "For the first time in its 103 years, the National Rifle Association recently registered in Washington, D.C., as a lobby. It did so to be able to counter effectively one of the most powerful anti-gun campaigns yet mounted, in the legislative halls and news media," read an article in the *American Rifleman* at the time.

The following year the NRA established an Institute for Legislative Action and made former NRA board member and past president Harlon Carter its executive director. It would be a momentous appointment. By then Carter was already the strongest advocate for gun rights within the Association, and he began trying to steer the NRA in a new direction. Within a year, the Institute for Legislative Action (NRA-ILA), as the Association's lobbying wing is still known, ran a double-page appeal to donors pointing out that NRA lobbying had helped defeat a federal bill that was intended to curb Saturday night specials but also would have declared illegal a Smith & Wesson K-38 Combat Masterpiece six-shot, double-action revolver.

The NRA's lobbying wing under Carter soon diversified, hiring two women and an African American man to represent the Association on Capitol Hill. They "were disarming new faces who destroyed stereotypes of NRA cynically fostered on the editorial pages of anti-gun newspapers such as the *Washington Post*," according to the NRA's second authorized history, *NRA: An American Legend*. The African American was Peter S. Ridley, an attorney and former army captain and Vietnam War veteran who had earned the Bronze Star; his American University law school alma mater still gives scholarships to African American students in his honor.

By this point the tensions between the old guard of NRA leadership, represented by Maxwell Rich, and the new guard, represented by Carter and Knox, were mounting. The more traditionally minded leaders wanted to expand the NRA's role as the nation's leading shooting organization and combine that with a focus on "activities like camping and wilderness survival training; conservation education; environmental awareness." They were even thinking of calling the proposed National Shooting Center in the Rocky Mountains the National Outdoor Center to make its appeal all the broader.

This was treason in the eyes of Carter and his allies on the board and staff, including Knox, and they began plotting a coup. But the old guard knew they were facing what was now an open struggle for power, and so late one Saturday afternoon in November 1976, in what became known as the "Weekend Massacre," Executive Vice President Maxwell Rich fired eighty employees, most of whom were allies of Carter. Carter himself, as the NRA lobbying chief, was too powerful to fire. But he resigned in protest.

Only the spring before, at the 1976 NRA annual meeting in Indianapolis (the last one to uphold the old guard), Carter had given his first major speech to the floor. Already leading the Association in a new direction, he emphasized the notion that a person is innocent until proven guilty, along with the idea that gun control could lead to overreaching government enforcement:

> There will be an awakening of the people to the dangers of impairing or perhaps losing the presumption that a man is innocent and may not be penalized until proven guilty of an offense, and of jeopardy of the Fifth Amendment right against self-incrimination. And there is a grave danger in gun control proposals, which presuppose the creation of a national gun control police force far larger than the FBI.

In his last point, Carter was picking up where NRA cofounder William Conant Church had begun more than a century before, defending the need for state control of militias as a check on federal power. Carter thus picked up an old line of thinking within the

Association's arc and gave it a tight new twist. In the early 1970s, more than ever before, Carter and a few more like-minded NRA leaders began to identify federal government agencies and their armed agents as a potential threat to the freedom of gun owners and the very liberty of the nation.

One particular incident seemed to validate their point. Kenyon Ballew was a gun collector in Maryland who was shot in the head and left paralyzed and further impaired during a botched raid by Treasury Department agents from the Alcohol, Tobacco and Firearms Division. One NRA board member who was also editor of the *Manchester Union Leader* wrote an article titled "Treasury Gestapo at Work" for that paper. Ballew, who had fired upon the armed agents with an antique revolver after they broke down the door and barged in, later sued the Treasury Department, but lost in court.

By then the NRA was already crafting another new narrative, one asserting that the right to bear arms is older than the Second Amendment. It was also arguing that both this "God-given right" and the Second Amendment protected an individual, as opposed to just a collective right to keep arms—a view upheld more than forty years later by the Roberts Supreme Court. By the winter of 1977, the new guard was looming, preparing to make its move at the spring meeting in Cincinnati.

"There have been charges that the National Rifle Association is being 'subverted'—that it is turning its back on the NRA Institute for Legislative Action—and abandoning its fight against gun control," read an unsigned editorial in the *American Rifleman* on the very eve of the convention. The old guard, knowing they were facing a challenge, asked NRA past president and board member Irvine Porter, from Alabama, to hold the gavel and preside in Cincinnati. They trusted Porter to ensure the meeting would be conducted according to NRA bylaws, which was unfortunate for them, because Knox knew these laws better than anyone else.

While Carter served as the leader whom the rebels wanted in power, it was Knox who was the architect of their revolution. He had used his columns in independent or non-NRA gun magazines to mobilize more than five hundred longtime NRA members who were eligible to vote and get them to travel to Cincinnati. There an army of his lieutenants, all wearing yellow tags indicating they were members of his faction, called "Federation for NRA," and carrying walkie-talkies, spread out among attendees on the convention floor, directing blocs of their loyalists how to vote.

They needed guidance, as some of the votes were on confusing procedural motions engineered by Knox to strip the old guard of its power. By sticking to the bylaws, Knox ended up making Irvine Porter a de facto ally; Porter's son Jim Porter, who would become NRA president in 2013, would later praise his father's historic role in support of the revolt. But Knox, a meticulous planner who rarely missed a trick, first pummeled the old guard with unexpected evidence of their alleged disloyalty to the Association.

"The event took on a Watergate-like atmosphere," reported *The New York Times*. The rebels used their motions to introduce secretly recorded conversations between themselves and members of the old guard. They revealed alleged financial improprieties that centered around the old guard's spending for the Association's planned move out of Washington to the Rockies to return the NRA to its roots in marksmanship and recreational shooting, and on what they claimed showed even worse disloyalty—the old guard's support for a gun control project led by the National Education Association. Knox and his lieutenants then went after every leader of the old guard one by one, including the EVP of the past seven years, Maxwell Rich.

"The effects were stunning: almost the entire NRA headquarters leadership was ousted, and Harlon B. Carter," then the Association's chief lobbyist, "was installed in NRA's top salaried post," reported the *American Rifleman* in the monthly magazine's July 1977 issue, which featured Carter's smiling image on the cover. "He had a shaved head ('bullet-headed' was one description) and vaguely resembled Nikita Khrushchev," reported *The Washington Post* decades later. "Concerned NRA Members Redirect Their Association" was how the *American Rifleman* more soberly characterized the meeting.

"The sweeping changes voted today were the result of a well-planned and executed strategy whose principal developer was Neal Knox, editor of *Rifle* magazine and *Handloader* magazine," reported *The New York Times*. The meeting became a marathon eight-hour session that began after dinner on a Saturday night and did not end until after three in the morning. In the end, "a crowd of well over 2,000 NRA members including more than 1,100 voting Life Members" permanently shifted the Association's life arc.

"When it was all over," the effort "had demonstrated the power of grass-roots organization, parliamentary skill, and a clear sense of purpose," approvingly noted the *American Rifleman*.

The rebels' voting blocs also approved changes in the Association's bylaws that for the first time in the history of the NRA gave voting members more direct power (although not all the changes would last). In fact, it was Knox's clever use of parliamentary procedure in changing the bylaws that enabled him to direct the vote to replace the old guard with Carter and soon also himself. In floor votes, Knox's bloc first passed an amendment affording the membership the power to fire the Association's professional or paid executive officers, and then voted to fire them. NRA past president Irvine Porter, presiding over the meeting, approved their floor motions and votes toward power.

"I have the distinct honor of being the first legacy president of the NRA, following my father, Irvine Porter, into the office 53 years after he held the chair," wrote outgoing NRA president James W. Porter II in May 2015. "Dad was one of 15 individuals to receive the NRA's highest honor, Honorary Life Membership. In 1977, in Cincinnati, when the members of our association re-established the core mission of NRA as safeguarding the Second Amendment above all else, my father chaired that historic assemblage."

The changes made at the meeting allowed for the nomination of board members by a petition of 250 voting members, provided that the Nominating Committee for NRA board elections be appointed by the board rather than by the NRA president, and mandated that at least three life members be voted onto the Nominating Committee, instead of having the Nominating Committee consist of just board members. Finally, the rebels tightened the bylaws to make it harder to change them thereafter, preempting future challengers. This was the start of practices that would be followed, if not strengthened further, by the leadership in the future.

Harlon Carter made his way to the rostrum to address the crowd after his election as the NRA's new leader. "I'm going to tell you one thing—that beginning in this place and this hour, this period in NRA history is finished. There will be no more civil war in the National Rifle Association," he said. Carter's remarks, reported the *American Rifleman*, "were greeted by a tumultuous ovation."

Seven

A GREAT RELIGION

Harlon Carter's victory in Cincinnati led to the largest reorganization of the National Rifle Association of America in its history. Out of it was forged the modern NRA.

Once in power, the rebels who had won revealed characteristics not uncommon to revolutionaries. The top man, in this case Carter, acquired more personal power than the predecessor he overthrew. He wielded this power to appoint his three closest associates to run the organization: Gary Anderson, a two-time Olympic gold-medal-winning rifleman, in charge of general operations; a big-game hunter, George Martin, as head of NRA publications; and gun rights advocate Neal Knox as the head of the lobbying institute. As with other revolutions, however, power proved "sticky": Carter was subsequently reelected executive vice president three years in a row. And, as in other revolutions, norms were upended: in 1981 Carter's supporters changed the organization's bylaws to elect him to an unprecedented five-year term.

And, not unlike in other revolutions, the new leaders soon turned on each other.

* * *

Carter and Knox were sixty-three and forty-one years old, respectively, in the spring of 1977 when they launched the NRA's gun rights revolt. Each defined himself as being uncompromising on the issue. Although Knox grew even more strident as he aspired to greater power over the Association, Carter, in his role as what was effectively the NRA's CEO, sought to find the right balance between ideology and pragmatism.

Knox recruited an assistant, Tanya Metaksa, a formidable lobbyist who would remain Knox's ally for a time before turning against him. Within eleven months, Metaksa—"That's *a-k* as in AK-47, and *s-a* as in semiautomatic" is how she introduced herself to reporters—hired a few young men. One of them was a former educator from New York and Virginia named Wayne LaPierre. He had also done a short stint as an aide to a Democratic representative in the Virginia statehouse, where he first worked on gun legislation.

Carter and his men remade the NRA—by then more than 106 years old—as a gun rights organization. And, as with any revolution, it is always illuminating to look at propaganda. The rebels who took over in 1977 soon gave the *American Rifleman* a makeover. Executive Vice President Harlon Carter's name became the only one at the top of the masthead, and the mission statement was replaced. Gone was the sentiment that NRA's purpose was to promote the accurate, efficient, and safe use of small arms for pleasure and protection among citizens, and to promote shooting skills among law enforcement agencies and the military. It was replaced by one proclaiming the NRA as "the foremost guardian of the traditional American right to 'keep and bear arms.'"

The editor of both the *American Rifleman* and the *American Hunter* until the end of 1976 had been Ashley Halsey Jr., an erudite writer who had come from the *Saturday Evening Post*. He left just as the war for control was escalating. Now every editor who survived was placed under the control of Carter ally George Martin, who ensured that no story contradicted the modern NRA's new views about gun rights.

The green-leaning "hunter-conservationist" angle grew harder to find. For a few years one might still see stories, especially in the *American Hunter*, on the restoration of game such as wild turkeys, or why human feeding of deer does more harm than good. But a reader would also see other stories seemingly incongruous with a hunter-conservationist view, such as one promoting the shooting of crows—an animal rarely killed for its meat—in Oklahoma and Texas. Or another story about using big handguns—like a .357 or .44 Magnum revolver, weapons an earlier generation of NRA leaders said should be restricted to police—to hunt deer. Articles like "Horsebackpack Hunting" soon gave way to articles about hunting with 4-wheel-drive vehicles.

In order to grow its membership and keep its members happy, the new leadership offered not just discounted insurance plans for guns but also health insurance options for members and their families—even including an option paying out in case of cancer. And the NRA lobbied Congress to sell surplus M1 Garand military rifles—which, by time of the Vietnam War, had been displaced by the standard-issue M16—to NRA members at discounted prices.

More important, in both the *American Rifleman* and its sister publication, the *American Hunter*, launched several years before, the new guard added a new section called "NRA Official Journal." While political updates and gun rights editorials had always been part of each magazine's editorial mix, the new section focused entirely on politics. At ten or more pages, the entire section was eventually set apart with colored or marked pages to make it easier for readers of either magazine to find.

During this period, the Cincinnati Revolt gave way to a radical experiment in member-driven, grassroots democracy within the nonprofit, nongovernmental Association. Different factions soon emerged, trying to influence eligible members to vote for their candidates for the NRA board. Beginning a pattern that would continue to the present day, there was little or no daylight between the factions when it came to gun rights. Instead the splits revolved around personalities and who would end up on top. Indeed, Neal Knox soon began mobilizing a movement that would allow him to take control.

But one clue that this would be a short-lived experiment was the disappearance of an item that had appeared yearly in the *American Rifleman* since 1926, but which now simply vanished, never to be seen again in any NRA magazine or online media outlet: the annual financial reports of the Association. With this, the NRA began another pattern, that of withholding information from its own members.

* * *

The "NRA Official Journal" section was compiled under the direction of the Association's new operations chief, Gary Anderson. In 1963 he had received the first United States Distinguished International Shooter Badge from President John F. Kennedy, and the White House ceremony had been attended by the NRA's executive vice president, Franklin Orth, then also serving as president of the U.S. Olympic Committee—the same Orth who five years later led the NRA to cooperate with Senator Dodd on gun control. Anderson had shot for Olympic gold in Tokyo in 1964 and in Mexico City in 1968, then won three NRA National Highpower Championships at Camp Perry in 1973, 1975, and 1976. Yet, notwithstanding his ties to the old guard, Anderson, like Carter's two other lieutenants, George Martin and Neal Knox, shared Carter's unyielding view on gun rights.

"Unyielding" indeed was Carter's preferred term. Full-throated and charismatic, Carter's writings and oratory spoke directly to the rank and file of the Association's members, telling them that it was *their* NRA. Two independent gun rights groups had emerged in the 1970s, the Citizens Committee for the Right to Keep and Bear Arms and Gun Owners of America, formed in opposition to the Gun Control Act of 1968. But the shift led by Carter in 1977 made the NRA the nation's largest gun rights vanguard literally overnight. Under his tutelage, membership rose, too—the Association claimed it had nearly doubled since 1975, reaching 1.7 million by 1980. Carter told members their gun rights were at risk in a way previous leaders hadn't. This view within the organization of being pinned in a corner, threatened by an unfriendly press and by government interference, soon became axiomatic.

A year after the Cincinnati Revolt, at the next NRA annual meeting in Salt Lake City, the Board of Directors had again relied upon the elder statesman Irvine Porter, who had been made chairman of the Nominating Committee, to preside over the elections of paid executive officers. Porter stepped onto the podium to nominate candidates for the NRA's executive positions, starting with the post of executive vice president. "That nominee was, of course, Harlon B. Carter to be returned," reported the *Rifleman*. "A standing and jubilant ovation followed Carter's unanimous election."

Porter went on to nominate the other incumbents, who, like Carter, were reelected one after the other by acclamation. "There is no substitute among men for the quality of decision, or for courage," Carter said about his team, receiving another standing ovation.

Next it was Carter's lieutenant, NRA chief lobbyist Neal Knox, who came onto the podium. Speaking with the twang of a man from the Cross Timbers region of the central Oklahoma and Texas plains, Knox, with only a touch of irony, greeted the seated members with "Good evening, gun lobby."

Four years after being first elected EVP of the NRA as the crowning act of the Cincinnati Revolt, Carter, after being confronted with evidence by United Press International and *The New York Times*, finally admitted that he had been arrested, tried, and convicted of Casiano's murder fifty years before, and then had that conviction overturned on appeal.

"I continue to regret the incident deeply as would anyone where a fatality is involved," he said in a statement released in 1981 by his office at the NRA.

* * *

These early years of the NRA's gun rights revolution established the creed, ethos, and practices that have persisted to this day, and perhaps even been strengthened. One of the first issues taken up by the new guard provides a window into their expansive vision of gun rights, going far beyond where the Association had gone before, and with implications beyond gun ownership.

During President Jimmy Carter's administration, NRA lobbying chief Neal Knox testified twice in the House against the placing of taggants, or chemical markers, in explosive or combustible agents, including black and smokeless gunpowder. Such taggants allow authorities to trace their origin or manufacturer in case of their misuse. Knox testified that taggants are expensive, unreliable, and an incomplete anti-terrorist measure. "Knox pointed out that bombs can be rigged using either gasoline or nitro methane, both available in quantities too large to tag, and exploded without a commercial booster," reported the "NRA Official Journal" in the *American Rifleman*.

Neither Knox nor the *American Rifleman*, however, explained the real, gun-rights-related reason the NRA opposed the use of taggants, which was that they could be used to trace the origins of smokeless or black gunpowder used by gun owners who hand-load their own ammunition—part of a long tradition in gun circles documented by the *American Rifleman* since the early 1920s. Through the use of taggants the federal government could conceivably track gun owners through the gunpowder in their hand-loaded ammunition.

In the spring of 2013, more than thirty years after Knox's testimony, two improvised explosive devices made with black powder packed with BBs, nails, and pellets into a pressure cooker with a simple detonator killed three people and wounded several hundred more, including sixteen people who lost limbs, along the path of the Boston Marathon. Within days authorities identified two suspects, a pair of brothers, through surveillance footage. But had there been no footage, it likely would have been more difficult to identify the perpetrators, as there were no taggants to trace in the black powder they used. This is directly due to efforts by the NRA that began with Knox's testimony to Congress.

* * *

The rebels, having taken control of the Association, soon recruited politicians across the nation to support their revolution, beginning the practice of having electoral candidates speak at NRA annual meetings. "[S]even key pro-gun legislators" addressed NRA members at the 1978 annual meeting in Salt Lake City, as the Association made inroads, especially into the GOP. They included Senators James A. McClure, Orrin Hatch, and Ted Stevens, Republicans from Idaho, Utah, and Alaska, respectively, each of whom would become invaluable allies of the NRA's new guard. Senator Stevens would later join the NRA's board. Senator Robert Dole, Republican of Kansas and future presidential candidate, and his wife, Elizabeth Dole, also attended the meeting and were photographed with Executive Vice President Carter. Senator Dole warned a room of gun collectors that President Carter's administration had a "backdoor campaign to make gun ownership not worth the trouble."

Carter and Knox shared the goal of repealing the Gun Control

Act of 1968, which had given rise to the Cincinnati Revolt, and they knew they would need more allies in Washington to prevail. Among Neal Knox's many contributions to the success of the modern NRA were his efforts as the head of NRA-ILA, the NRA's lobbying wing, to endorse Ronald Reagan for president in the 1980 election. But, much like other NRA leaders today, Knox soon found himself a victim of his own success.

Two months into President Reagan's first term, a disturbed man attempting to impress a female celebrity shot and wounded the president with a Saturday night special, a German .22-caliber blue steel revolver, and wounded three others, including Reagan's press secretary, James Brady, leaving him permanently impaired. The NRA reacted cautiously, not directly responding itself but having an ally make its case instead, and in doing so laying out the basic principles of the Association's new creed. It was not an NRA official but the Republican governor of Oregon, Vic Atiyeh, an NRA life member, who was quoted by The Associated Press in newspapers across the country saying, "In every instance in which we find such a terrible act taking place, gun control itself would not have made a difference."

The assassination attempt opened up a fissure among Republican leaders. James Brady remained permanently incapacitated. His wife, Sarah Brady, a former official of the Republican National Committee, joined the group Handgun Control Inc., which began recruiting supporters on Capitol Hill for a bill to regulate access to handguns and other firearms.

While Carter was interested in working with a wide swath of leaders, including relative moderates such as Kansas senator Bob Dole, Knox clashed with nearly anyone who did not share his own zealotry for gun rights. He revived his old faction, "Federation for NRA," the same group that had brought him and Carter to power in Cincinnati. Another group, called Patriots for NRA, appeared to oppose Knox.

Carter himself lamented the "bitterly-partisan, campaign-type" of infighting. After the 1982 annual meeting in Philadelphia, where he alone was recognized as "the symbol of the struggle against oppressive firearms legislation," Carter fired Knox as NRA chief lobbyist. Carter himself had proved resilient and still popular; even after the news broke that he had once been convicted for murder, his supporters changed the NRA bylaws to vote him a five-year term.

The NRA's new leaders knew full well that their success depended on generating more of two things: members and revenues. The Association's claimed membership grew threefold during Carter's tenure, reaching 3 million by 1984. The year before, Carter had shared the stage in Phoenix with President Ronald Reagan, who became the first sitting president to attend an NRA convention. Reagan and Carter were pictured together on the cover of the *American Rifleman*.

Carter chose a man named J. Warren Cassidy, a former insurance salesman and U.S. Marine who had more recently served as mayor of the city of Lynn, Massachusetts, to run the Institute for Legislative Action. Another beneficiary was Wayne LaPierre. At thirty-four, he was now second-in-command of the NRA's lobbying wing.

At the same meeting in Phoenix in 1983, fourteen new directors were elected to the board. One was a thirty-seven-year-old congressman representing western Idaho, Larry Craig. A family rancher and a former private first class in the Idaho Army National Guard, Craig would go on to become a United States senator. Another was a forty-four-year-old small-framed woman from Florida named Marion P. Hammer. Born in South Carolina into a family of subsistence farmers and hunters, Hammer would eventually become not only the NRA's first woman president but one of the organization's most formidable figures ever. She was also—crucially, it would turn out—an ally of Neal Knox, who in his former position of power had authorized a grant to support her fledgling gun rights group in Florida.

Later that same year Wayne LaPierre was authorized by Carter to write a letter to members asking them to support the Firearms Owners' Protection Act—now cosponsored in the House by a Democratic congressman from Missouri, Harold Volkmer—by writing letters to their own representatives. This began a practice that would grow exponentially and ultimately prove invaluable to the NRA's long-term success.

The NRA also established two tax-exempt structures that for the first time allowed it to accept funds from donors, including gun manufacturers, as reported by the *American Rifleman*. One, eventually named the NRA Civil Rights Defense Fund, was designed "to defend gun owners" who use their weapons in self-defense. As of this writing, these nonprofit entities associated with the NRA (which is still chartered in New York) are under investigation by the state of New York over matters including alleged tax evasion.

* * *

Carter was in command, but Neal Knox was not about to go away. Just one year after being fired, Knox used his columns in *Guns and Ammo* and other gun glossies to successfully campaign to get himself elected to the NRA's Board of Directors—made easier in part because of bylaw changes allowing members to vote by mail. From there he continued his "one-man lobbying effort against the amended McClure-Volkmer Bill," which Knox claimed was bad for gun rights but which Carter supported.

Within a year the board voted forty-five to twenty-four to expel Knox, making him the first NRA director ousted by fellow directors in the Association's 113-year history. Before the vote, Knox was excoriated on the floor by a fellow board member and gun rights activist named Allan D. Cors. "'Neal, you have caused irrevocable harm to this organization,' Cors said, his voice quavering," reported the *American Rifleman*. "'I don't know why you do it,' Cors added, looking directly at Knox."

In 1985 Senator McClure introduced a marked-up version of the federal firearms act, backed by others including Senator Orrin Hatch of Utah. In the House, Representative John Dingell, a Democratic representing Dearborn and other parts of Michigan, who had been elected to the NRA board in 1968—supported parallel legislation in the House to reform the act. A big-game hunter, Dingell would for years be one of the NRA's best allies on Capitol Hill during a time when the organization sought support from both major parties. Crucial to this outreach was the ILA's Wayne LaPierre.

LaPierre had worked at the NRA's lobbying arm under Knox and Metaksa since 1978. Named after his father, an accountant for General Electric, LaPierre was born in Schenectady, New York, in November 1949. A descendant of seventeenth-century French immigrants from Brittany, LaPierre was the younger of two children and was raised Catholic and attended two colleges run by priests. His family arrived in Virginia during segregation in the 1950s, when LaPierre was five. "LaPierre father and son would attend all-black high school football games on Thursday nights, the only evening when the white schools did not use the stadium," the *Los Angeles Times* reported in a 1995 profile of LaPierre.

He studied political science at Siena College, a Franciscan school, choosing a college back near where he was born, and graduated in 1972. Although eligible for the draft once he turned eighteen, LaPierre received a student deferment after enrolling at Siena College, a common occurrence at the time, and later a medical one, although the reason was never specified.

LaPierre volunteered for the ill-fated 1972 presidential campaign of Democrat George McGovern, a fact he managed to keep out of the press until *The New York Times* reported it in 2013. It can only be inferred that the twenty-three-year-old LaPierre identified with the campaign's anti-war, anti-poverty platform. LaPierre then attended Boston College, a Jesuit university (and my undergraduate alma mater), where he earned a master's degree in political science in 1975, concentrating on American government and politics.

He began his professional career as a substitute special education teacher, first in Troy, New York, and then in Roanoke, Virginia. "I concluded that a lot needs to be done to give those kids hope," he said in a rare interview in 1995 for the *Los Angeles Times* profile. In 1977 LaPierre became a legislative aide in Richmond to State Representative Vic Thomas, a Democrat representing Virginia's Seventh District, which included Roanoke. It was here that he first worked on firearms legislation before being hired by Metaksa.

Described as shy, soft-spoken, and sometimes absent-minded, LaPierre, who had little more than a pedestrian knowledge of firearms himself, excelled as a political strategist: he knew how to read a room, and he could navigate the labyrinth of a legislative body. His acumen was complemented by his charm, as LaPierre became known for being gracious in person even with his antagonists. He worked to make friends, avoiding confrontations, and it served him well.

* * *

No one had more influence in establishing the NRA as the vanguard of the nation's gun rights movement than Harlon Carter. After riding the crest of the Cincinnati Revolt, Carter centralized power within the leadership, eventually lending his clout to change the bylaws as a way of deterring future challenges to their control. He argued more strongly than any other NRA leader before him that gun owners must be given a robust defense whenever they use their arms for protection, and that the federal government itself posed a threat to gun owners. He saw gun rights as being part of the culture wars and a struggle going beyond gun ownership—much as the NRA does today.

In the spring of 1984, Carter informed the board that, out of def-
erence to his wife, he wished to retire to Arizona even though he
had more than one year still left in his five-year term. According to
the bylaws, his ally Gary Anderson, the Olympic gold medalist and
NRA operations chief, was next in line until an election could be
held. But Anderson declined the post, so the board, instead of using its
own Nominating Committee, at Carter's suggestion hired an outside
consulting firm, Ackerman McQueen, to search for suitable candidates. Although no one knew it at the time, Ackerman McQueen
would end up playing an even greater role over time.

Ackerman McQueen recommended, and the board chose, G. Ray
Arnett, an assistant secretary of the interior for fish, wildlife and
parks who was also a personal friend of President Reagan. He was
made acting executive vice president, and at the 1985 annual convention in Seattle, board member Alice Bull nominated him to assume the position on a full-time basis. Another director nominated
Neal Knox, who of course had already been expelled from the board.
Arnett won his five-year term by a landslide, 2,014 to 881.

Then NRA board member Joe Foss, a World War II Marine
fighter pilot who had received the nation's highest honor, the Medal
of Honor, for his role in providing air support for the Guadalcanal
Campaign in the Pacific, introduced a motion to postpone indefi-
nitely a proposed suite of mostly petty bylaw amendments that had
been introduced by Knox's allies, led by Metaksa, in an effort to
strengthen Knox's hand. The motion passed, stymieing Knox again.

But Knox, nothing if not dogged, would soon try again.

* * *

In certain ways the incoming NRA executive vice president, Arnett,
and the new president, Howard W. Pollock, seemed like throw-
backs to an earlier era of public service and conservation. Arnett

had served two terms as president of the National Wildlife Federation and had been director of California's fish and game department under Governor Reagan. He belonged to a half dozen other conservation groups, including Ducks Unlimited and Game Conservation International. Arnett had also served as a Marine in the Pacific during World War II and in the Korean War. Pollock was a lawyer and former congressional representative from Alaska who had been wounded as a seaman in World War II.

In truth, neither of these men was a hunter-conservationist of the first rank. "Arnett was known in hunting circles as a 'slob hunter,' one who placed conservation and the standards of ethical hunting second to his own personal enjoyment," wrote Josh Sugarmann, a former journalist and leader of a research-oriented gun control NGO. In the fall of 1985, Arnett was in a motorized boat being filmed for an "I'm the NRA" television commercial. Game wardens observed him fire at clapper rails (birds also known as marsh hens) while his motorboat was under power—violating federal game laws, along with the NRA's own Hunting Code of Ethics. He ended up paying a $125 fine.

The year before, NRA president Pollock and four others were cited by game wardens in Delaware for hunting waterfowl in an area that had been baited with more than two hundred pounds of cracked corn, in violation of federal game laws. The defendants, including Pollock, got the violation overturned on appeal. The lead U.S. agent on the case later complained, "I know of no judicial district in which these defendants would not be charged."

* * *

Despite the turmoil, during this period the NRA was successful on its own terms, and especially in its legislative goals. Wayne LaPierre was largely responsible for this success. Even though he was still only second-in-command of the lobbying wing, it was he who had guided passage of the Firearms Owners' Protection Act.

"You have been on board this ship since it left port, Captain. It must feel nice to finally bring her home," wrote Senator Orrin Hatch in a personal letter to LaPierre. The Firearms Owners' Protection Act passed the Senate in the summer of 1985 and the House by spring of the following year. Over the winter, LaPierre was promoted to executive director of the Institute for Legislative Action. After the bill became law, LaPierre was photographed in a celebratory pose with Senators Hatch and Dole, and shaking the hand of President Reagan.

The Firearms Owners' Protection Act reversed some but not all the provisions of the Gun Control Act passed eighteen years before. It included four major changes favored by the NRA. First, it re-legalized the interstate sale of long guns, such as rifles and shotguns, under a number of limitations. It required that the sale comply with the laws of the home jurisdictions of both the buyer and the seller, and that the weapons be shipped through federally licensed dealers (that is, unless the buyer and seller from different states were to physically meet to conduct the transfer in person). Background checks were required only for those sales made through licensed dealers. This proviso remains in effect.

Second, the 1986 act removed the requirements for record-keeping by ammunition dealers and also allowed for mail-order sales of ammunition (with the exception of some types of armor-piercing ammunition).

Third, the act loosened regulation of federally licensed firearms dealers, limiting unannounced inspections by federal officials to no more than one a year, imposing a higher standard of proof for demonstrating violations, and reducing penalties if a dealer was found in violation.

Fourth, the act explicitly forbade any government entity from creating a list or registry of gun owners using records from licensed

dealers, and also forbade "the establishment of any system of registration of firearms, firearm owners, or firearm transactions." This
provision in particular lent the NRA a bona fide victory that ended
up being far more important than it looked, as the same seemingly
symbolic language buried in the law erected an inviolable barrier to
any future gun control in America modeled upon the kind of controls in place today in every other developed nation on the planet.
Never since has a sitting president raised the issue of a federal registry for firearms.

The act also included one eleventh-hour provision: it banned the
production and sale of new machine guns to civilians, making it
unlawful—with some exceptions—to possess or transfer fully automatic weapons. This measure was the result of a last-minute amendment introduced by New Jersey Democratic congressman William
Hughes, and LaPierre himself quietly supported this provision to
make sure the bill passed. This provision, too, is still on the books,
and it means that machine guns may be sold only to the military or
law enforcement agencies, and may be kept by only a relatively few
civilians with de facto grandfathered licenses.

Three months after allowing the amendment through without
applying any pressure, LaPierre announced the NRA would now
make repealing the machine gun ban "a top priority." The Institute
for Legislative Action weighed in as well. "The National Rifle Association supports the right of law-abiding individuals to choose to
own any firearm, including automatic firearms," read an NRA-ILA
statement. "The Second Amendment is not limited by its language to
the type of arms which the people have a right to own." Knox never
forgave LaPierre for this mistake, and he always made it clear that
when the time was right, the ban on fully automatic weapons must
be repealed.

Such a position would have been inconceivable coming from the
old guard, but it was consistent with the new guard's vision that cit-

izens require unlimited firepower in small arms or handheld weapons to both exercise and, if necessary, defend their gun rights. Yet the same NRA—much to the chagrin of the most unyielding gun rights activists—never compelled any lawmaker to even introduce a bill that would re-legalize fully automatic weapons. This kind of pragmatism on LaPierre's part would soon be wielded by Knox against him.

* * *

The very morning after the 1986 act finally cleared Congress, following nine years of struggle, Arnett fired the entire staff of the NRA's public education section, ordering all fifteen employees to clear out their desks by noon. Their duties were being transferred to the outside public relations firm Ackerman McQueen—the same firm that had recommended Arnett's hire.

The tension that led to the mass dismissal was over the promotion of a woman. One of NRA EVP Ray Arnett's frequent traveling companions was a competitive clay target shooter named Tracey Attlee. "Both . . . denied rumors that their relationship was anything more than a friendship based on a common love of shooting," reported Josh Sugarmann. Arnett eventually promoted Attlee out of the public education division to the eighth floor of executive suites, putting her in charge of publicity for international shooting competitions and giving her a salary more than 50 percent higher than was authorized for the position. It was not long after the section head complained that Arnett fired him and his staff.

By then Arnett had made other enemies as well. These included a married couple, Theodore and Francoise Gianoutsos, who were NRA benefactor members. Theodore Gianoutsos had in fact been a whistleblower at the Interior Department under Arnett, bringing attention to allegations that Assistant Secretary Arnett had engaged in financial mismanagement. Within the NRA, the same couple organized a petition to recall Arnett over matters including his citation for violating game laws. Even his ally Pollock could not help him, as it was the NRA president who had informed Arnett that he was being charged with six general categories of abuse of power, failure to comply with board directives, and negligence.

Arnett was suspended without pay. His top three aides were let go as well, including his chief of staff, Morton C. Mumma III, along with Tracey Attlee. Eight of the fifteen formerly fired employees were reinstated, either in other divisions of the Association or as staff members at the outside agency Ackerman McQueen—by now already well on its way to becoming nearly an in-house wing of the NRA.

Neither the *American Rifleman* nor the *American Hunter* ever mentioned a word of any of this. Nor did Arnett refer to this in his final message in the *American Rifleman*, in which he conveyed his "best wishes for continued success, good hunting and good shooting." Most NRA members were left wondering what happened.

Following Arnett's ouster, the leadership promoted Warren Cassidy, the chief lobbyist who had taken over the ILA after the firing of Knox, to be the acting NRA executive vice president. Four months after that, the board nominated Cassidy to fill the vacancy permanently, and he was later elected by the members.

Carter, out of office but still exercising power thanks to a lifetime post on the Executive Council, decided it was time for a change. Continuing to vest electoral power in the membership had become too unpredictable. The NRA's experiment in grassroots democracy would come to a close ten years after it began, and Harlon Carter would be largely responsible for both beginning the experiment and shutting it down. In 1987 the organization managed to pass bylaw amendments to return the election of the executive vice president from the membership to the board. Carter and Cassidy together had outmaneuvered Knox.

Yet EVP Cassidy would soon face his own challenges. A veteran employee who was also an NRA life member filed a civil suit over alleged sex discrimination. He denied the allegation. The Association ended up settling with the employee out of court.

Cassidy was accused of other misdeeds, including by a former NRA spokesman who charged that he was responsible for "a host of unprecedented legislative, financial and program fiascos."

Indeed, it could be argued that the NRA of the late 1980s was an organization beginning to decline. The momentum of the 1986 legislative victory had faded quickly. The NRA lost a quarter million members between 1986 and 1990. By the early 1990s, "the NRA spent about $60 million more than it took in, depleting its ready assets from $102 million to $40 million."

All this proved beneficial for Knox. He was again using his own gun magazine columns to try to build a personal following that would help get him back on the NRA board.

* * *

Harlon Carter, still occasionally writing in the *American Rifleman*, sometimes addressed other matters—not unlike one of his predecessors, C. B. Lister. Take, for example, his column on the "war on drugs." Beginning with the premise that "there is no link between possession and use of drugs and the use and possession of guns," Carter volunteered a plan to win the war on drugs.

"Weaklings will consider it tough, but it is humane," he wrote in September 1989. "The emergency powers of the president should be invoked. . . . Let us temporarily suspend the privilege of the writ of habeas corpus as done by President Lincoln during the War Between the States and after his death by the authorization of Congress." Suspected drug traffickers "would be arrested without warrant" and delivered "to a place prepared for internment . . . located in the desert . . .

surrounded by double rows of concertina wire . . . with lookout towers, armed guards and searchlights."

Between the concertina fences "would be a patrol of trained Doberman pinschers. . . . No access would be permitted attorneys, congressmen or sob-sisters . . . except at some time in the future as the victorious end of the drug war would permit." The incarcerated would be segregated by gender, with isolation available for "trouble makers." "There would be no limit to the number of internees. Space for expanding numbers would be easily and economically provided by more concertina and more acres. . . . There would be no limit to 'wilding' in the desert inside the concertina."

Many thoughts and questions may spring to mind when reading this passage. Among them surely is the strangeness of the notion that to be free of detainment without a warrant is a privilege, while having access to the unlimited firepower of small arms is a right.

* * *

In January 1989, eight months before Carter's column on the war on drugs and during President Reagan's last three days in office, a man described as a drifter, armed with a semiautomatic version of a Chinese-made Kalashnikov military rifle, killed five schoolchildren and wounded thirty-two others in Stockton, California. Most of the victims were from refugee families from the Southeast Asian war-torn nations of Vietnam and Cambodia. The shooter had been arrested two years before for shooting a semiautomatic pistol along with his half brother while carrying a book about the Aryan Nations in the Eldorado National Forest in California's Sierra Nevada.

The NRA was slow to respond to the Stockton tragedy. One NRA lobbyist in California concentrated in his public response on the resolve of the NRA's own members to protect their guns. "A lot of these people take it very seriously," David Marshall told The Associated

Press. "It's a very important part of their lives." Two weeks later a higher-ranking NRA official responded. "We share the grief of the tragedy in Stockton," NRA lobbyist James Baker told The Associated Press. "But the answer does not lie in restricting the rights of law-abiding citizens. The answer lies in getting criminals off the streets."

Not everyone was satisfied with the NRA's position. "I want to hear it again," wrote Scripps Howard News Service syndicated columnist Stephanie Salter. "I want to hear some high-placed, articulate, long-practiced official of the National Rifle Association explain why Americans must protect their right to buy, carry and use AK-47 semiautomatic assault rifles."

The NRA ended up losing ground in the aftermath of the shooting. California banned about sixty different types of "assault" or military-style weapons. The Bureau of Alcohol, Tobacco, and Firearms under President George H. W. Bush cited the lack of "sporting purposes" for such weapons, leading the Bush administration to ban further imports.

Two years earlier, in 1987, the Brady Act had finally been introduced in Congress—six years after the assassination attempt on President Reagan. It had taken so long in part because the NRA and the Reagan administration were closely allied, and in part because of the inroads the NRA had already begun making on both sides of the aisle on Capitol Hill. The NRA kept the bill from advancing for years, demonstrating the clout that would only swell in the future.

And while the bill had languished after its introduction, the Stockton shooting seemed to mark a turn. Sarah Brady became Handgun Control's chair. Even worse for the organization, three weeks later former president Reagan, shortly after leaving office, gave a brief address at the University of Southern California and received "extended applause" when he answered a question about over-the-counter sales of military weapons like the one used in the Stockton shooting by saying, "I do not believe in taking away the right of the citizen for sporting, for hunting and so forth, or for home defense. But I do believe that an AK-47, a machine gun, is not a sporting weapon or needed for defense of a home."

Two years later, in 1991, Reagan broke with the NRA again by writing an op-ed in *The New York Times* titled "Why I'm for the Brady Bill."

* * *

But the Association and its leadership remained undaunted. As the scandal-plagued Warren Cassidy told *Time* magazine in 1990 shortly before he stepped down, with the debate over how to respond to Stockton still raging, "You would get a far better understanding if you approached us as if you were approaching one of the great religions of the world."

At the annual meeting that year in San Antonio, the members of the Nominating Committee chosen by the board recommended Wayne LaPierre to replace Cassidy as EVP, and the board voted him into power. At forty-one, Wayne LaPierre was realizing his dream.

As LaPierre took the office that he still enjoys today, it might have seemed that the longest period of turmoil in the history of the National Rifle Association of America was over. But a new crisis—Neal Knox's last stand—was about to start.

PART THREE

THE FOCUS

Around the world and throughout history, gun registration schemes have one thing in common: registration virtually always precedes mandatory and compulsory gun surrender or confiscation. Yet too many Americans say, "It can't happen here" or "You don't have anything to worry about." But it can happen here. It *has* happened here. And it is happening here.

—Wayne LaPierre, executive vice president, The National Rifle Association of America, "Standing Guard," *American Rifleman*, **March 2015**

Eight

THE POLITBURO

Several events in the early 1990s drew the attention of millions of Americans concerned about their gun rights, and at first their grievances went underreported by the press. The Rodney King riots in the spring of 1992 stoked fear in Americans of all kinds across the country. The iconic images of store owners and others on the roofs of their buildings armed with 9 mm pistols and AR-15 rifles, along with footage of four young black men beating truck driver Reginald Denny, one hitting him with a piece of brick in the head, were aired live by freelance journalists for Los Angeles's KCOP television station, filming from a helicopter. Afterward, Marion Hammer wrote a piece in *American Rifleman* titled "You Loot—We Shoot."

Less than four months later, on isolated Ruby Ridge in rural northern Idaho, a federal siege took place at the house of a family of white separatists who homeschooled their children. In the eyes of many both within and outside the NRA, this was the start of a larger war in the culture. The suspect, who had a bench warrant out for his arrest, was a forty-five-year-old man named Randy Weaver. He had come onto the federal law enforcement radar when he encountered a federal informant during a local meeting of a group called Aryan Nations. "Weaver invited the informant to his home to discuss forming a group to fight the 'Zionist Organized Government,' referring to the U.S. Government," according to a report prepared by the U.S. Department of Justice in 1994. Weaver sold the informant two illegal sawed-off shotguns, and later missed his court date over weapons charges brought by the Bureau of Alcohol, Tobacco and Firearms. The U.S. Marshals Service then spent eighteen months "gathering information about Weaver and developing a plan to arrest him. . . . Weaver had made statements about his intent to violently confront federal law enforcement officials. . . . [The marshals service] concluded that an undercover operation would be the most prudent way to proceed."

Weaver and his family, along with a friend staying with them, were placed under government surveillance. "The marshals observed that Weaver and his children responded to approaching persons and vehicles by taking armed positions over the driveway leading to the Weaver cabin."

The surveillance team was eventually detected and chased by one of the family's dogs, resulting in a firefight that left fourteen-year-old Sammy Weaver and the dog dead, along with a U.S. marshal. Randy Weaver's wife, Vicki Weaver, was killed by a federal sniper the next day. Randy Weaver and the family friend were also later shot and wounded. After a standoff lasting a total of eleven days, the raid finally came to an end. Before it did, the governor of Idaho had declared a state of emergency in the county and mobilized the Idaho National Guard, which deployed with armored personnel carriers and was backed up by state police, both supporting federal agents already deployed from the ATF, the FBI, and the U.S. Marshals Service.

"'Here you had federal agents come into a little county in northern Idaho, suspend state law and then say they had the right to eliminate anyone with a gun,'" the *American Rifleman* quoted Randy Weaver's defense attorney in its first mention of the tragedy fifteen months afterward, in the November 1993 issue.

By then, another incident had pervaded the national consciousness to an even greater degree. On February 28, 1993, federal agencies launched a siege near Waco, Texas, at the compound of a religious sect over the alleged presence of illegal fully automatic weapons. Named for their founder, the Branch Davidians were led by a man credibly accused of felonious misconduct including the physical and sexual abuse of children. Four federal agents and six Branch Davidians were killed in the initial strike. More agents moved in, and the resulting nationally televised standoff lasted fifty-one days, until Clinton administration attorney general Janet Reno ordered an assault on the compound with tear gas. Hours later a fire began inside the compound, and by the time it was over, at least seventy-six more people including twenty children had died. Autopsies later showed several children had been shot and one toddler had been stabbed in what may have been "mercy killings" carried out by adults in the cult during the fire.

These federal actions in the early 1990s fueled an anti-government fervor already smoldering both inside and outside the NRA. But the NRA's flagship magazines said nary a word about the Ruby Ridge tragedy for more than a year, and Wayne LaPierre's "Standing Guard" column waited more than three years. Why would LaPierre lead the NRA to ignore for so long what to many of his followers and other gun rights activists were patent examples of government overreach, if not tyranny?

LaPierre, like everyone else active within America's gun rights movement, knew one thing: white nationalists, white supremacists, neo-Nazis, and other white power advocates were out front in talking about the Ruby Ridge debacle, and the NRA's credibility on Capitol Hill and around the country would suffer if the Association were tied to white power groups.

LaPierre faced a challenge: he had to balance the constant specter of voices like Neal Knox's claiming he was weak on gun rights with the dangers to the mainstream credibility of the Association if it were perceived as harboring extremists. LaPierre's success balancing this tightrope showed a mastery of the skills that have long marked his leadership.

* * *

The Brady Handgun Violence Prevention Act, named for President Reagan's former press secretary, was signed into law by President Bill Clinton in 1993. It soon became the nation's most important gun control law since the 1986 bill, establishing mandatory federal background checks along with a five-day waiting period before the purchase of a firearm. In 1997, however, the Supreme Court ruled that the federal government may not mandate state participation, making the waiting period voluntary for state and local officials to impose. A year later the establishment of a federal instant background check system eliminated the waiting period, but most states still declined to participate.

A year later, President Clinton signed the Federal Assault Weapons Ban—the nation's fifth federal gun law of note, and unprecedented in several ways. The Democrats agreed to limit its duration to exactly ten years, in order to garner enough votes to get it passed. Furthermore, the ban defined assault weapons less by their firing mechanism than by their largely cosmetic accessories, prompting gun manufacturers to design innovative weapons that circumvented the ban but had the same kind of semiautomatic capacities that the law was intended to outlaw.

Passage of the law was a defeat for LaPierre, but he quickly turned it to his advantage by allying the NRA with a new wave of right-leaning House candidates who ended up being led by Georgia congressman Newt Gingrich.

Two months after President Clinton signed the ban, in the 1994 midterm elections, the Republican Party reclaimed both the House and Senate for the first time in forty years. The GOP-led Congress quickly passed a bill, the "Dickey Amendment," that limited the Centers for Disease Control from conducting research on gun violence or from treating it like an epidemic affecting health. The same legislative package permanently barred the placement of taggants in black and smokeless powders. The GOP also went on to deny the ATF the ability to create searchable databases of gun dealers' records. As a result, when trying to trace back to their origins guns that were seized from crime scenes or criminals, the federal agency responsible for firearms and explosives must often resort to paper-and-folder files, whose contents are not searchable, even today.

The specter of the botched, bloody raids at Ruby Ridge and Waco combined with anger at the limited ban on assault weapons to give rise to a new "patriot" or militia movement. Many of these people had no other agenda whatsoever apart from "exercising their Second Amendment rights." Others were white power advocates of one kind or another, including some who had been charged with violent crimes. Out of 224 militias identified in thirty-nine states in 1995 by the Southern Poverty Law Center, 45 had ties to white power groups. What united all these modern-day minutemen was opposition to gun control and the perceived overreach of federal authority—rooted in the faith that gun rights themselves are a test not unlike the canary in the coal mine. By some measures, the nation's militia movement, estimated at up to 5 million strong, was bigger in the mid-1990s than the NRA, with 3.5 million members.

The same events that galvanized the militia movement eventually led Timothy McVeigh, a decorated former soldier, to bomb the Alfred P. Murrah Federal Building in Oklahoma City on April 19, 1995, killing 168 people and injuring hundreds. While initial speculation focused on the idea that the bombing must have been carried out by terrorists from the Middle East, the press—prompted by law enforcement sources—soon noted the bombing coincided with the second anniversary of the end of the Waco siege.

* * *

Crime through the early 1990s was rising steadily, too, giving rise to the era of "three strikes" laws, which mandated lengthy prison sentences for anyone previously convicted of two serious felonies, regardless of the nature of the third major crime they were convicted for. In this atmosphere of penal retribution, the NRA had a major influence on the nation's biggest crime bill in a generation. The modern NRA had long known that gun rights was not necessarily a popular issue. So the lobbying wing under Knox protégé Tanya Metaksa began allying with other conservative political action groups to forge coalitions focused largely on two issues: getting tougher on crime to put criminals in jail, and passing tort reform to make U.S. firms including but not limited to gun manufacturers less vulnerable to lawsuits.

In the Crime Bill of 1994, the NRA was hoping to shift the legislation's focus to putting more criminals in jail while leaving assault weapons alone. They accomplished the former but not the latter. By trying to focus on crime but not guns, the NRA ended up helping to stop an amendment that would have let first-time nonviolent drug offenders out of prison. Yet the bill that ultimately passed still included the assault weapons ban. The number of inmates in federal prisons soon swelled by more than a third. Many states, which collectively hold far more prisoners than the federal government, followed suit and largely defeated mandatory sentencing reform.

In 1991, in an incident that flickered only briefly in the national spotlight, a man drove his pickup through the plate-glass windows of a Luby's Cafeteria in Killeen, Texas, pulled out two semiautomatic 9 mm pistols, a Glock 17 and a Ruger P89, and killed twenty-three people and wounded nineteen before killing himself. It was America's largest modern mass shooting up to that point. One survivor was Suzanna Gratia Hupp, whose parents were shot and killed. Later appearing as an independent gun rights advocate in a Senate committee hearing chaired by Senator Chuck Schumer, she testified, "The Second Amendment is not about duck hunting . . . but it is about our rights, all of our rights, to be able to protect ourselves," she said, pointing to herself and other NRA witnesses, "from all of you guys up there"—and she pointed to the members of the committee.

* * *

By the early 1990s, the NRA was sanctioning nearly twelve thousand competitive shooting events annually, involving up to a quarter million participants in all fifty states. By then there were no fewer than 13,827 hunting and shooting clubs across the country affiliated with the Association; those clubs had a combined membership of 1.2 million, and many if not all of them were also NRA members. There were also more than 1,800 affiliated Junior Clubs, teaching over thirty-five thousand young people about safe, responsible gun ownership. For years the NRA had provided four- and five-figure grants to gun clubs in nearly every state. In other words, nearly everyone across the nation involved in recreational shooting was most likely involved on some level with the NRA—and still is, to a large degree.

As Wayne LaPierre knew well, the shooting programs were blocks that had been added to the Association structure over the course of many years. They were the first elements in what, three decades later at the 2018 board meeting in Dallas, LaPierre would refer to as the NRA's then-emerging "business model."

A patient leader, LaPierre always kept an eye on the horizon. Firmly at the helm, finally steadying the course of the NRA in the wake of the shift, the EVP introduced changes to the *American Rifleman*. As if foreshadowing trends in the media to come, there began to appear short, stand-alone glossy sections that had as much graphics as text, if not more. One that ran during 1992 reads "Let Armed Criminals Be Warned," and alongside photographs of actual criminal suspects is the glib warning that "law-abiding Americans everywhere" will work "to *put you away*."

LaPierre was a pioneer in other ways as well. Previous leaders had instituted a clever "Lie-Ability Award" given to media types such as Herblock, the syndicated *Washington Post* political cartoonist. But the NRA under LaPierre began to avoid tangling with specific media outlets and journalists, instead concentrating on finding new and innovative ways to be heard. In its January 1996 issue the *American Rifleman* introduced members to the notion of "electronic-mail messages." By then the NRA had already launched *On Target*, a weekly live show on America's Voice, a small, conservative cable network.

The always redoubtable Tanya Metaksa had been brought back to the NRA by LaPierre as lobbying chief. Even though she had been a Knox ally, she was a gun rights activist first. Also, she was the one who had first hired LaPierre, and he knew well her capabilities. Then fifty-six, Metaksa—a Smith College alumna whose father was the conservative writer John Chamberlain and whose mother was the modern dancer Ernestine Stodelle—soon strategically reached out in two directions at once. She made headlines by meeting with members of the Michigan Militia, in an apparent effort to show the gun rights movement's more radical wing that the NRA was on their side. At the same time she was reaching out, as she told members plainly at a lobbying meeting in Phoenix in 1995, to mainstream conservative groups such as the U.S. Chamber of Commerce to continue building the kind of electoral alliances that had already borne fruit in the previous midterm elections.

Although he never let on in public, Wayne LaPierre himself got together with rivals from time to time to talk about gun rights. Among these was a man called Larry Pratt, who ran the nation's largest gun rights group after the Association: the Gun Owners of America. Pratt met with LaPierre and other "NRA guys" several times a year in Washington, D.C., in the Embassy Row apartment of Richard Feldman, a former NRA lobbyist who by then was lobbying for a gun industry association. Wrote Feldman:

> I remained on good personal terms with Jim Baker [then the NRA's chief lobbyist], Wayne LaPierre, as well as with all the key Second Amendment groups. At least three times a year we held secret meetings in Washington at my suite in the Park Terrace Hotel across from the NRA's headquarters. These "quilting bees" were frank (no-notes-taken), free-ranging discussions of gun politics and industry trends. Alan Gottlieb [of] the Citizens Committee for the Right to Keep and Bear Arms, Larry Pratt of the Gun Owners of America, Joe Tartaro of Gun Week, Mike Saporito, my chairman [at the gun industry group American Shooting Sports Council], and even Neal Knox joined the NRA guys.

In the fall of 1992, two months after the Ruby Ridge siege, Pratt had traveled to Estes Park in Colorado's Rocky Mountains to meet white power activists from at least fourteen states. "This is the fight of the decade," an attorney named Kirk Lyons, who called himself "a Christian Confederate Southern American," told the group. "This is the crucible. This is the turning point." Lyons, reported *Rolling Stone*, wanted to work side by side not just with other white supremacists but also with people more in the mainstream, like Pratt and the Gun Owners of America.

Pratt, for his part, defended the NRA at the white power meeting in the Rockies. "The NRA is an organization that does a lot of good work. And I want to make sure that I make the record clear. . . . [But] for too long they tended to perceive the whole issue of firearms freedom as one of recreation, as one of the right to hunt." Pratt noted, too, "that the NRA was beginning to pursue a broader and more hard-line strategy and that new board members had been elected who favored 'a more aggressive approach.'"

Pratt was right about the more aggressive approach, at least in the pages of the *American Rifleman*, where LaPierre, just months later, marked the contentious era by calling it "an electrifying time." In his "Standing Guard" column in January 1993, LaPierre wrote that the "energy" was "like a current that spans centuries, uniting us with the citizen soldiers who stood at Concord Bridge," where armed American militia engaged in the first battle of the American Revolutionary War, "and all great patriots in between."

In that same issue of the magazine, David Kopel, a legal scholar whose institute would soon begin receiving five- and six-figure grants from NRA foundations, also referenced the famed Concord Bridge battle, "the shot heard round the world." "Today," Kopel went on, "the forces that want to take away your guns wear three-piece blue suits instead of red coats, and the combat arena is the legislature rather than the battlefield."

* * *

In the spring of 1994, LaPierre had been in power for three years as EVP. At the annual meeting that year in Minneapolis, the Saturday evening banquet boasted an African American gospel group from New York City, and celebrities including the film actors Richard Roundtree and Paul Sorvino. Unbeknownst to most of the twenty-four thousand NRA members and gun enthusiasts milling about, Neal Knox was about to launch his next putsch.

By this point in his wilderness years, Knox had begun saying of his fellow founding father Harlon Carter that "Carter had nothing to do" with the Cincinnati Revolt; rather, Carter "was only the beneficiary." Knox also compared the NRA Board of Directors to the

Kremlin. "If you want to understand the NRA Board," he had told a journalist in 1990, "you study the Politburo."

"The Leon Trotsky, if you will, of the gun revolution" is how *The Washington Post* described him. To others, however, Knox may seem more reminiscent of the noble but deluded Don Quixote or, in a darker view, the vengefully obsessed Captain Ahab from *Moby-Dick*. However one might like to characterize him, by this point Knox was again on the rise.

In the spring of 1994 Knox, who had long been a columnist for other gun magazines, got his first column in the *American Rifleman* and the *American Hunter*. "Knox's Notebook" was placed to follow the "Standing Guard" column by LaPierre. He also continued writing in independent gun magazines.

A few months later, Knox would float what might be called his grand theory of gun control. "Someone has said: 'Once is happenstance; twice is coincidence; three times is enemy action,'" he would write in the December 1, 1994, issue of *Shotgun News*. Knox would go on to make the claim that the assassinations of President John F. Kennedy, Senator Robert F. Kennedy, and Martin Luther King Jr. might have all been staged for the purposes of passing gun control measures. "With drugs and evil intent, it's possible," he would conclude.

But this particular column still lay in the future when in Minneapolis at the NRA's board meeting in the spring of 1994, the NRA's eight paid executive officers took their seats at tables on a raised dais, looking down on seventy-one attending volunteer directors of the NRA board. The printed agenda called for reports by each executive officer. All but the treasurer, however, said they were unprepared. It seemed another matter was on their minds: everyone was awaiting the report of the board's Nominating Committee and its recommendation for the NRA presidency. Rumors had grown so loud over the weekend that even *USA Today* reported there might be a surprise.

Tradition dictated that the first vice president, Thomas L. Washington, a large, rotund man, should be next in line to be president. A big-game hunter from Michigan and a true hunter-conservationist, Washington had worked with liberal environmentalists in his home state to conserve natural lands. He had even organized the establishment of a trust there to use state mining earnings to expand state parks, in addition to helping pass a law restricting highway billboards. His greatest legacy to his home state is probably the Michigan bottle bill, immortalized in an episode of *Seinfeld*, which imposed a ten-cent tax on most beverage bottles, reducing litter and taking an early step toward recycling. But to his critics, this was only more evidence that Tom Washington was just a Fudd.

The chairman of the board's Nominating Committee was T. J. Johnston, a tall and muscular firearms instructor and martial arts expert from California. (After the Rodney King riots, Johnston founded a militia called the Orange County Corps, of which he remains commander.) Johnston was among the newer group of board directors whom Knox had helped get elected to the board. Knox chose him to start the putsch.

Johnston nominated the second vice president, Florida gun rights activist Marion P. Hammer, for the presidency, in effect meaning she would be leapfrogging over Tom Washington. Then a fifty-five-year-old grandmother, four feet eleven inches tall with straight brown bangs, Hammer preferred to be photographed with a steely-eyed, straight-lipped stare.

The motion to nominate Hammer was seconded by another board director and opened to discussion. Wearing a sky-blue jacket over a ruffled white blouse, Hammer listened without expression as her nomination provoked audible outrage from many directors.

The first to speak was James W. Porter II, then forty-five, part of an NRA family legacy begun by his father. "When you open my veins, NRA blood runs out," he began. He was upset that the leadership would nominate Hammer over Washington, who had rightfully earned the post. Worst of all were what he called the "scurrilous accusations" that had been spread over the weekend about his "good friend" Tom Washington (whatever these accusations were was not repeated at the microphone that day). Porter said he'd reported the gossip and infighting to his mother, a lifelong NRA member like his ailing father. She had replied, "'That's not the organization I know.'"

Johnston defended the Nominating Committee's choice, saying the board directors on the committee had paid no attention to rumors against Washington. He was "unacceptable," Johnston went on, because he had "made statements" against the executive director, Wayne LaPierre. This was a bombshell revelation, but LaPierre said nothing at all as the debate unfolded; though Knox was still claiming to be one of LaPierre's allies, LaPierre was acting as though he was waiting to see which side would come out on top.

Not only was Knox back again and grasping at power, but he had new allies, including both Hammer and even LaPierre. According to some of the directors, Knox could count on as many as fifty-six of the board's seventy-six directors to support him. This had allowed Knox to place his loyalists on the Nominating Committee, which chose Hammer to leapfrog over Washington.

After a while, board member Wayne H. Stump got his turn at the mike. An Arizona state legislator, he had once advocated abolishing the Federal Reserve Board, and he was a leading member of the emerging "English Only" movement in Arizona. Speaking in defense of Hammer, Stump said, "She has fire." Having a woman president, he went on, would only help raise the profile of women in the organization. "Marion can take on Hillary," he said, referring to the current First Lady, Hillary Clinton.

Several of Hammer's supporters followed suit, repeating the same notion that, by nominating a woman, the NRA would be in a better position to take on "Hillary and Sarah [Brady]," focusing on the latter's role in particular as the Brady Bill, requiring background checks, had just three months earlier become law. "The Brady Campaign is here, in this room," warned Hammer, making her only comment of the debate. (I myself was in the room to hear her make this statement, having bought a luncheon ticket—for which NRA membership was not required—that came with a pass for the weekend convention. Very early that morning, I had arrived to the room for the board meeting with my convention pass to take a seat hours before it began.)

A turning point seemed to come when Lee Purcell, a petite, auburn-haired actress from the TV movie *Secret Sins of the Father* and one of seven women directors in the room, spoke. "We must remember we were put here by the membership," Purcell said calmly, "and I think that is sometimes forgotten." She did not believe that the membership wanted Hammer to make the jump. "I'm a woman, but I support Tom Washington." Purcell pointed out that the press was aware of a dispute within the leadership, and she suggested that word might get out—a point that Hammer had made as well with her comment about the Brady Campaign being in the room. Soon after, a director asked the Executive Committee to close the ballroom door. By now there were NRA staffers checking IDs at the door.

Joe Foss stepped to the mike. Born in 1915, he was later profiled among other notable contemporaries of his era by Tom Brokaw in *The Greatest Generation*. In addition to receiving the Medal of Honor, Foss had also been the governor of South Dakota and the commissioner of the American Football League (later absorbed into the NFL). Even though he had joined the NRA after the Cincinnati Revolt, Foss was a gun rights activist who simultaneously espoused the riflery and outdoor traditions of the old guard. From 1988 to 1990 he had served as the Association's president, a voluntary post. "Words alone can't express the magic of our marshes, mountains and woods. Suffice to say it's something in the blood, something that ties us to our ancestral past, that binds us even closer as Americans," Foss had written in 1989.

Joe Foss was no friend of Knox's, and during the debate over whether Hammer should leapfrog over Washington, he spoke like a man raised on a small family farm not far from the Big Sioux River. He looked around at his fellow board directors and said, "Whatever we do, this jerkin' around has got to end." Although he did not say so during that meeting, a year later Foss said of Knox in an interview with me for the *Village Voice*, "That's always a bad situation, when you have somebody that has a group that more or less, if he just raises his hand, they wait till he does, and they're gonna vote that way."

A motion was soon made to go into executive session, meaning that all observers—including NRA staff, media, rank-and-file NRA members, and others, including myself—would have to leave the ballroom. Fearing a closed session would only help Knox, Washington and seventeen of his supporters voted against it, but in vain. Everyone except the Board of Directors and executive officers (at the board's behest) then left the room.

According to one insider, in this closed session the board discussed the "accusations" against Washington, as well as new issues. "They complained about his weight," said the insider. "Petty things like that." The night before, Knox had convened "a secret meeting" of fellow allied board directors. "I spoke with directors who attended Knox's customary 'secret meeting' the night before the elections," another longtime NRA director, Robert K. Brown, a former Green Beret and Vietnam veteran who is the publisher and editor of *Soldier of Fortune* magazine, said later. "Knox had at some length gone through the list of allegations against Tom," Brown went on, adding that at least two directors objected, one telling Knox: "You'd never go to print with a story that sounds as bull— as this one because you'd get sued . . . and I'm not prepared to destroy a man's career and his life work on the basis of what amounts to hearsay."

When the board reconvened in open session and the results of a secret ballot were announced, Washington had won—"by a wide margin," said NRA board member Jim Porter days later in a telephone interview with me, though other directors later said Washington had won by only one vote. Nonetheless, Tom Washington and his allies, led by Porter and Purcell, had convinced a majority of their fellow directors that they would not be bullied by Knox and his bloc.

Knox was defeated, but LaPierre and Hammer both came out unscathed. LaPierre had managed to stay out of the fray, and Hammer was willing to bide her time, knowing that the board would no doubt elect her president next.

It would not be long, of course, before the infighting would arise again, and some of the principals would end up switching sides.

* * *

The following spring, Wayne LaPierre was presented with just the kind of crisis he had no doubt long dreaded: the Oklahoma City bombing.

Timothy McVeigh, motivated by Ruby Ridge, Waco, and the assault weapons ban, got the idea to bomb the Federal Building in Oklahoma City from the plot of a novel, *The Turner Diaries*, written in 1978 under a pseudonym by William Luther Pierce, the leader of the National Alliance, then the nation's largest neo-Nazi organization. This organization, like most other white supremacist groups across the nation, saw themselves as being in opposition to "ZOG," or the "Zionist Occupation Government" (though some both in and outside the white power movement adopted the newer term "New World Order," appropriated—strangely enough—from remarks made by President George H. W. Bush before the 1991 Gulf War).

In the novel, the protagonist and his supporters bomb the FBI headquarters in Washington, D.C., in revenge for the federal government's confiscation of firearms two years before. This right-wing terrorist attack sparks a massive race war lasting a decade. The escalation of conflict begins with the "Day of the Rope," when the corpses of "race traitors" are left hanging from streetlamps throughout the city of Los Angeles.

> *One famous actress, a notorious race-mixer who had starred in several large-budget, interracial "love" epics, had lost most of her hair, an eye, and several teeth—not to mention all her clothes—before the rope was put around her neck. She was a bruised and bloody mess. I wouldn't have known who she was if I hadn't asked. What, I wondered, was the point in publicly hanging her if the public couldn't recognize her and draw the a proper inferences [sic] between her former behavior and her punishment?*

(More recently, a copy of this novel's first printing in 1978, in "very good" condition and autographed by the author with both his real name and pseudonym, was advertised on Amazon for $888.88. The pricing seems curious until one remembers how "the number 88 represents the phrase 'Heil Hitler,' because H is the eighth letter in the alphabet.")

McVeigh frequented gun shows and mixed with white power activists. Some of his grievances were congruous with many views of the gun rights movement at large. His favorite movie, which he watched "over and over," was *Red Dawn*, about a takeover of America by communist forces. In the film, which was written and directed by NRA board member John Milius, one of the invaders' first acts is to use local lists of gun owners to go and seize citizens' firearms.

The Oklahoma City bomb went off at 9:02 a.m. Central Time on the second anniversary of the Waco siege. Larry Pratt of the Gun

Owners of America had already been planning to protest the Waco siege that day in front of the FBI headquarters in Washington, D.C., and he went ahead and did so that afternoon. Three days later, Pratt attended a meeting in Branson, Missouri, of about six hundred adherents of Christian Identity, a white supremacist group.

The presence of militia-minded members at the NRA's next annual meeting in Phoenix—one month after the Oklahoma City bombing—was palpable. Tanya Metaksa felt it necessary to tell the assembled membership in Phoenix that there were not, in fact, any black helicopters from the United Nations flying over America in preparation for some kind of takeover. She was not kidding. The incident showed that the NRA leadership is—when they need to be—more sophisticated than their own base. Then as now, many gun rights activists both inside and outside the NRA are a conspiracy-minded community both in-person and online who sometimes lean toward either paranoia or extremism.

LaPierre himself found some of his own recent statements newly unpalatable. In a fundraising letter dated little more than a week before the bombing, he wrote that the Clinton administration's assault weapons ban "gives jackbooted Government thugs more power to take away our constitutional rights, break in our doors, seize our guns, destroy our property and even injure and kill us." The same letter also referenced both the Ruby Ridge and Waco sieges. It ended up being a low moment for LaPierre: the letter led one of the NRA's most prominent supporters, former president George H. W. Bush, to resign his life membership in the NRA. LaPierre, after initially defending his words, apologized, saying, "I really feel bad. . . . If anyone thought the intention was to paint all federal law enforcement officials with the same broad brush, I'm sorry, and I apologize."

The bombing had revealed a fissure within the NRA leadership over how to handle extremists. Knox, in his electronic newsletter to his own supporters three days after the attack, denounced those responsible as "maggots," adding they must be "insane" if they thought "they were defending liberty" and that they should be "quickly caught, quickly tried and quickly hung." Yet Knox still defended the larger militia movement, within which many white power groups operated, telling *The Washington Post*, "Unless those people have committed a violation of the law, I'm not going to say we can't have anything to do with those people."

LaPierre drew a line on the floor at the NRA annual meeting in Phoenix. Looking out over the members seated in the packed hall thirty-one days after the Oklahoma City bombing, LaPierre said he was now speaking to anyone here in the room "who supports—or even fantasizes about—terrorism [or] insurrection." There is "a difference between 3.5 million united NRA members, and some scattered band of paranoid hatemongers," he said. "And if someone in this room doesn't know the difference, then there's the door!"

LaPierre spoke almost as if he suspected that members of the National Alliance, whose violent, neo-Nazi ideology had been another factor motivating McVeigh, were in the room quietly passing out fliers to potential recruits—as indeed they were. The next day I met an elderly white man with platinum hair and thick white whiskers seated in the back of the hall. He shook my hand, but when he saw an NRA-issued press pass hanging on a lanyard around my neck he recoiled and said, "Well, journalists are the enemy." But after I showed him my New Jersey firearms ID card and told him that the gun I had used it to buy was a Glock, he said, "Well, you must be one of us." He then handed over a pamphlet from the National Alliance.

"There is hardly a more significant difference than that which exists between the people who want gun control and those who don't," the trifold pamphlet began, striking a chord designed to resonate with NRA members and other gun rights activists. The National Alliance pamphlet concluded, "Keep your firearms out of sight, but within reach. The day will come for using them. The day for a great cleansing of this land will come. Until that day, keep your powder dry."

"People have passed out literature, they could pass out literature for the communists. It doesn't mean we support communism," Tanya Metaksa told me in an interview shortly after this incident.

But that spring in Phoenix, the fissure broke through the convention floor. A motion was raised by an NRA member for a resolution favoring the re-legalization of fully automatic weapons. Coming within five weeks of the worst terrorist act on American soil up to that point, it was an untimely move. None other than Neal Knox rushed to a mike to put it down. "I do not want to kill this motion" or "vote against it," he said. "But there is a time and place for everything." Then he used his clout to get the motion tabled.

Within the NRA board there were notably different takes on the matter. Lee Purcell, then forty-seven, had been shooting, sometimes competitively, since she was a child. Raised on army bases, she said she supported the NRA because of its concern with gun safety, its promotion of the shooting sports, and its training of women to use firearms in self-defense. "I have to think about this," Purcell told me in Phoenix when asked whether she supported the re-legalization of machine guns. "I just don't think that . . . I can't see any reason for them to want one." This opinion labeled her a Fudd. Purcell was gone from the board within a year, her candidacy dropped by the Nominating Committee.

The editor of the "Endangered Tradition" column for *Field & Stream*, an NRA benefactor member named David E. Petzal, wrote a column in which he—briefly—broke with the NRA. "Gun owners— all gun owners—pay a heavy price for having to defend the availability of these weapons," he wrote. "The American public—and the gun-owning public; especially the gun-owning public—would be better off without the hardcore military arms, which puts the average sportsman in a real dilemma."

As Petzal later acknowledged in an interview with the *Village Voice*, writing that column "took tremendous courage." No other major gun magazine columnist ever followed suit. Petzal kept on writing for the top-selling gun glossy, and is now *Field & Stream*'s rifles editor; he also coauthors the column "The Gun Nuts" in its pages. Petzal's pieces later sometimes criticized matters like the "militarism" on display at large gun shows for dealers. But rarely if ever did he again criticize the NRA or advocate for compromise on gun rights. Instead Petzal did what can only be described as a complete turnaround. In 2017 he even wrote an online piece for the *American Rifleman* called "Media Mysteries Explained" that launched a broadside against journalists in general for being allegedly unaccountable, prone to groupthink, ignorant about and fearful of firearms, and so on. He went on to say that what the NRA needs to do in the face of their shortcomings is "tell the truth." He ended his piece with the kind of words that would have made men like Harlon Carter and Neal Knox proud: "Long live the revolution."

* * *

In 1993, after eighty-five years in Washington, D.C., the Association crossed the Potomac River and settled in Fairfax, Virginia, in a modern glass building with 304,770 square feet, eventually including a 15,000-square-foot NRA National Firearms Museum, along with an indoor gun range in the basement.

The expensive move to Virginia came at a difficult time for the organization. Despite Wayne LaPierre's prowess in many respects, the NRA's finances declined measurably in the 1990s, lending Knox and his allies a hard issue with which to attack him. The Association's cash and investment portfolio had waned from $80.6 million in 1991, when LaPierre took over, to $50.9 million in 1996, and of that remaining amount, $35 million had been pledged as collateral to cover the mortgage for the new headquarters.

Knox had two experienced allies draft a report on the Association's money problems that he could use to try to oust LaPierre. At the time Knox was living off donations from followers of his newsletters, making his detractors wonder aloud if what he really wanted was LaPierre's salary of around $190,000 a year (his annual salary alone has since swelled to more than $2.2 million). Knox went on using his newsletters and gun-magazine columns to advance his cause, while LaPierre got his own radio show, *The Wayne LaPierre Show* on the NBC Radio Network, to advance his. LaPierre was learning that he needed to accumulate both more influence and more funds.

In late 1995 Tom Washington died of a heart attack, and Marion Hammer became the first woman president of the NRA. She paid tribute in the *American Rifleman* to Washington's "legacy of good works."

* * *

The final straw that led LaPierre to finally dispense with Neal Knox began as a skirmish over Ackerman McQueen, the firm that had been recommended by Harlon Carter more than a decade before, and which in turn had recommended the hiring of former Reagan administration official Ray Arnett in the 1980s, though he wound up resigning in disgrace. But that does not account for Knox's intense antipathy to the company. Rather, he seemed to see the firm and its influence more as obstacles to his attempts to claim power within the Association. In 1996 Knox used his influence on the board to demand that LaPierre cut ties with Ackerman McQueen over alleged overbilling. LaPierre did so, but then established a relationship with a firm called Mercury Group, which turned out to be an Ackerman McQueen subsidiary.

LaPierre had had enough from Knox, who at the time was first vice president—an unpaid position—and seemed to be angling for LaPierre's job. LaPierre reached out to an ally, Hollywood director

John Milius, who had joined the board two years before, and to an Ackerman McQueen executive named Anthony Makris, who had his own ties to Hollywood, to help him defeat Knox.

Described by one observer as "a Zen anarchist with Republican libertarian tendencies," Milius had written the screenplay for *Dirty Harry* and its first sequel, along with co-writing *Apocalypse Now*. Milius's movie *Red Dawn*, a favorite of the Oklahoma City bomber, starred Patrick Swayze and Charlie Sheen. In the film, the United States is invaded by a Soviet-led, Cuban- and Nicaraguan-supported communist force. In a small Colorado mountain town, the invaders' first action is to get a list of gun owners and then go door-to-door confiscating arms and executing resisters.

It became clear later that LaPierre and his allies violated many common norms in their internal effort to dislodge Knox. "We used our best techniques: lying, cheating and disinformation. I didn't tell the truth for weeks," Milius later told *The Washington Post*, recounting how they tried to compel a Knox ally to openly turn on LaPierre in an attempt to discredit Knox.

At a board meeting at the Key Bridge Marriott Hotel in Arlington, Virginia, in February 1997, I was surprised to see photocopies of an op-ed I'd written for *The Washington Post* in 1995 titled "Gunning for His Enemies: Neal Knox, the Real Power at the NRA, Sees Diabolical Plots Everywhere." The piece was on a table of NRA literature being handed out to reporters. In a rare step, they had been invited to the meeting by Tanya Metaksa, who was now with LaPierre and Hammer against Knox.

As Hammer later told *The Washington Post*: "Knox had an arrogance like I've never seen, so we chopped his head off." But Knox was still popular among members, so LaPierre needed star power of his own to defeat him. Luckily, he had a star in mind.

* * *

It all came to a head by the spring of 1997 at the annual meeting in Seattle. "Good morning, gun lobby" is how a confident Knox, first vice president of the NRA, began his speech to members on the floor. They were the same words Knox had used in his victory speech after the revolt in Cincinnati. But instead of celebrating, Knox this time used the dais to complain about the "scurrilous attacks" that had been made against him. "The truth," he went on, "is that NRA must get its financial house in order. The truth is that our EVP has spent millions of dollars at variance with board policies without a contract. The truth is we are not winning on Capitol Hill."

In his own address, LaPierre said nothing about Knox at all. Instead LaPierre said, "It is Americans who have proven to the dictators and despots of history that freedom works. People like us have proven to the Communists, Fascists—the tyrants of history—even the Clintons, Renos and Schumers, that once and for all, liberty is a better idea and that democracy works." He then went on to defend his record. As if to preempt Knox, he revived some language he had shied away from for a few years, saying that "when a few maverick federal agents with jack-booted attitudes" had abused their authority, he had spoken up. He repeated how he had "stood in the blistering spotlight to defend our honor and draw the line between American patriots and terrorists scum," while at the same time repeating his "There's the door!" line for any "paranoid hatemongers" in the room. In other words, he performed another balancing act.

But he had something else this time. He had a movie star waiting in the wings.

With the support of Makris and Ackerman McQueen, LaPierre had recruited Charlton Heston to join the board. The iconic actor was already known to NRA members. The year before, in Dallas, he had given the keynote address marking the Association's 125th anniversary. Since his participation in the 1963 March on Washington, Heston had continued to drift right, and he had been a vocal supporter of Ronald Reagan. An eloquent, charismatic celebrity, Heston was the figure LaPierre and his allies needed to finally defeat Knox for good.

While seventy-five of the seventy-six directors are elected before the annual meeting by mail by life members and by others who have been NRA members for five consecutive years, one director is elected annually from the convention floor. Getting elected from the floor is almost the only way to get on the board without the support of the Nominating Committee, and volunteers for candidates pass out fliers at every board meeting to try to reach voters. Though Heston had done no prior campaigning, with LaPierre's support—and thanks to his own celebrity—he was elected as the seventy-sixth board member that year.

But LaPierre had an even bigger plan in mind. The Monday morning after the weekend convention, at a board meeting that was closed to the press but open to NRA staff and members, LaPierre and his allies nominated Heston for first vice president, to run against Knox. LaPierre was breaking tradition by backing Heston to leapfrog over the second vice president to challenge the first vice president—the way Knox had done three years earlier by pushing Marion Hammer to leap over Tom Washington. The vote was close, but tradition was in fact broken—Heston won by four votes. Knox would later complain they brought out Moses to defeat him.

LaPierre continued to engineer Heston's ascent, as it would ensure continuation of his control. That summer the *American Rifleman* celebrated with a photo of LaPierre, Hammer, Metaksa, Heston, and others on its cover. In the fall Heston again appeared on the cover, this time surrounded by five young, diverse children. The photo was accompanied by the caption "Are Gun Rights Lost on Our Kids?"

Heston spoke at the National Press Club in 1997. Striking another chord common to the modern NRA, he painted gun owners in starkly racial and socioeconomic terms:

> *Heaven help the God-fearing, law-abiding, Caucasian, middle class,*
> *protestant, or even worse evangelical Christian, midwest or southern*
> *or even worse rural, apparently straight or even worse admitted*
> *heterosexual, gun-owning or even worse NRA-card-carrying,*
> *average working stiff, or even, worst of all, a male working stiff,*
> *because then, not only don't you count, you're a downright nuisance,*
> *an obstacle to social progress, pal.*

The following year, the board elected Heston NRA president, and reelected him again the next year. Then the board changed the Association's bylaws, amending them again and again to extend to Charlton Heston—and only Charlton Heston, not any other future NRA president—an unprecedented cumulative five-year term.

Even so, the infighting and accusations had taken their toll. Membership dipped again, hitting another low of 2.6 million in 1998.

Charlton Heston, more than any other individual of the era, preserved LaPierre's leadership and beat back Knox. But in order to keep Knox down, Heston—despite all his gun rights credentials—had to keep proving he was nobody's Fudd. "The individual right to bear arms is freedom's insurance policy, not just for your children, but for infinite generations to come," he said in Denver in 1999—nine years before the Supreme Court, for the first time, upheld an individual's right to keep arms in the home.

Neal Knox never regained his momentum. Near the end, LaPierre's camp smeared Knox as (of all things) a "gun nut" in (of all places) *The New York Times*. By the time of the spring meeting in 1999 in Denver, Knox was all but defeated. Yet his eldest son, Chris Knox, reported that his father was not bitter at all in the end, saying on his deathbed, "It's been a great run." It was an inarguable point.

"The NRA's biggest reluctance is" to acknowledge Neal Knox, says Jeff Knox, his youngest son, who today runs *The Firearms Coalition*, the newsletter founded by his father. "They have made concerted efforts to erase him from the history, to minimize his role in the history."

Throughout his own exhausting rout, Knox ceaselessly accused his peers of being less committed than he was to gun rights. In so doing, he surely further radicalized the NRA, or at the very least ensured that the moderations shown before the Cincinnati Revolt would never be repeated in the wake of what could credibly be called the Knox wars—or what his oldest son dubbed "the Gun Rights War."

"[Knox] is motivated simply by power," commented a former ally, NRA board member Robert K. Brown, who broke with Knox years before LaPierre did—and who more recently, in 2019, broke with LaPierre. Of Knox, Brown added, "I despise his ethics."

Knox left another unfortunate legacy within the Association. He was the chief protagonist of nothing less than decades of internecine conflict, the author of a litany of false ad hominem smears against anyone who stood in his way—and he was also the herald of reckless conspiracy theories, including, as we have seen, the notion that the assassinations of both Kennedys and King in the 1960s might have been staged to impose gun control. This set the stage for other conspiracy theories, nearly as or even more outlandish, to be floated more recently by the NRA and even more so by other, extremist advocates of gun rights.

* * *

Had things gone differently, had Neal Knox won and taken over the NRA, the Association would have gained support on the fringes, but it would have lost muscle on Capitol Hill. LaPierre, the tightrope balancer, managed to hang on to power, and one way he did so was to make sure he never got outflanked on gun rights again.

The spring after Heston's ascent, an iconic image of both confidence and defiance would come to mark the Association. At the

2000 NRA annual meeting in Charlotte, North Carolina, Charlton Heston spoke with the gravitas of his most iconic performances in his legendary sonorous voice, pacing each line to let it sink in, using language as lyrical as it was potent to leave his own timeless stamp on the NRA's vision of gun rights.

"When loss of liberty is looming as it is now, the siren sounds first in the hearts of freedom's vanguard. The smoke in the air of our Concord bridges and Pearl Harbors is always smelled first by the farmers who come from their simple homes to find the fire and fight. Because they know that sacred stuff resides in that wooden stock and blued steel. Something that gives the most common man the most uncommon of freedoms. When ordinary hands can possess such an extraordinary instrument, that symbolizes the full measure of human dignity and liberty. That's why those five words issue an irresistible call to us all," he said before raising a Revolutionary War–era flintlock rifle over his head, and, addressing Vice President Al Gore, then the Democratic front-runner for president, concluding, "From my cold, dead hands!"

So spoke the president of the NRA. Watching him, the executive vice president, Wayne LaPierre, might have felt no small measure of gratification. At the dawn of the new millennium, he finally had full, unrivaled control over the Association.

Nine

THE BUSINESS MODEL

Wayne LaPierre turned the NRA into a peerless force in Washington. The 2000s saw a newly empowered Association, where infighting had finally faded, and a White House where a "pro-gun" president was back in office. LaPierre made sure to integrate the NRA's gun rights message into nearly every Association activity. This would be a long period of unprecedented unity, growth, and influence.

It is hard to overestimate LaPierre's sophistication in terms of creating content that furthered the mission of his NRA. Of course, as usual, the *American Rifleman* ran constant reminders of the creed. "The Second Amendment guarantees us the absolute ability to defend ourselves from anyone who would take away our liberties or our lives, whether it be King George's Redcoats or today's criminal predators," went a representative column by none other than Charlton Heston.

Other methods of communication were more subtle. NRA writers renamed the entire family of AR-15s—high-capacity semiautomatic rifles firing small rounds with extra velocity—as "modern sporting rifles," a term soon also adopted by the gun industry as a whole.

The Association expanded its publishing program to include new glossy magazines beyond the flagship *American Rifleman* and

American Hunter. InSights focused on a junior audience, highlighting youth competitions; *Shooting Sports USA* profiled competitive shooting; and *America's 1st Freedom* aimed "to cater to a more mainstream audience, with less emphasis on the technicalities of firearms and a more general focus on self-defense and recreational use of firearms."

The *American Rifleman* and the *American Hunter* were the nation's number two and three ad-revenue-generating magazines in 2001, behind only the men's magazine *Maxim*, according to *Advertising Age*. Glossy gun ads in the NRA's monthly magazines, the youngest being *America's 1st Freedom*, all still generate millions for the NRA. A love of guns inspires its fellowship. Ackerman McQueen coined the phrase: "The NRA, Freedom's Safest Place."

Ackerman McQueen by now was the Association's "'in-house' ad agency, literally on the second floor where public affairs used to be." LaPierre and company CEO Angus McQueen often spoke daily. Among the projects no doubt discussed was the NRA's new online video network, NRA Live. In 2002 the NRA established NRA Country, hosting country music concerts "powered by pride, love of country, respect for the military, and our responsibility to protect our great American lifestyle." Longtime NRA Country performers include the Charlie Daniels Band, Hank Williams Jr., and Travis Tritt.

By the early 1990s, Richard Feldman, the former lobbyist for first the NRA and then a gun industry association, was criticizing Ackerman McQueen for enjoying "a no-contract monthly retainer" from the NRA that he considered "a blatant conflict of interest" as the arrangement allowed for neither other competitive bids nor any other real check on costs. But the occasional carping about their role did little to curb their growing influence. By then Ackerman McQueen was already making aggressive television commercials urging viewers to "defend your right to defend yourself," or asking, "Should you shoot a rapist before he cuts your throat?"

Meanwhile, Ackerman McQueen's wholly owned subsidiary Mercury Group, on behalf of the NRA, placed interviews and stories in "earned media," as opposed to "paid media," said Angus McQueen in 2002 in a legal deposition. His firm provided the NRA with "ongoing collaboration in strategic thinking, and [the] access to news organizations that—not just the access but the coordination with the earned media efforts that often are part of the overall communications strategy."

As early as 1999, the NRA's yearly budget for combined publications and public affairs was nearly $30 million. Much of that went, one way or another, to Ackerman McQueen. A report to the Association's Board of Directors noted that "during the summer, Public Affairs staff also coordinated media interviews and publicity for Charlton Heston for the release of the new film, 'Planet of the Apes,' worked with John Richardson, senior writer for *Esquire* magazine, on a feature story profiling Mr. Heston, and provided assistance and media support for appearances by Wayne LaPierre and Charlton Heston at various venues nationwide."

Language is power, as the NRA board knew well. A subcommittee of the board suggested the need for a review of "the language currently being used in all our communications," according to a 2001 report by the Special Committee on Language to the NRA board. "[O]ur communication media" should no longer use "the following terms, 'gun violence, assault weapon, gun show loophole, or gun control,'" as each of these terms is "misleading" and "damaging to our cause because they shift the terms of the debate onto our opponents' ground." Instead, "[w]e should develop a lexicon of our own." Over time the NRA and Ackerman McQueen together redefined the terms of the nation's gun violence debate.

* * *

Stories, images, and displays can be powerful, too. The NRA began curating historical materials focused on NRA shooting matches at least as early as the 1930s. But the National Firearms Museum that opened in 1998 at NRA headquarters has never provided any information whatsoever about the rich history of the Association, and very little about any of its own leaders, whether they be world-class marksmen or war heroes. Instead, the museum "details and examines the nearly 700-year history of firearms with a special emphasis on firearms, freedom, and the American experience," according to its website.

The National Firearms Museum profiles the use of firearms by gunslingers to frontiersmen, and presents the role of firearms in every conflict the United States has been involved in, down to a display of "America's Rifle," the AR-15. It freely mixes facts and fantasy, too—the popular exhibit "Hollywood History" is juxtaposed with the exhibit "Real Guns of Real Heroes." One film even boosted sales: in 1971, after the release of *Dirty Harry*, "there was a run on the Model 29 revolvers" and Smith & Wesson .44 Magnums like the one carried by Clint Eastwood's character, "the likes of which the firearm industry has seldom seen." The museum's Hollywood display even includes a few foreign gunmen, like the sniper defending Stalingrad played by Jude Law in the film *Enemy at the Gates*.

More recently the publication *American Rifleman* has featured guns in history. In 2013 it ran an article focusing on the FBI's early long guns; in 2014 there was one on the Battle of Blair Mountain, the largest labor uprising in American history; and in 2015 it featured a piece on the Battle of the Bulge. Another story that year appropriated the memory of Tecumseh, a Native American leader whose name means "Panther Across the Sky," focusing on the British rifle he wielded against U.S. forces during the War of 1812.

The *American Rifleman* revived the apologue of the American rifleman on the frontier. Since its founding, the NRA has sought to bring "the American rifleman," to borrow the words of cofounder General George Wood Wingate, closer to "the legendary stature" many always thought he deserved. In late 2004, the publication ran a cover story about the "Rifleman's Rifle," the Winchester Model 70. An artist's watercolor rendition shows a man with a wide-brimmed brown hat and a polka-dotted red neckerchief astride a white horse; the man is drawing a Model 70 rifle from his leather saddle holster as he twists around to look back at a grizzly bear baring its teeth. A portion of the sales of one of the rifles in the Model 70 line, the "limited edition Rocky Mountain Elk Foundation rifle," was even being donated to support "improving elk habitat and engaging in elk research nationwide."

The NRA still supported some elements of its old hunter-conservation heritage. The Migratory Bird Treaty Reform Act made it illegal "to take migratory birds by the aid of baiting," and the NRA under LaPierre supported the act. Many other positions taken by the NRA in the 2000s on wildlife issues, however, centered around one issue: access for hunters to state and federal lands where livestock might be grazing, or within the protected borders of designated wildlife refuges for threatened and endangered species. In 2008 the NRA launched a new website devoted to "hunter's rights" that complained of "restrictive regulations" and that prioritized access over conservation.

Whatever they were doing seemed to work. As early as 2001, the NRA achieved a new threshold: a record four million members.

* * *

In 1999, in Columbine, Colorado, two teenagers armed with an arsenal of small arms killed twelve fellow students and one teacher, wounding dozens more, before killing themselves.

Columbine posed the greatest challenge yet to LaPierre. Gun violence of course had long been rampant in America, taking over thirty thousand lives a year—nearly two-thirds from suicide, mostly white men, and the rest concentrated largely among young black and other minority men. And of course there had been horrific mass shootings before. But Columbine was different. The scale of the violence, the shock of it occurring in a suburban school, the fear of the "trenchcoat mafia"—all struck a raw nerve throughout the country.

The NRA convention that year was held only two weeks later, and by happenstance it was in Denver. Thousands of people demonstrated outside the Adams-Mark Hotel, fifteen miles from Columbine. The tragedy presented the NRA with a challenge over how to respond, and the Association developed a playbook still largely in use today: Stall by saying as little as possible. Deflect by saying this is not the time to discuss politics but a time to mourn. Deflect more by claiming that any proposed solution simply doesn't work. Overwhelm interlocutors by "gunsplaining," delving into the minutiae of firearms. Deflect more by asking, "Where would you draw the line? Would you outlaw cars, too?" Then, if pressed, wrap your argument in the Second Amendment, but avoid getting bogged down in explaining exactly how or why it is incompatible with gun control. And if it comes to that, say that the measures that some people say work in other nations would be unconstitutional here, so the issue of whether they actually work or not is moot. All the while reassuring your base you will never compromise. Or, as Charlton Heston told NRA members in Denver while protesters chanted outside, "Each horrible act can't become an ax for opportunists to cleave the very Bill of Rights that binds us."

In the spring of 2000, a year after Columbine, the first truly mass protest against gun violence, the Million Mom March, took place, drawing close to a million people in cities around the country. A new outrage was evident, even if it had not yet (and has not yet) led to change. Columbine also saw Wayne LaPierre blinking before Congress. "We think it's reasonable to provide mandatory instant background checks for every sale at every gun show. No loopholes anywhere, for anyone," he testified before a House committee that included Representative Bob Barr from Georgia, who had been elected to the NRA board the year before. LaPierre's remarks suggest that Columbine overwhelmed the leadership and that he decided a good-faith attempt to show moderation would help.

By the time LaPierre testified before Congress again, more than a decade later, he had turned 180 degrees. He now opposed universal background checks, saying that he and the NRA no longer supported background checks at gun shows "because the fact is, the law right now is a failure the way it is working." In other words, he cited the failures of the nation's current background check system, which fewer than half the states even bother to report to, as a reason not to fix it.

* * *

LaPierre had demonstrated great patience as he awaited the expiration of the assault weapons ban in 2004. Meanwhile, he and his team continued their attacks on "radical" Democratic politicians such as Senators Dianne Feinstein and Charles Schumer, the author and one of the cosponsors, respectively, of the ten-year ban. Meanwhile, a new, young, bona fide rifleman named Chris Cox was promoted by LaPierre in 2002 to run the Association's lobbying wing. He had learned how to shoot with his father and brothers in west Tennessee, and like LaPierre, he had been an aide to a Democratic elected official, Congressman John Tanner from his home state, before being hired by the NRA.

LaPierre and Cox's top priority was to ensure that nothing like the assault weapons ban, about to expire, would ever happen again.

There was no chance of renewal after Republicans gained control of both houses of Congress in 2002 during President George W. Bush's first term. But LaPierre and Cox each set their sights on the long term as they worked to bolster the NRA's message and clout.

As they went about their work, the lesson of Charlton Heston was not forgotten. Celebrity and spectacle became part of the recipe. Take the NRA board candidates in 2001. Oliver North, at that point already a household name thanks to Iran-Contra and his failed Virginia Senate campaign, was in the running. So was the actress and screenwriter Susan Howard, best known for playing the character Donna Krebbs on *Dallas*. Candidate Joaquin Jackson, first elected in 2001, was a storied former Texas Ranger turned Hollywood actor who had played alongside Tommy Lee Jones in the 1995 film *The Good Old Boys*. (After Jackson was elected, NRA activists led a failed effort to oust him from the board, calling him a Fudd for having once told *Texas Monthly* that a hunter should never need to carry more than five rounds of ammunition.) Dave Butz was a retired All-Pro football star and defensive tackle for the Washington Redskins during their glory years in the 1970s and 1980s. He had also recently won top awards in the NRA-sponsored Charlton Heston Celebrity Shoot.

President Heston himself was, of course, still on the board that year. Another successful candidate was Karl Malone, record-scoring basketball star for the Utah Jazz who had been on two gold-medal-winning Olympic basketball teams. One NRA board director whose involvement in the NRA dates back to the Cincinnati Revolt later told me that he could not recall ever seeing Malone at a board meeting. Four years later, in 2005, the actor Tom Selleck was elected to the NRA board. He later donated firearms to the NRA's National Firearms Museum, appeared in NRA print ads saying "Shooting teaches young people good things," and has been twice a keynote speaker at the NRA's annual Women's Leadership Forum, including in 2017 alongside President Donald Trump advisor Kellyanne Conway.

In addition to the celebrities, lawyers became more common. In 2001, the Texas trial lawyer Charles Cotton, who had testified before the Texas Senate in favor of what soon became the state's concealed handgun license, was a candidate. So was the trial attorney Sandra Froman from Tucson, by then NRA second vice president. An alumna of Stanford University and Harvard Law School, Froman had similarly helped pass Arizona's law allowing residents to carry concealed weapons with a permit. Another candidate recommended by the Nominating Committee who won was Patti Clark, a smallbore rifle champion from Newtown, Connecticut, where she helped train junior shooters how to safely handle and operate. Another fresh face elected to the board that year was the conservative tax-cut advocate and Republican Party figure Grover Norquist.

Every one of the aforementioned candidates was recommended by the Nominating Committee, which was controlled by the board and loyal to LaPierre.

* * *

Celebrity board members, glossy materials, new methods of outreach in media—these all served their purpose. Today's NRA is much more than its marketing, however. The Association under LaPierre built one of the most active grassroots networks of voters in the nation on either side of the political divide, one that combined volunteers with professional lobbyists and field operations supported with resources in nearly every state. By 2002 the NRA had forty-one paid field representatives and about three hundred election volunteer coordinators (EVCs). As the director of ILA's Grassroots Division wrote in a memo to the Board of Directors, "EVCs work with the various pro-gun campaigns in their areas to provide them with critically-needed volunteer support for a variety of activities, such as: phone banks, precinct walks, literature drops, voter registration drives, and Get Out the Vote & Election Day activities, etc. In 'off election years,' we also work with the EVCs to promote our legislative agenda at the federal and state levels. This program is an ongoing, year-round venture."

The NRA and its allies soon learned another valuable lesson: supporting candidates aligned with its goals was good, but sometimes attacking detractors was even better for its purposes. The NRA is "very strategic with its war chest, going after vulnerable candidates early and often, inciting fear in members of the House and Senate who are up for reelection and worried about losing their seats," wrote one journalist. Best yet, of course, is if no fingerprints or other sign of the Association was left behind.

The NRA became skilled at establishing and funding proxies to run attack ads against targeted candidates without the Association's fingerprints. Take Kirk Watson, a Democrat and former mayor of Austin who back in 2002 ran for Texas attorney general against Republican Greg Abbott. When a colleague interviewed Watson for the *Texas Observer*, he described the time during his campaign when he first saw an ad sponsored by a police group he had never heard of before, the Law Enforcement Alliance of America (LEAA). It was early on a Sunday morning, more than a week before the November 2002 election, and Watson was in a hotel room in Dallas shaving with the television on in the background. A somber voice intoned, "Personal injury lawyers like Kirk Watson have made millions suing doctors, hospitals, and small businesses, hurting families and driving up the cost of healthcare. Greg Abbott is different." By this point Watson was standing before the television, holding his razor, his face still lathered. "A respected Supreme Court justice," the voiceover in the ad continued, "Greg Abbott believes in commonsense lawsuit reform, and Greg Abbott supports the swift and aggressive prosecution of sexual predators and child pornographers. Greg Abbott has a plan for Texas. To learn more, log on now."

Founded in 1991, reportedly with seed money from the NRA, in 2002 the LEAA spent about $1.5 million for ads that ran in every major media market in Texas, running down Watson and lifting up the GOP's Abbott. Abbott won that election and later won the race for governor of Texas. In 2017, after a shooting at the Sutherland Springs, Texas, First Baptist Church during a Sunday service, Governor Abbott proclaimed the next Sunday after the attack a day of prayer in the state. He did not argue for any changes in the gun laws of Texas or the nation.

The LEAA spent millions for commercials against candidates in other states as well. Also in 2002, a Republican named Jerry Kilgore was elected attorney general of Virginia after the LEAA ran ads in his favor. Kilgore's campaigns have also received $11,000 directly from the NRA. Attorney General Kilgore later overruled the Virginia Department of Conservation and Recreation, saying the agency could not ban concealed handguns in state parks.

The NRA went on funding the LEAA, giving it at least $2 million between 2004 and 2010, according to NRA tax filings. The LEAA has claimed it is "the largest coalition of law enforcement officers, crime victims and concerned citizens," and it takes positions on gun access, gun rights, and related matters that are distinct from those of other police groups—many of which have much larger numbers of law enforcement professionals in their membership. "It's absurd to suggest that LEAA represents the law enforcement community," Jim Pasco, then head of the Fraternal Order of Police and a retired Bureau of Alcohol, Tobacco and Firearms special agent, told me for a *Texas Observer* article in 2004.

The LEAA briefly stepped up its efforts after the election of President Barack Obama in 2008. Two years later, in Michigan, the LEAA ran attack ads helping to elect a Republican named Bill Schuette attorney general. The following year he allowed Michigan gun owners to use silencers if they meet the requirements for a permit from the federal government. Attorney General Schuette's press release on the matter quoted an NRA spokesperson describing silencers as "useful safety devices" because they allegedly serve to protect shooters against hearing loss.

* * *

The NRA's ability to mobilize voters on command is the fruit of Wayne LaPierre's labor and the very measure of his and the modern Association's success. Supported by both transparent and undisclosed efforts, the NRA has long been able to lead lawmakers to repeatedly pass laws wholly incongruous with the views of most voters. And nothing better shows the modern NRA's influence and success of its business model than the proliferation of laws permitting the carrying of concealed handguns. These laws have spread like wildfire in recent decades across the United States, and the NRA paved the way by setting up extensive field operations in nearly every state.

As recently as the mid-1980s, only six states—Vermont, Washington, Indiana, Maine, North Dakota, and South Dakota—allowed concealed carry, either with or without a permit. Today, only eight states—California, Connecticut, Delaware, Hawaii, New Jersey, New York, Maryland, and Massachusetts—do *not* allow permissive forms of concealed carry. As a result, the number of Americans carrying concealed handguns is estimated to have reached nearly thirteen million. Close to a quarter of that number, or three million people, legally carry concealed handguns daily.

The NRA is the principal architect of this change. Or as the former lobbying chief Chris Cox, since forced out by LaPierre, put it to NRA members in the spring of 2019 in Indianapolis, "No one else has accomplished so much for so many for so long."

Jeff Cooper was a retired Marine colonel who was first elected to the NRA board in 1988 after being endorsed by the Nominating Committee. In 1972 Cooper had written a book, *Principles of Personal Defense*, later dubbed the "Gun Rights Bible," focusing on the mind-set required to survive an attack. Influenced by rising crime in the late 1960s and early 1970s, Cooper, who also wrote for the *American Rifleman* and *Gun Digest* and was editor-at-large at *Guns and Ammo*, blamed the victims in many cases for not being ready and able to defend themselves. This thread was picked up and amplified by the NRA in its post–Cincinnati Revolt incarnation.

The tipping point came in Florida. Marion Hammer formed the group she still runs today, Unified Sportsmen of Florida, in the late 1970s, and she was elected to the NRA board in 1983 on the basis of her lobbying in Florida. By 1987 her efforts had helped Florida pass a concealed-carry law requiring the state to issue permits on demand to anyone who did not fail a required background check for the permit. Within three years more than sixty-five thousand Floridians were licensed carriers of concealed handguns. In 1988 a total of 468 people in Florida were killed with handguns. A year later the number killed rose to 722. "It doesn't make me feel a whole lot warmer to think that many weapons are out there in people's hands," said Sheriff Nick Navarro of Broward County. "I've always thought the criteria should be tighter."

Five more states—Oregon, Pennsylvania, West Virginia, Georgia, and Idaho—passed concealed-carry laws in 1989 or 1990. Another sixteen states—Mississippi, Montana, Alaska, Arizona, Tennessee, Wyoming, Arkansas, Nevada, North Carolina, Oklahoma, Texas, Utah, Virginia, Kentucky, Louisiana, and South Carolina—followed suit by 1996, at which point twenty-seven states allowed concealed carry, with or without permits. The trend continued through the aughts, when Michigan, Colorado, Minnesota, Missouri, Ohio, New Mexico, Kansas, Nebraska, Iowa, Wisconsin, Alabama, and Illinois all passed similar laws. New Hampshire also has permissive concealed-carry procedures.

The example of Missouri shows the tenacity of the NRA at work. In the late 1990s, after lawmakers attempted to pass a concealed-carry law and failed, they turned to a referendum on the same matter. "After four or five years of filibustering from a few senators, and assurance from this governor that he will not sign the bill, we decided to have the people speak," State Senator Marvin Singleton, a Republican from Seneca, told the *Joplin Globe*. But a 1999 referendum about concealed carry still failed. Four years later, Republican majorities backed by the NRA in the Missouri House and Senate finally passed a law establishing concealed carry. In 2017 Missouri legalized the open carry of firearms in most cases.

The spread of concealed carry has, of course, been a boon to gun manufacturers. "The gun industry should send me a basket of fruit," NRA chief lobbyist Tanya Metaksa told *The Wall Street Journal* in 1996. "Our efforts have created a new market." Records of firearms sales are not kept in the United States due to restrictions imposed during the Reagan administration by the 1986 Firearms Owners' Protection Act, but records are kept of the number of firearms manufactured. A total of 1.4 million handguns (including both revolvers and pistols) were made in the nation in 1986. In 1994, 2.5 million were produced. In 2015, 4.4 million guns were manufactured in the United States.

In at least some of the states that have allowed for concealed carry, people with criminal records have ended up carrying handguns. "This includes individuals who have been convicted of violent misdemeanors (some of which may have originally been charged as felonies prior to a plea bargain), have multiple drunk driving violations, a history of multiple arrests, and those who had restraining orders for domestic violence issued against them that expired," according to the Johns Hopkins Bloomberg School of Public Health.

Other scholars disagree, particularly NRA-funded scholars. They argue that the expansion of concealed carry reduces rather than adds to violent crime. "Whenever a state legislature first considers a concealed carry bill, opponents typically warn of horrible consequences," noted NRA-funded scholar David Kopel. "But within a year of passage, the issue usually drops off the news media's radar screen, while gun-control advocates in the legislature conclude that the law wasn't so bad after all."

But in states with concealed-carry laws, violent crime has showed an increasing upward trend for every year the carry laws have been in place, with one study showing an increase of 11 to 14 percent after seven to ten years of such laws, and another showing a more than 10 percent increase in homicides committed with handguns in states with concealed-carry laws. This rise in gun violence in concealed-carry states comes as crime has dropped overall across the nation, falling by nearly half or more over the past quarter century.

Moreover, other studies debunk the notion that concealed carry affords citizens the opportunity to effectively defend themselves from harm. Concealed-carry laws trigger a 13 to 15 percent increase in violent crime a decade after the typical state adopts them, according to one recent study of thirty-three states. Of course, the "Armed Citizen" column in the *American Rifleman* includes one anecdote after another about men and women successfully using firearms in self-defense.

One of the most celebrated recent cases came in 2017 when a former NRA firearms instructor, Stephen Willeford, used his own AR-15 to wound the AR-15-equipped shooter at Sutherland Springs, stopping the slaughter that had killed twenty-six, including one infant, and wounded twenty more. Statistics suggest that the successful use of firearms for legal defense is rare. But for the NRA and its supporters, the issue is not one of probability but one of belief.

The NRA's "dream" goal is to establish a national concealed-carry reciprocity law. This would require every state to honor any concealed-carry permit issued by any other state the way they recognize a driver's license, allowing gun owners to carry concealed sidearms across state lines. Such a bill passed the House in 2018, but its momentum has since waned.

* * *

Charlton Heston resigned from the NRA in 2003 after being diagnosed with Alzheimer's disease. He died at the age of eighty-four in the spring of 2008. "It's a lot easier to play a leading man than it is to be a leading advocate like Charlton Heston," fellow NRA board member and actor Tom Selleck had said in a video tribute five years earlier at the NRA annual meeting in Orlando.

Heston's appearance in the 2002 film by Michael Moore, *Bowling for Columbine*, where Moore surprised him with a photo of a six-year-old girl, Kayla Rolland, shot dead by a six-year-old classmate in Moore's hometown of Flint, Michigan, seemed to tarnish his image with some. But to the leadership and activists within the NRA and countless other conservatives, Heston's legacy is intact.

The Clinton-era assault weapons ban expired on schedule in 2004. It achieved mixed results in terms of curbing either gun violence or mass shootings across the nation. The use of assault weapons in crimes did in fact drop in six cities examined in one U.S. Department of Justice–funded study carried out at the University of Pennsylvania, with the decline attributed largely to a reduction in the use of assault pistols. But the same study concluded that "the ban's impact on gun violence is likely to be small." A Rand Corporation study similarly found "inconclusive evidence" for the ban's impact on gun violence.

As we have seen, however, because of the way the law defined assault weapons, the ban backfired: the gun industry produced equally powerful weapons that were not covered by the legislation, leading to a record rise in assault-rifle production by the late 1990s, even as the ban was still in effect. The NRA incorporated AR-15 rifles into its "high power" shooting competitions, helping to make their possession, transport, and use ubiquitous, and this had both political and legal ramifications. Writing about the National Matches at Camp Perry in 2001, the *American Rifleman* (using the AR-15's nickname) reported that "the 'Black Rifle' is becoming more and more common in the hands of both military and civilian shooters."

* * *

The NRA continued to find new ways to engage its members. Under LaPierre, that would always be the first and foremost task. The NRA partnered with Visa to issue a credit card. Director Marion Hammer developed the NRA Eddie Eagle gun safety program for children— "If you see a gun, don't touch it. Go get an adult"—as an alternative to proposed regulations for gun storage. This program was deplored by critics for ignoring other aspects of gun safety, including trigger locks, the use of gun safes, and the statistically undeniable premise that keeping a gun in a home where children live makes it far more likely that the weapon will be used in an accident than in self-defense. (Children from five to fourteen years old are eleven times more likely to be killed with a gun in the home in the United States than in other developed countries, according to a 2011 study.)

LaPierre's attention was consumed by two federal laws, but at first glance neither had an obvious link with the stated concerns of the Association. One was a campaign finance bill, the McCain-Feingold Act. "There has never been a legislative concept as dangerous to our ability to protect the Second Amendment as this," wrote LaPierre about this legislation. The reason? The act limited issue advocacy ads before elections, and these had become the trademark tool of groups like the NRA. The Association joined with other groups in filing a suit against the Federal Election Commission over the act. The Rehnquist Supreme Court largely ruled against them, although this ruling was later overturned in the *Citizens United* case against the same FEC.

The other issue that drew the NRA's attention was tort reform. The NRA worked with the U.S. Chamber of Commerce to pass the Protection of Lawful Commerce in Arms Act in 2005. The law had the effect of protecting firearms manufacturers and dealers from being held liable when people use their weapons in crimes—to "stop the tyranny," as LaPierre had put it, "of the greedy trial lawyers and big-city mayors" like New York City mayor Michael Bloomberg, who backed lawsuits against gun manufacturers.

In 2005, Sandra Froman, a Harvard-trained lawyer who was also a longtime member of the conservative legal group the Federalist Society, was made the second female president of the NRA. Froman had had no childhood experience with firearms at all. However, late one night in 1981, a man tried to break into her home in Los Angeles while she was inside alone. Although the invader fled, "I freaked out," she later told *Stanford Magazine*. She bought a gun the next day and soon took up target shooting and eventually even big-game hunting. LaPierre and Froman used their *American Rifleman* columns to stoke the NRA's base, arguing that the Second Amendment would be destroyed should the Democrats prevail in the 2006 midterm elections.

"Only by voting can we stop the Schumer-Emanuel gun-ban machine from taking power and destroying the Second Amendment we've fought so long and so hard to protect," thundered LaPierre. "If we lose control of the Senate, then we lose control of the judicial nomination process and the Second Amendment is at the mercy of those who think it is a relic of history," claimed Froman. That year Democrats won in a sweep, retaking control of the House and Senate along with governorships and state legislatures around the country.

Yet with a Republican president, no major gun control laws would be passed.

The next spring, a twenty-three-year-old South Korean immigrant who was a legal U.S. resident and an undergraduate student at Virginia Tech killed thirty-two people and wounded seventeen others in the worst school shooting in American history. All of them were students or faculty members. Six others were injured from jumping out windows to escape. The shooter, who was armed with two semiautomatic pistols, a Glock 19 and a Walther P22, committed suicide as police were closing in.

The Virginia Tech shooting inspired new calls for gun control in Virginia and briefly revived the debate over gun policy in the nation. The shooter, who had received mental health treatment for depression, selective mutism, and social anxiety disorder, had made a video manifesto praising the teenage Columbine shooters and comparing them to Jesus Christ. Two years before, in 2005, a judge had ordered him to seek outpatient treatment.

Yet he still managed to pass a background check and purchase both weapons legally, even though federal law should have prohibited him from doing so. The federal background check system requires the states' cooperation, and only twenty-two states submit mental health records to the federal National Instant Criminal Background Check System. Virginia does submit mental health records, but its laws are relatively lax, barring firearms purchases only by those who are involuntarily committed or deemed mentally "incapacitated." The discrepancy was one reason his purchases fell through the cracks.

The NRA's initial response in the wake of the shooting was: "Our thoughts and prayers go out to the families and friends who lost loved ones to this senseless act." But eight years later, after the Association and its leaders seemed besieged by school shooting survivors from Connecticut to Florida, uglier language was employed. From the pages of *America's 1st Freedom*: "Some Virginia Tech victims and survivors, several no doubt coached by gun control lobbyists, responded to the tragedy by demanding harsher gun laws."

If these victims and survivors were pleading, they were pleading in vain.

Ten

HIDDEN HANDS

The 2008 presidential election presented the National Rifle Association of America with a new foil, one they wasted little time in taking advantage of. The group's chief lobbyist, Chris Cox, warned in the *American Rifleman*'s final issue before the 2008 elections: "It's no stretch to say that Barack Obama would be the most anti-gun president in U.S. history." Cox went on to point out that Obama had voted for no fewer than fifteen different gun regulations in less than four years as the junior senator from Illinois.

The NRA's practice of endorsing presidential candidates is a relatively recent phenomenon given the organization's long history. The first time the NRA endorsed a candidate was 1980, three years after the Cincinnati Revolt. Led by Executive Vice President Harlon Carter and lobbying chief Neal Knox, the leadership penned twin editorials in the October 1980 issues of both the *American Rifleman* and the *American Hunter* with the headline "NRA Endorses Reagan."

The NRA was even quieter in its support for President Reagan's Republican successor. Neither the NRA as an organization nor its lobbying wing, the Institute for Legislative Action, officially endorsed Vice President George H. W. Bush for president in 1988, but both NRA EVP Warren Cassidy and president Joe Foss favored him over his Democratic challenger, Michael Dukakis, in their respective columns in both the *American Rifleman* and the *American Hunter*. The NRA withheld its support from President Bush's 1992 reelection campaign, however, after his administration stopped the importation of foreign-made assault weapons. The NRA declined to endorse anyone in the 1996 presidential election, too, after the Republican candidate, Bob Dole, flip-flopped from saying he would overturn the Assault Weapons Ban to saying he would leave it in place.

In 2000, the NRA Board of Directors voted not to endorse former Texas governor George W. Bush for president. Although Wayne LaPierre early on had cochaired a Republican black-tie fundraiser for him, Governor Bush had not sought the NRA's endorsement. "Polls suggest that the NRA, while popular in many Republican areas, is viewed negatively by large numbers of the independent suburban voters whom Mr. Bush is trying to court, particularly women," observed *The New York Times*. But the NRA did back President Bush's reelection bid—its second official endorsement of a presidential candidate—less than three weeks before the 2004 election, when it endorsed the combined Republican ticket by saying, "President Bush and Vice President Dick Cheney both love to hunt and fish. They know the Constitution gives people the personal right to bear arms. And, they want to pass the values of our Nation on to a new generation."

The NRA made its third official endorsement for president in 2008, choosing Arizona senator John McCain, the former Navy fighter pilot who had been held as a prisoner of war by the North Vietnamese. Despite the Association's differences with McCain about matters ranging from gun show rules to campaign finance regulations, he was the only choice for the NRA when compared with Obama. The Association made its fourth official endorsement in 2012, endorsing both former Massachusetts governor Mitt Romney and his running mate, Wisconsin congressman Paul Ryan. All of these endorsements were made on the eve of the election. The 2016 election would play out rather differently.

* * *

As a "social welfare group," the NRA cannot accept or make tax-deductible donations. But both of the NRA's two "educational foundations" can. In the aughts, under LaPierre, the NRA Foundation and the NRA Civil Rights Defense Fund each gave millions of dollars in grants to several key legal scholars and their institutions. These scholars and institutions in turn disseminated "pro-gun" views throughout the press, academic journals, and courts without leaving NRA fingerprints. The same foundations spread hundreds of small grants a year around the country, providing money to youth shooting clubs like 4-H groups; gun, pistol, and rifle clubs of all kinds; and local hunters' groups as well as conservation groups. These donations bring the members of the receiving groups closer to the fellowship centered around the Association and bonded by its creed. To advance its views, the foundations also give small grants each year to law students around the country for "pro-gun" law review articles.

The modern NRA's legal strategy may well be the most successful case of strategic advocacy in any field in terms of its impact on American jurisprudence. Take the debate over whether the Second Amendment protects a collective right to keep arms that is limited to militias versus an individual right of citizens to keep arms. "From 1970 to 1989, twenty-five articles adhering to the collective rights view were published (nothing unusual there), but so were twenty-seven articles endorsing the individual rights model," wrote the historian Carl Bogus. "However, at least sixteen of these articles—about 60 percent—were written by lawyers who had been directly employed by or represented the NRA or other gun rights organizations, although they did not always so identify themselves in the author's footnote."

The impact of the NRA's quiet support of these "pro-gun" scholars cannot be underestimated. "It's hard to convey fully the circular nature of these writings. One after the other, they plumbed the same material, extracted the same quotes, and piled up citations to one another," noted the author and legal scholar Michael Waldman. "Soon they began to include self-congratulatory explanations of how many other articles made the same point."

One of the NRA's most effective advocates is David B. Kopel, who for years did not volunteer that he received NRA funding but has also never denied it when asked. Born in 1960, Kopel began writing columns about gun laws along with occasional forays into early American history in the *American Rifleman* in 1988, when he was three years out of law school and twenty-eight years old. Kopel has been backed by the NRA or its grant-making foundations since 1998, and it has been an investment of immeasurable gain for the Association.

Only a few men have done more, in fact, to advance an expansive view of gun rights both in the press and within American legal jurisprudence. One of the most prolific and most-often-quoted scholars on gun issues across the nation, Kopel has both written for and been quoted in the nation's top-circulation and most-respected newspapers, testified before Congress, and filed amicus briefs with the Supreme Court as well as with many state courts.

Kopel graduated from Brown University and Michigan Law School. He has since worn a number of hats, only one of which by itself would seem to pay him enough to make a living—the one funded by NRA research grants. Kopel is an adjunct scholar at the Cato Institute in Washington, D.C., as well as an adjunct professor of advanced constitutional law at the Sturm College of Law at Denver University—both of which are part-time positions. More recently Kopel became a contributor to *The Volokh Conspiracy*, a conservative legal blog, and his pieces often ran in *The Washington Post* and the conservative scholarly journal *National Review*—each of which offers writers a national platform for their views without offering any significant compensation.

As a young man Kopel was an assistant district attorney in New York. His career since has been that of a dogged freelancer, writing pieces favoring expanded gun rights (along with some earlier pieces on environmental law) and placing them in law reviews and other academic journals throughout the country.

Kopel's most lucrative position is with the Independence Institute, one of a growing number of politically active nonprofit 501(c)3 groups. The institute reveals not a single one of its donors ever since an executive order by the Treasury Department under President Trump lifted disclosure requirements as of 2019. "We do not name our donors," said Independence Institute donor relations manager Josh Williams by telephone from Denver. "We are committed to our donors' privacy."

But prior tax records of the NRA's two grant-making arms show that together they donated $3.1 million to the Independence Institute from 1998 through 2016, an average of over $172,000 year. And David Kopel has been the Independence Institute's highest-paid employee for at least twenty years, earning $93,169 in 1997 and $209,906 in 2017.

For decades Kopel said nothing about his receipt of NRA funds, and no one asked. But in 2014 *The New York Times* in response to my prodding finally disclosed Kopel's receipt of NRA funds by adding that fact to the author ID running with one of his many opinion pieces in that paper. When asked if the belated, forced disclosure was accurate, Kopel replied to me in an email, "Writers and editors make their own decisions, which I don't second-guess."

Early in his career Kopel wrote often about why the gun laws of other advanced nations allegedly would not work in the United States. That was also the theme of his first major book, *The Samurai,*

The Mountie, and The Cowboy: Should America Adopt the Gun Controls of Other Democracies?, released in 1992. The author Tom Clancy, on the back of the book's jacket, described it as providing "the fresh air of reason in a national debate too often marked by acrimony and prejudice."

In 1999 Kopel, with another longtime *American Rifleman* writer and NRA-funded legal scholar, Stephen P. Halbrook, wrote about the right to keep and bear arms in the early republic, which was published in the *William and Mary Bill of Rights Journal*, put out by the Virginia law school of the same name.

But Kopel went on spreading the NRA's message by himself as well. The next year he wrote "Treating Guns Like Consumer Products" for the *University of Pennsylvania Law Review*. In 2003, he wrote "Gun Ownership and Human Rights" for his alma mater's *Brown Journal of World Affairs*. Kopel wrote "Is Resisting Genocide a Human Right?" for the *Notre Dame Law Review* in 2006.

Kopel began testifying before Congress as early as 1988. After Senator Howard Metzenbaum, a Democrat from Ohio, introduced legislation that year to make it illegal for anyone to sell or transfer a gun without a seven-day waiting period before delivery, David Kopel testified against the legislation, identifying himself as a former district attorney in New York.

But the best return on the NRA's quiet investment in David Kopel has come from his amicus briefs to higher courts in a half dozen states as well as federal courts, including five to the Supreme Court. In 2008 the Supreme Court reached a benchmark decision on gun rights in *District of Columbia v. Heller*. The lead plaintiff, Dick Anthony Heller, was a special police officer and guard at a federal government building, and he was licensed to carry a weapon on the job. He sued to be able to keep the same weapon for his own protection in his D.C. home. The decision, written by Justice Antonin Scalia, established for the first time that individuals have the right under the Constitution to keep a gun for self-defense in their home. Kopel—presenting himself as an independent expert without disclosing that the Independence Institute, where he is the top researcher and employee, had by that time received $1.8 million in NRA funding—was part of the team that made oral arguments before the panel of nine justices.

Kopel was the counsel of record for an amicus brief filed to the Supreme Court in the *Heller* case on behalf of a number of mostly small or obscure law enforcement groups, including the Law Enforcement Alliance of America, in which he only identified himself as being with the Independence Institute. This brief by Kopel was cited four times in the Roberts Court's opinions in *Heller*, including Scalia's.

Two years later, in *McDonald v. Chicago*, the Roberts Court established that the same individual right recognized in *Heller* for the District of Columbia was in effect throughout the nation. Kopel filed a brief in the *McDonald* case on behalf of many of the same groups, including this time also the Congress of Racial Equality, led by NRA board member Roy Innis. Kopel's brief in the *McDonald* case was cited in Justice Samuel Alito's plurality opinion, and twice in Justice John Paul Stevens's dissent.

This amicus brief included a corporate disclosure statement affirming that each of the groups on whose behalf the brief was filed was a legally chartered nonprofit corporation in its state, and that the lead amicus party in this case, the International Law Enforcement Educators and Trainers Association, is an S corporation chartered in Wisconsin. Supreme Court rule 29.6 requires that any corporation filing an amicus brief disclose any parent corporations or publicly held companies that own more than 10 percent of the amicus corporation's stock. Supreme Court rule 37.6 requires any nongovernmental nonprofit amicus to identify any parties who contributed to the preparation or submission of the brief.

But the Supreme Court rules include no requirement that either counsel or amici disclose potential conflicts of interest in terms of who may have funded their research including but not limited to the brief. The lack of comprehensive disclosure requirements in the courts, legislatures, and even the press, combined with the NRA leadership's clever use of conduits to channel funds to proxies, has allowed them to amplify their message without the justices, legislators, press, or the public ever knowing it.

Kopel was hardly the only NRA-funded scholar who influenced *Heller*. Stephen P. Halbrook, born in 1947 and a Florida State undergraduate alumnus and Ph.D. and a Georgetown law school graduate, has been described even by his critics as "the nation's leading expert on the right to keep and bear arms." A frequent contributor to the *American Rifleman* and other NRA publications since 1983, Halbrook either directly or through the California-based Independent Institute (not to be confused with Kopel's Independence Institute) received $293,831 from the NRA between 1999 and 2010. Much of that support, such as two grants from the NRA Civil Rights Defense Fund, was earmarked by name for research on his book *The Founders' Second Amendment: Origins of the Right to Bear Arms*.

Halbrook filed an amicus brief in *Heller* on behalf of 250 members of the House of Representatives, 55 senators, and the president of the Senate (Vice President Dick Cheney) without making any mention of having received NRA funding. Justice Scalia's decision cited this brief twice. And in 2010 Halbrook was one of the attorneys representing the NRA in *McDonald v. Chicago*, which extended the Court's ruling in *Heller* throughout the nation.

Scalia's *Heller* decision drew scorn from some other legal scholars. "The Court's ruling overturned two centuries of precedent," wrote Michael Waldman, president of the Brennan Center for Justice at New York University's School of Law, going on to criticize Justice Scalia for writing his watershed decision in the name of the legal concept of "originalism," meaning Scalia's impulse to seek the intent of the Founding Fathers when they crafted the Bill of Rights. "[A]fter engaging in hyper-literal reading of words, and after pages of highly selective historical readings from two hundred years ago that ignore the history of the past hundred years—suddenly the opinion veers away from originalism altogether."

Waldman later explained: "Justice Antonin Scalia called the *Heller* case the 'vindication' of his philosophy of originalism—the idea that the only legitimate way to look at a constitutional provision is to ask what it meant to the framers. I think that's really not the right way to understand the Constitution. In *Heller*, I suggest Justice Scalia skipped over the motivating force behind the Second Amendment. Only two pages out of his 64-page opinion dealt with the militias, which was what the entire debate in the House of Representatives was about" before passage of the Second Amendment as part of the Bill of Rights.

Another effect of the unprecedented national victory for gun rights that emerged from the Court's decision in *McDonald* was that it gave the NRA a new platform on which to rewrite its own history. A narrative that had been proffered before, mainly by a few African American conservatives in small forums, was deftly embraced by LaPierre and the NRA.

Otis McDonald, the lead plaintiff in the Chicago case, was a former soldier and retired maintenance engineer who had come to the city as a teen from Louisiana as part of the Great Migration of African Americans. Twenty years later he bought a home in Morgan Park on Chicago's South Side. But more recently he had seen the neighborhood where he had raised his family deteriorate, "the quiet nights he once enjoyed replaced by the sound of gunfire, drunken fights and shattering liquor bottles." Once he called the police to report gunfire only to find himself quickly threatened for having done so. "I just got the feeling that I'm on my own," he said. So he decided to buy a handgun for his and his family's self-defense.

"Mr. McDonald felt strongly that he had a duty to stand up for the rights that had been taken away from African-Americans during slavery," reported his hometown paper, the *Chicago Tribune.* "He had come to understand more about his ancestors and the . . . 'black codes' that kept guns out of the hands of freed blacks." McDonald was a gun rights activist in his own right, even though he never joined the NRA. LaPierre himself would write: "With our unyielding dedication to preserving the Second Amendment, the NRA has long been fighting the covert racism of 'gun control.'" He went on, "In our 146-year history, open doors for minorities, and defense of our common rights, has been at the center of the NRA's existence."

In 2019, at the annual meeting in Indianapolis, the NRA honored McDonald's surviving family members with the Roy Innis Memorial Award, presented by board member Allen West. West, an African American himself and a retired army lieutenant colonel, had been brought onto the board through a petition by members instead of by the usual route via the Nominating Committee. In 2018 he wrote on the conservative website CNSNews.com, "As an American black man, the history of the National Rifle Association has a special meaning for me. . . . When faced with the threats, coercion, intimidation, and yes, violence of an organization called the Ku Klux Klan, it was the NRA that stood with and defended the rights of blacks to the Second Amendment."

During the ceremony onstage with the McDonald family, West addressed both the McDonald family and NRA members on the floor when he said, "Know the history. The NRA, this organization, stood with freed slaves to make sure they had their Second Amendment rights." He drew a strong round of applause.

This is all a fantasy, spun from thin air. The notion that the early NRA maintained open doors for minorities seems incongruous with cofounder William Conant Church's use of a pejorative stereotype to characterize free black men. After the war ended, he wrote, "Tickling Sambo's fancy, or his shins, will be likely to prove as shrewd an electioneering [device] as harping on that 'sweet Irish brogue'; for political parsnips *are* buttered with fine words, and office-seekers well know that a vote is a vote, and counts *one*, whether it is registered by a Caucasian or an African."

Leaving aside Church's advocating the use of torture against Native Americans, it's true that, from New York City, Church, Wingate, and other early NRA leaders supported President Grant's efforts to crush the Klan in order to put an end to southern resistance. But neither the Association nor its leaders ventured much farther south than New Jersey, as Church himself of course loudly complained. The use of "black codes" to outlaw gun ownership by freed slaves in the South was painfully real. But it was never a concern of either the early NRA or the men who founded and led it.

Church, the most respected military writer of the era, wrote a book covering the Civil War and its aftermath titled *Ulysses S. Grant and the Period of National Preservation and Reconstruction*. At 574 pages, the tome was exhaustive. In it, Church dealt explicitly with the challenges faced by freed slaves, including violence by southern groups and authorities:

> *The negroes had ceased to be slaves, but they had not yet become free men, and there was no guaranty that they might not be subjected to some new form of oppression. . . . [O]ne Southern State after another passed laws designed to perpetuate the scheme of enforced labour by establishing a system of apprenticeship, more heartless and cruel than slavery had ever been, and lacking the ameliorating features of the "patriarchal institution." . . . . Negroes were killed in large numbers throughout the South without even an attempt to hold any one responsible for their murder.*

Church was aware, too, of the efforts for racial equality led by the former escaped slave and public intellectual Frederick Douglass.

He pointed out that in 1872, one year after the NRA was founded, "a National Convention of coloured men . . . under the Presidency of Frederic[k] Douglass, passed a series of resolutions in which they joined the names of [Senator Charles] Sumner and Grant in the special recognition of their services to the coloured race." Church, an unabashed Grant admirer, in the same volume remarked on the importance of former Confederate soldiers receiving pensions equal to those of former Union soldiers, the need for former southern slave-owners to receive compensation for their lost slaves, and concerns about former Union soldiers living in the South after the war ended who lost their homes and farmlands to "partisan courts and judges."

In the same comprehensive work, Church made no mention whatsoever of any group, whether private or governmental, coming to the aid of freed slaves by helping to arm them. (Although he did mention the Union Army's decision during the war to start "arming the negro" to add "a powerful ally" and "make good soldiers.") Nor did he mention any need to arm freed slaves, or even any discussion about the matter. As a matter of fact, Church did not mention the National Rifle Association, which he and Wingate had founded and of which they were still eminent elders, at all in this extensive book.

Eighty years after Reconstruction, however, at the start of the civil rights era, there was a case that involved the NRA and the KKK. A black man named Robert Williams, who had served as a Marine in a segregated unit during World War II, after returning home became the president of the local chapter of the National Association for the Advancement of Colored People in Monroe, North Carolina. He helped integrate the town library, but trouble started when he and other activists tried to desegregate the town's swimming pool after several black children drowned in swimming holes.

The local KKK mobilized in response. "So we started arming ourselves. I wrote to the National Rifle Association in Washington which encourages veterans to keep in shape to defend their native land, and asked for a charter, which we got. In a year we had sixty members." They called themselves Monroe's Black Armed Guard.

In 1957 a group of hooded Klansmen fired shots at the home of a black doctor who was another local NAACP leader. They were surprised when "Williams and the black men of Monroe fired back from behind sandbags and covered positions," wrote Nicholas Johnson, a Fordham University law professor and the nation's leading African American scholar favoring gun rights.

The firefight was covered by newspapers as far away as Norfolk, Virginia, with the headlines "Citizens Fire Back at Klan" and "Shots Exchanged Near Residence of NAACP Head." But the *American Rifleman* said nary a word, and the NRA did nothing subsequently to support its black Monroe chapter, either. Williams and others later hosted Freedom Riders from the Congress of Racial Equality, who did try to assist. Williams later said he protected a white couple inside his home from an angry black mob. But he was eventually charged with kidnapping them, and in 1961—never relinquishing his support for the right of black Americans during segregation to be armed—went into exile in Cuba and China for ten years.

Black men arming themselves for self-defense was simply not on the NRA's agenda.

* * *

In 2012, the NRA took its message of "unyielding" gun rights to the world via the United Nations. The Association had gotten itself recognized as an observing nongovernmental organization at the United Nations in New York City in 1996. Over the next six years, the NRA began warning about "the U.N. global gun-ban movement."

This issue gave the NRA the opportunity to claim that it was out front "protect[ing] our firearm freedoms from foreign and domestic threats," as David Keene, elected NRA president in 2011, wrote about the proposed UN Arms Treaty. He claimed that treaty "could destroy private gun ownership in this country in spite of our Second Amendment." He offered no proof. But by this point such a claim would no doubt sound plausible to many NRA members.

* * *

In 2011, a young man whose writings espoused anti-government views and who was armed with a semiautomatic Glock 19 pistol with two extended thirty-three-round magazines killed six people and injured thirteen more, including Representative Gabby Giffords as she was meeting in Tucson with some of her constituents in Arizona's Eighth District. After the shooter dropped one of the magazines to reload, he was subdued by several people nearby, including a wounded army colonel and one person who had a permit to carry a concealed weapon but never drew his weapon. The shooter was later determined to be mentally unfit to stand trial.

* * *

By the end of the year, during President Obama's reelection bid, NRA executive vice president Wayne LaPierre wrote in the *American Rifleman* of "Obama's Secret Plan to Destroy the Second Amendment," without offering any evidence of the alleged "dangerous conspiracy."

The same issue included the story "It Will Never Happen Here," about how rioters had rampaged through London and other cities the summer before. Although the article did not mention it, the riots began after the British police shot and killed a twenty-nine-year-old black man in North London.

The story—reflecting what could be accurately called the American gun rights creed—lamented how the United Kingdom had passed strict gun control laws nearly a quarter century before, after the nation's worst mass shooting, known in Great Britain as the Hungerford massacre, and how "shocking" it was that so many hunters and other gun owners in the British Isles had supported the same restrictive gun laws, violating the notion of keeping gun owners united against all restrictions at all costs.

"The rioting in England last August should serve as a reminder to gun owners not to take their Second Amendment rights for granted," said Chris Cox in a pullout quote accompanying the same piece. "Not long ago, the British enjoyed much the same access to firearms that we enjoy today, but all that has changed."

* * *

One Friday night in an Aurora, Colorado, movie theater, a young man equipped with tear gas and armed with a semiautomatic .40-caliber Glock pistol, a pump-action 12-gauge Remington 870 shotgun, and a semiautomatic Smith & Wesson MP15 AR-15 rifle—while listening to techno music via earphones—killed twelve people and injured seventy more at the midnight premiere of the film *The Dark Knight Rises*. The shooter was eventually determined to be mentally unfit to stand trial.

* * *

By the time President Obama won reelection in 2012 over former Massachusetts governor Mitt Romney, the Roberts Court's decision in the *Citizens United* case had rendered moot proxy groups such as the Law Enforcement Alliance of America, through which the NRA for nearly thirty years had quietly directed funds to influence elections. From here on out the NRA could largely raise and spend money however it chose.

Today it appears the LEAA is inactive. For years, starting even before *Citizens United*, the only content one could find on the group's website, leaa.org, were long passages taken from President Abraham Lincoln's Civil War–era Gettysburg Address. But after *Huff-Post* reported on the matter, the language was replaced by the "lorem ipsum" text—a string of gibberish, used as dummy text for layout purposes, that is a corrupted version of a Latin text written by the Roman statesman Cicero back in 45 BCE. As of this writing, the LEAA website is still up and still contains nothing but the same gibberish.

* * *

The 2000s were of course the years of the great conflicts in Iraq and Afghanistan involving U.S. troops. These wars fueled demand back home for weapons not dissimilar to those the troops carried.

The AR-15 stems from the same lineage of weapons as the M16 automatic rifle. The family of AR-15 rifles, in fact, includes both progenitors of and descendants from the M16 military rifle. What these two types of weapons—one semiautomatic and the other fully automatic—have in common, among other things, is the kind of round each weapon fires. Most weapons in both the AR-15 and the M16 rifle groups fire either a .223-caliber or a similarly sized 5.56 × 45 mm (diameter and length) round. Relatively small and fast-moving, the .223 round in particular is designed to fragment upon impact and tumble, causing maximum damage.

"The injury along the path of the bullet from an AR-15 is vastly different from a low-velocity handgun injury," recently wrote a doctor who had treated casualties from the February 2018 shooting at Marjory Stoneman Douglas High School in Parkland, Florida. "The bullet from an AR-15 passes through the body like a cigarette boat traveling at maximum speed through a tiny canal. The tissue next to the bullet is elastic—moving away from the bullet like waves of water displaced by the boat—and then returns and settles back. This process is called cavitation; it leaves the displaced tissue damaged or killed. The high-velocity bullet causes a swath of tissue damage that extends several inches from its path. It does not have to actually hit an artery to damage it and cause catastrophic bleeding. Exit wounds can be the size of an orange."

Not dissimilarly, an AR-15 is capable of penetrating a Level IIIA (so-called bulletproof—or, more accurately, bullet-resistant) body armor vest commonly worn by police, which provides protection against handguns up to even Dirty Harry's famed Smith & Wesson Model 29 .44 Magnum. In the spring of 2019, in Arkansas, a pair of men wearing bulletproof vests intentionally shot each other with a .22-caliber rifle, causing bruises but no serious injuries. Had the men attempted the same stunt with an AR-15 rifle, firing nearly the same caliber round but with far more velocity behind it, the very first shot would have almost certainly caused a critical if not fatal injury, possibly leading them to bleed out within minutes.

For years the NRA and its supporters, including many TV talking heads, have claimed that use of the term "assault weapons" for AR-15 rifles and similar weapons is a misnomer, and that even to use the term for anything other than fully automatic military firearms is a sign of ignorance if not malicious intent on the part of the speaker. The phrase is a "make-believe unicorn term used to demonize certain kinds of semiautomatic rifles by conflating them with their military-issued model relatives," wrote Dana Loesch, a gun rights radio personality, later a paid special advisor to Wayne LaPierre, and formerly the host of her own show, *Relentless*, on NRATV. "If the goal is to sound like the most unintelligent person in the room when it comes to the subject of civilian-use firearms, by all means, use the term."

Loesch went on, "What 'assault weapons' actually are is a term commonly given to rifles that are black and have scary-looking, cosmetic components attached, which anti–Second Amendment advocates believe magically and dramatically alter the function of the rifle to make it 'shootier' once affixed." Similarly, the National Shooting Sports Foundation, an industry trade and lobbying group based in Newtown, Connecticut, and founded by the late NRA board member and local gun range owner Charles E. Lyman III, stated categorically online in a piece titled "Understanding America's Rifle" that "AR-15-style rifles are NOT 'assault weapons' or 'assault rifles.' An assault rifle is fully automatic, a machine gun. Automatic firearms have been severely restricted from civilian ownership since 1934. If someone calls an AR-15-style rifle an 'assault weapon,' then they've been duped by an agenda."

However, independent gun trade publishers and journalists have flatly disagreed. Phillip Peterson is a certified gunsmith and federally licensed firearms dealer with more than twenty-five years in the industry; he is a columnist for *Gun Digest* magazine and author of at least five *Gun Digest Buyer's Guide* books. "The main criteria for inclusion in this guide are that the firearms be semi-automatic and accept detachable magazines that hold more than ten rounds of ammunition," he wrote in *Gun Digest Buyer's Guide to Assault Weapons*, released in 2008. "The popularly-held idea that the term 'assault weapon' originated with anti-gun activists, media or politicians is wrong. The term was first adopted by the manufacturers, wholesalers, importers and dealers in the American firearms industry to stimulate sales."

In a phone interview, Peterson told me that "the NRA refused to put the title [*Gun Digest Buyer's Guide to Assault Weapons*] with 'assault weapons' on their website." No such guide was released in 2009 at all. In 2010, Peterson and his editors renamed the same annual review the *Gun Digest Buyer's Guide to Tactical Rifles*.

After the assault weapons ban expired, the NRA conjured up another name for the AR-15: "America's Rifle." Statistics for sales of AR-15 rifles remain unavailable due to Reagan-era laws prohibiting any national registry of firearms. Nonetheless, statistics are available for the combined *production* of M4 military rifles and AR-15 civilian rifles, and they provide some indication of trends. A record 4.6 million rifles, including both M4 and AR-15 weapons, were produced between the ban's expiration in 2004 and 2013. While these rifles accounted for 3 percent of all guns and 6 percent of all rifles manufactured in the United States in 2004, by 2013 their share had increased to 19 percent of all guns and 29 percent of all rifles.

Similarly, the estimated revenues generated from rifle sales were between $70 million and $93 million in 2004, rising eightfold or more by 2012 to reach nearly $1 billion. The following year, after both the reelection of President Obama and fear of a possible new assault weapons ban in the wake of the Sandy Hook Elementary School shooting, demand for the same rifles increased, raising prices and generating between $2 billion and $3.5 billion in 2013.

A new AR-15 rifle starts at around $500 and can easily run up to $3,000 or more with accessories. The rifle itself is a modular platform, with options for add-on features such as muzzle breaks or compensators to reduce recoil, or a scope or laser sight to improve targeting. One can also swap out "the uppers," or the barrel and chamber parts, with "the lowers," or the grip and stock parts, to create different configurations of the same weapon. Popular among consumers, the AR-15 family of rifles—also now commonly called "modern sporting rifles" by both the NRA and gun manufacturers—and their accessories have generated record revenues for a dozen or more firms.

"Bushmaster was one of the first companies to introduce modern sporting rifles to the consumer market, a market that is growing faster than the general firearms industry," reads the annual report for 2012 from Remington Outdoor Company, also doing business as Freedom Group. In that year Freedom Group alone—America's top-earning rifle maker—generated nearly $1 billion in sales.

The total economic impact of the firearms and ammunition industry in the United States nearly doubled from $19.1 billion in 2008 to $37.7 billion in 2013, according to the National Shooting Sports Federation. In aggregate this is greater than the annual sales of major individual companies, such as Delta Air Lines, Inc., Deere & Company, Sprint Nextel Corporation, American Express Company, News Corporation, and General Dynamics Corporation.

The gun industry also knows that more restrictive regulations, even if they are just proposed but never enacted, could have "a material adverse effect" on both their sales and their profits, as Freedom Group noted in 2012. Companies in the firearms industry donated between $19.3 million and $60.2 million to the NRA over seven years from 2005 to April 2011. The minimum annual donation to become a "Corporate Partner" is $25,000. Large donations today compose up to 60 percent of the NRA's total revenues; declining members dues make up the rest.

* * *

In the summer of 2012, five months before the Sandy Hook Elementary School shooting, EVP Wayne LaPierre gave a speech at the United Nations in New York opposing the proposed Arms Trade Treaty. In his address, LaPierre used some of the NRA's strongest language to date to articulate a now-global creed: "We will not stand idly by while international organizations, whether state-based or stateless, attempt to undermine the fundamental liberties that our men and women in uniform have fought so bravely to preserve—and on which our entire American system of government is based," said LaPierre.

"Our Founding Fathers wrote the Second Amendment so Americans would never have to live in tyranny," LaPierre went on. "Our Second Amendment is freedom's most valuable, most cherished, most irreplaceable idea. History proves it. When you ignore the right of good people to own firearms to protect their freedom, you become the enablers of future tyrants whose regimes will destroy millions and millions of defenseless lives." LaPierre said the NRA opposed the treaty because it included civilian firearms within its scope, even though the language of the treaty, which ultimately passed in 2013, was focused on curbing arms to regimes or insurgents engaged in abusing civilians. LaPierre in his speech said that even incorporating language that excluded civilians' arms would not be enough to satisfy the organization, although he never explained why.

Wayne LaPierre on behalf of the NRA seemed to be saying that more arms were better than less, and that people everywhere must have access to arms to protect themselves. This is a view with which few observers with much time on the ground in many conflictive places around the world would agree. But it is a view that LaPierre would have occasion to repeat on an even more freighted stage five months later.

Eleven

A FAMILY SPORT

"The Zen of riflery" would be one (anachronistic) way to describe the instruction for rifle practice that master rifleman and NRA co-founder George Wood Wingate outlined in his voluminous writings and later perfected on the NRA's first range at Creedmoor. Anyone who has never fired a weapon, or who has never practiced doing so for any length of time, may find it difficult to appreciate the art of shooting on target—especially under pressure.

In the biathlon competition held every four years in the Winter Olympics, the athletes ski for miles before suddenly stopping to swing their rifles around, take aim, and fire. They ski on for more miles, shoot, and then repeat again. To be successful, every biathlete practices what many call "controlled breathing." This is pretty much the same technique that many elite soldiers might call "tactical breathing" and what Zen masters call "mindful breathing." Within the world of shooting, it is a technique employed by top shots around the world—from military snipers to sports shooters—to calm themselves before firing.

"The physical things are difficult—using all your muscles and pumping your heart as fast as you can. But the mental piece is the biggest challenge," American biathlete Clare Egan told *The New York*

Times. "When preparing to fire a single shot, or a string of shots, our first priority is to bring all of our awareness to the present," wrote the author of *Zen, Meditation and the Art of Shooting.* "The routine processes of taking our stance and focusing on our breathing should act as the triggers that automatically bring our thoughts fully to the moment at hand."

Smallbore rifle competition is no different. In 2019, on a rather warm winter's day at a gun range in southern Connecticut, I saw one young shooter after another take the time to put on their padded synthetic coat and trousers and to prepare their weapon and ammunition before going into the indoor range with about ten firing lanes fifty feet long. Taking different positions, they fired at their own pace. One of the younger boys in a lane had been there longer than anyone else. His coach—an older man—came out and told the boy's father he was having trouble, but that, as with any discipline, practice pays off.

A healthy spirit of competition, comradery, and excellence infuses NRA competitions, the pinnacle of which remains the National Matches still held annually at Camp Perry. The NRA leadership cut out smallbore competition from the National Matches in 2014. But the nation's Civilian Marksmanship Program—the former federal government program that had sustained the NRA for decades through the first half of the twentieth century, but which is now maintained through private organizations, shooting clubs, and state associations—led the effort to get smallbore competition finally reinstated at Camp Perry in 2018.

Southern Connecticut has produced many smallbore junior competitors (as shooters from fourteen to twenty are called within NRA-promoted shooting matches) on every level, including NRA National Matches at Camp Perry, National Collegiate Athletic Association (NCAA) competitions, the International Shooting Sport Federation World Cup, and the Olympic Games. One woman, Emily

Caruso, was a four-time All-American in both the air rifle and the smallbore rifle, and she also won a gold medal in the Pan American Games in 2011 in Guadalajara.

Southern Connecticut has riflery roots dating back to before the Revolutionary War, and the region helped give rise to the smallbore rifle—despite its French origins—as a signature American sporting weapon. In 1920, two Connecticut riflemen, P. E. Littlehale and J. F. Rivers, finished in first and second place in the smallbore Wimbledon rifle category at the annual NRA National Matches at Camp Perry, taking twenty shots at two hundred yards and earning scores of 100 and 99, respectively. Nine years later, right before the start of the Great Depression, Connecticut rifleman Eric Johnson won the national smallbore title.

In 1981 two Connecticut riflemen won trophies at Camp Perry—a junior shooter and David Lyman. Lyman, second in line in an NRA family legacy and owner of the Blue Trail Range, was an NRA Certified Rifle Instructor who trained nearly twenty thousand junior shooters in southern Connecticut. His father, Charles Lyman III, was an NRA board member and founder of the gun industry's National Shooting Sports Foundation, based in southern Connecticut, who himself also trained thousands of junior shooters. David Lyman, his wife, Debbie Lyman, and their son, whom they named after their favorite brand of rifle, Remington, and who has been shooting since he was three, have all been NRA Double Distinguished National Smallbore Rifle Champions.

Nor were they alone in the region. Patti Clark is an NRA Certified Firearm Instructor and Training Coach who was long based in Newtown. First elected to the NRA Board of Directors in 1999, Clark was elected chairman of the Nominating Committee in 2011. The smallbore champion has also served as chairman of the Air Gun Committee and the Youth Programs Committee. Like the late David Lyman, Patti Clark has been one of the leading mentors of juniors in southern Connecticut for more than thirty years, and "she has developed shooters who have competed nationally and internationally, won championships, earned collegiate shooting scholarships and received numerous honors."

* * *

It was into this healthy, family-oriented milieu in Newtown, Connecticut, that a former stockbroker named Nancy Lanza introduced her son to target shooting. Nancy had grown up around guns, and in the aughts, after her separation and divorce, she had developed a greater interest in target shooting and collecting different types of firearms. She took both of her sons to a number of gun ranges in southern Connecticut, and then after the older one moved away to live on his own, she went with just her younger son, Adam. She suggested he try shooting guns like her smallbore .22-caliber Savage Mark II rifle, a type popular with junior shooters throughout the area.

"Both the mother and the [son] took National Rifle Association (NRA) safety courses. The mother thought it was good to learn responsibility for guns. Both would shoot pistols and rifles at a local range and the [son] was described as quiet and polite," according to a report of the Connecticut state's attorney for the area. "Guns require a lot of respect, and she really tried to instill that responsibility within him, and he took to it. He loved being careful with them. He made it a source of pride," said a family friend, speaking specifically about Adam.

Nancy's younger son was by all accounts a very troubled young man. By 2005 he had been diagnosed with Asperger's syndrome and "was described as presenting with significant social impairments and extreme anxiety," according to the state's attorney report. "It was also noted that he lacked empathy and had very rigid thought processes. He had a literal interpretation of written and verbal material. In the school setting, [he] had extreme anxiety and discomfort with changes, noise, and physical contact with others."

He had been a student at the Sandy Hook Elementary School, about five miles from his home, for six years, from first grade through fifth grade. His educators identified him as having "Pervasive Developmental Disorder (PDD) spectrum behaviors." They noted that "his high level of anxiety, Asperger's characteristics, Obsessive Compulsive Disorder (OCD) concerns and sensory issues all impacted his performance to a significant degree, limiting his participation in a general education curriculum."

Dana Loesch, the NRA's special assistant to the EVP for public communication, has accused law enforcement authorities of failing to respond to "red flags" that she claims have been clearly displayed by troubled shooters before school shootings like the one that took place in Parkland, Florida, in 2018. But if that were true, and if one were to apply the same logic here, then the shooting carried out by Adam Lanza in 2012 at Sandy Hook Elementary School was a case where the same kind of "red flags" or worse were ignored and not reported to police by southern Connecticut's own NRA-supported smallbore rifle community, including the shooter's mother, Nancy Lanza—although she was fully aware of her son's condition and deteriorating behavior.

"Over the years his mother consistently described the shooter as having Asperger's syndrome. She had a number of books in the home on the topic. She also described the shooter as being unable to make eye contact, sensitive to light and couldn't stand to be touched. Over time he had multiple daily rituals, an inability to touch door knobs, repeated hand washing and obsessive clothes changing, to the point that his mother was frequently doing laundry." Adam Lanza also only communicated with his mother via email, even though they lived in the same home. He taped black plastic garbage bags over all the windows in his bedroom, too, so no one could see in—and to block out sunlight. Yet while the young man was shooting alongside his mother in lanes at local gun ranges, he never did anything to draw attention to himself.

While at home Adam spent much of his time playing video games, some violent and some not, even traveling to arcades and other venues to play outside his home. He told one of his video game companions about his interest in mass shootings, but neither the companion nor anyone else reported anything to police.

This young man's lack of empathy seems to have resulted in him having absorbed some of the technical riflery skills he learned alongside his mother without attaching any emotion—if his final act is any indication—to the techniques and their potential conse-quences.

On a Wednesday in December 2012, eleven days before Christ-mas, he walked into his mother's bedroom sometime before nine in the morning and shot her four times with her own smallbore Savage Mark II rifle, the one she had encouraged him to learn how to shoot. According to his mother's autopsy report, he shot her once in the center of the forehead and three more times nearby. In target shoot-ing, four such holes in a paper target would be called a good "shot group" or "tight pattern"—a mark of basic competency, at least.

He left the smallbore rifle on the floor by his mother's bed and then took a drive of about thirteen minutes to his old school, Sandy Hook Elementary. He entered the school armed with a Bushmaster XM15-E2S 5.56 mm semiautomatic rifle, a Glock 20 10 mm semi-automatic pistol, and a Sig Sauer P226 9 mm semiautomatic pistol, while leaving an Izhmash Saiga 12-gauge shotgun in the trunk of his car. Each weapon, and most likely the ammunition too, had been legally purchased by his mother.

* * *

The ineffable carnage inside Sandy Hook Elementary School in Newtown, Connecticut, struck a chord of trauma, even in a country as inured to gun violence as the United States of America. "What was happening?" witnesses including children asked, reported *The New York Times*. "'Some people,' a little girl said later, searching for words, 'they got a stomachache.'"

The tragedy posed the greatest challenge to the National Rifle Association of America since the Cincinnati Revolt, one even larger than the Stockton elementary school shooting more than twenty years before, or the Columbine high school shooting thirteen years before. It presented an existential crisis to the modern NRA, along with the rest of America's gun rights movement.

In that atmosphere of mass grief, Wayne LaPierre would have recognized the grave threat to the organization he led. He must have felt the mantle of great responsibility. It would be on his shoulders to hold in place and repel any attempted executive, legislative, or judicial action by Congress and the states.

LaPierre and his team took shelter in the immediate aftermath, as they had done before in the wake of mass shootings. But LaPierre decided that the NRA had to do something it had never done before: hold a press conference after a mass shooting—seven days later.

It was an odd kind of press conference, held before a live audience and nationally televised, but one in which neither LaPierre nor other NRA officials took questions. Rather, LaPierre laid out in plain language before the American public—for the first time—a principal tenet of the NRA worldview and creed, saying he had a plan to keep America's children safe.

"While some have tried to exploit tragedy for political gain, we have remained respectfully silent. Now, we must speak for the safety of our nation's children," said LaPierre. "It's now time for us to assume responsibility for our schools. The only way—the only way to stop a monster from killing our kids is to be personally involved and invested in a plan of absolute protection." He went on, "The only thing that stops a bad guy with a gun is a good guy with a gun. Would you rather have your 911 call bring a good guy with a gun from a mile away or from a minute away?"

The suggestion was hardly a surprise to activists in the NRA. In fact, while LaPierre had long avoided making this argument so plainly before, no doubt knowing it would draw intense criticism, many gun rights activists in and outside the NRA had long been quietly clamoring for him to finally make such a case.

LaPierre had prefaced these remarks by making an anti-elitist, comparative case. "We care about our money, so we protect our banks with armed guards. American airports, office buildings, power plants, courthouses, even sports stadiums are all protected by armed security. We care about our president, so we protect him with armed Secret Service agents. Members of Congress work in offices surrounded by Capitol Police officers. Yet when it comes to our most beloved, innocent, and vulnerable members of the American family, our children, we as a society leave them every day utterly defenseless, and the monsters and the predators of the world know it, and exploit it."

LaPierre blamed evil deranged monsters—not a new theme, either, but one he attacked with more verve than before. "The truth is, that our society is populated by an unknown number of genuine monsters. People that are so deranged, so evil, so possessed by voices and driven by demons, that no sane person can ever possibly comprehend them. They walk among us every single day. And does anybody really believe that the next Adam Lanza isn't planning his attack on a school he's already identified at this very moment?"

How many more insane killers are out there? he asked. "A dozen more killers? A hundred? More?" Going on, he lamented what he described as "our nation's refusal to create an active national database of the mentally ill." Apparently the irony of this call was lost on the public as well as the press: it showed that the modern NRA's embrace of civil liberties was selective at best, protecting law-abiding gun owners while broadly targeting the mentally ill. The EVP then widened his message to "the much larger, more lethal criminal class—killers, robbers, rapists, gang members who have spread like cancer in every community across our nation"—striking the modern NRA's theretofore most familiar chord.

LaPierre dropped several seeds into what was still a boiling argument. "Add another hurricane, terrorist attack, or some other natural or manmade disaster, and you've got a recipe for a national nightmare of violence and victimization." Then he fired at the video game industry, right after blaming the media, again, for allegedly "try[ing] their best to conceal" the role played in American society by "vicious, violent video games with names like Bulletstorm, Grand Theft Auto, Mortal Kombat, and Splatterhouse. And here's one, it's called Kindergarten Killer. It's been online for ten years. How come my research staff can find it, and all of yours couldn't?" he added, addressing the reporters in the room.

LaPierre went on to target the Hollywood film and music video industries, too, although he spoke like he had to treat the former cautiously and quickly lest he be called out for the NRA's own past endorsements of violent Westerns and cop movies—and for the exhibit of these in the National Firearms Museum at NRA headquarters in Fairfax, Virginia. "I mean we have blood-soaked films out there, like *American Psycho*, *Natural Born Killers*. They're aired like propaganda loops on Splatterdays and every single day.

"A thousand music videos—and you all know this—portray life as a joke, and they play murder, portray murder as a way of life. And then they all have the nerve to call it entertainment. But is that what it really is? Isn't fantasizing about killing people as a way to get your kicks really the filthiest form of pornography?" The irony of the NRA EVP making these charges—including this one in particular,

given that John Milius, whom the *American Rifleman* called "the father of *Dirty Harry*," had been reelected to the NRA's board just the
spring before—similarly escaped notice.

Liberal critics and TV pundits panned the "tone-deaf" nature of
LaPierre's remarks. But on its own terms, the NRA's Sandy Hook
press conference was a success. The EVP had defended the Association by deflecting criticism away from gun owners and in the process
secured the loyalty of both his board and his base. Five weeks later,
in the first major congressional hearing on gun violence in eighteen
years, the NRA pulled off nothing short of a masterpiece, one so
perfectly executed that no one who watched or heard this nationally
televised hearing knew that of the three witnesses expressing pro-
gun perspectives, although two were tied to the NRA, the ties of
only one, Wayne LaPierre, were disclosed. One of the allegedly independent witnesses, David Kopel, representing the Independence
Institute, had received for his research over the past fourteen years,
through 2012, no less than $2.4 million from two different NRA
foundations, according to tax filings. This breaks down to an average
of $174,514 a year. Kopel's average salary, according to the tax filings
of the Independence Institute, where he had been over the same
period its highest paid-employee, was $145,071.

Another witness who testified before the same committee not
long afterward, David T. Hardy, had received nearly half a million
dollars from one of those NRA foundations over the same period.
Hardy—who as a witness identified himself as a private attorney
from Tucson, Arizona—had received $446,902 directly from the
NRA Civil Rights Defense Fund from 1998 through the end of 2012.
Like with Kopel's, Hardy's NRA funding was not disclosed during
the hearing. "They did not ask, I did not tell them," he told me at the
time. "Most of it is for research and writing in law journals, some
amicus briefs."

The Senate's Democratic leadership was concerned about the

hearing's optics, as their majority in the Senate was still too thin to pass any meaningful gun regulation without the support of at least some Republicans. A staff aide to Vermont senator Patrick Leahy, the chairman of the Senate Judiciary Committee, which held the hearing, told me that the committee wanted a "balanced witness panel." One irony is that the Democratic leadership, in what would prove in the end to be a failed effort to appease some of their Republican colleagues, put together panels during the extended hearing that were dominated by pro-gun witnesses, many of whom did not disclose that they were financed by the NRA.

The first witness to testify was Captain Mark Kelly, the former astronaut and Gulf War Navy combat pilot, who with his wife, former congresswoman Gabby Giffords, had founded the gun control group Americans for Responsible Solutions after she was injured in the 2011 gun attack in Tucson. Kelly said that he and his wife were both gun owners who supported the Second Amendment. Adding that we as a nation "are not taking responsibility for the gun rights our founders conferred upon us," he went on to endorse universal background checks, research on the effects of gun violence, the enactment of strong federal penalties for arms trafficking, and limitations on the lethality of firearms in order to best protect "our rights and communities alike."

The next witness was David B. Kopel, who identified himself as research director of the Colorado-based Independence Institute, associate policy analyst at the Cato Institute in Washington, D.C., and adjunct professor of advanced constitutional law at Denver University's Sturm College of Law.

"Today police and law-abiding citizens choose semi-automatic handguns and rifles such as the AR-15 for the same reason," Kopel testified. "They are often the best choice for the lawful defense of self and others. To assert that such firearms and their standard capacity factory magazines are only meant for mass murder is truly to libel law-abiding citizens and the many law enforcement officers who choose these guns not for hunting, not for collecting but for the purpose for which police officers always carry firearms, for the lawful defense of self and others." Kopel made the case that no one wants to be outgunned in a firefight, and that this explained why semiautomatic tactical firearms—what the gun industry itself previously called assault weapons—are needed by law-abiding citizens to effectively defend themselves and others.

News of Kopel having received $1.39 million in NRA grants from just one foundation would come to light a few months later in a report by Fox 31, the Fox News–affiliated television station in Denver. In the spring of 2013, Kopel led the Independence Institute to file a lawsuit on behalf of fifty-four out of Colorado's sixty-four elected sheriffs challenging the state's new gun control laws, passed after the Sandy Hook shooting. The day of the press conference at which the lawsuit was being announced, a Colorado resident named Tom Mauser called the Independence Institute to ask whether it had received any money from the NRA. Mauser has been a well-known Colorado gun control advocate for years, ever since his fifteen-year-old son, Daniel, was one of twelve students murdered along with one teacher in the 1999 Columbine High School shooting. He managed to get someone at the Independence Institute on the phone who was not David Kopel. "I asked them if they got money from the NRA, and they wouldn't tell me," Mauser told Fox 31. "They said, 'Look it up for yourself.'"

At the hearing in Washington, the next witness was Baltimore chief of police James Johnson, who was also chief of the National Law Enforcement Partnership to Prevent Gun Violence. Like Kelly before him, Johnson urged Congress to "require background checks for all firearm purchasers; ensure that prohibited purchaser records in the National Instant Criminal Background Check System (NICS) are up-to-date and accurate; and limit high capacity ammunition feeding devices to ten rounds." He went on, "Seven of our nine groups, including the largest organizations among us, also support Senator Feinstein's assault weapons ban legislation."

The fourth witness was Gayle Trotter of the Independent Women's Forum. "Guns make women safer," Trotter testified. "Guns reverse that balance of power in a violent confrontation. Using a firearm with a magazine holding more than 10 rounds of ammunition, a woman would have a fighting chance even against multiple attackers."

The Independent Women's Forum had had a total income of $4.4 million the year before. Of that, salary costs accounted for $337,285, and $3.4 million had been devoted to lobbying, paid advertisements, and other expenses. In prior tax filings the group listed its expenses as "communications and earned media," using some language not unlike that used by Ackerman McQueen's CEO about the company's (and its subsidiary's) work for the NRA: "support, advance and promote conservative public policies based on the principles of limited government, free markets and personal responsibility through a strategic earned media and communications program that works in tandem with every domestic policy and economic, foreign policy, and international women's human rights project that the organization's scholars are working on."

The Independent Women's Forum, which shared its downtown Washington address with dozens of other small nonprofits and firms, is "a right-wing policy group that provides pseudofeminist support for extreme positions that are in fact dangerous to women," wrote *The New York Times* in an editorial. In her testimony, Trotter said nothing at all about the link between domestic violence and firearms that nearly every other group focused on women and gun violence seems to make. More than half of all women murdered in America are killed by their intimate partner, and a firearm is the cause of death about half the time. While many groups focused on preventing violence against women have called for people credibly accused of domestic violence to lose their firearms, the NRA maintains this would be a violation of citizens' gun rights. Trotter simply ignored the matter in her testimony.

Wayne LaPierre was the last witness to speak, and the third of the five to make a pro-gun argument before the Democratic-controlled Senate committee. Of all of LaPierre's remarks, the most telling was his response to a question by Democratic senator Richard Durbin of Illinois. Senator Durbin said he had spoken to an NRA member in his state who told him that the Second Amendment goes beyond hunting, target shooting, and self-defense. Durbin recounted that the person had told him, "We need the firepower and the ability to protect ourselves from our government, from our government, from the police—if they knock on our doors and we need to fight back."

Senator Durbin asked LaPierre what he thought of that notion, lending the longtime NRA leader a perfect opportunity—or so it seemed—to finally promote before the nation the NRA's worldview and creed. But LaPierre chose instead to just briefly reference the notion that such a belief was part of the Founding Fathers' original motivation, and then pivoted back to the point he had made a little more than two weeks before: that what people all over the nation feared most was the possibility that the government might be unable to protect them in the event of a sudden lawless situation, anything from a disaster to a riot.

> Senator, I think without any doubt if you look at why our Founding Fathers put it there, they had lived under the tyranny of King George and they wanted to make sure that these free people in this new country would never be subjugated again and have to live under tyranny. I also think though that what people all over the country fear today is being abandoned by their government. If a tornado hits, if a hurricane hits, if a riot occurs, that they're going to be out there alone, and the only way they're going to protect themselves in the cold, in

*the dark, when they're vulnerable, is with a firearm. And I think that
indicates how relevant and essential the Second Amendment is in
today's society to fundamental human survival.*

LaPierre seemed to be saying, oddly, that the first notion, about
the Second Amendment existing to protect people's right to check
and overthrow the government if necessary, was either no longer relevant or not as relevant as his point about how keeping arms is the
key to survival.

LaPierre and his advisors such as Angus McQueen seemed to
know that, if openly embraced on Capitol Hill, the NRA belief that
the Second Amendment affords citizens the right to keep firearms
so as to be able to resist the government—a view that no U.S. court
has ever upheld, and which is unrecognized as a norm or right in
any other nation around the world—could seem like an extremist
position even though it may well remain popular among America's
gun rights base. Once again, though, he was walking the tightrope.
If for any reason LaPierre ever publicly betrayed the creed, he would
face scorn if not a revolt from his own board and base.

Chief lobbyist Chris Cox reportedly advised LaPierre to be more
cautious about his words than he had been in his response to Sandy
Hook. There is no daylight between any NRA leaders today on gun
rights, and there has not been for decades, since the Knox wars. But
Cox's exhortation about a cautious response underscores the balancing act the leadership must perform no matter who is in charge.

* * *

LaPierre, as always, instinctively grasped the importance of the Association's leader expressing sadness for the loss of the America so
many members pine for, while demonizing and scapegoating political opponents, sketching them into caricatures, and stoking fears

about matters from crime to tyranny. But the climate after Sandy Hook seemed to shove the redoubtable NRA against the wall in a new way. The grisly details of this senseless crime fast seeped into the public's consciousness.

Sandy Hook's heartbreak may have aroused LaPierre and his advisors' worst fear—what the late Neal Knox once referred to as people "'waving the bloody shirt' of emotionalism." One month after the tragedy, the organizers of the largest outdoor gun show in the country, in Harrisburg, Pennsylvania, decided to exclude tactical rifles from the show. (Pressure from the gun industry soon ensured that this boycott of "America's Rifle" and others would not be repeated.) LaPierre, NRA president David Keene, and lobbying director Chris Cox, meanwhile, each turned up the alarm over their clarion call: any attempt to regulate guns after Sandy Hook must be stopped lest it lead down the "slippery slope": registration, confiscation, tyranny.

There was a convenient bogeyman in dramatizing this dire scenario: New York City mayor Michael Bloomberg, the "elitist without peer," as NRA president Jim Porter called him, who six years before had founded the group Everytown for Gun Safety. He was the scapegoat, the straw man, and the face, it seemed, of all of America's gun control efforts. "Bloomberg and his billionaire buddies spent millions upon millions of dollars" on gun control efforts, posing a "nightmare for every law-abiding gun owner," wrote LaPierre in the *American Rifleman*. "Michael Bloomberg is using his billions to fund bogus research" on gun violence, wrote Cox in a story that was accompanied by a full-page caricature of Bloomberg looking like the Mad Hatter pulling a stuffed rabbit out of his hat.

"Are you as sick and tired as I am of being blamed for the unspeakable crimes of insane killers?" LaPierre asked in the *American Rifleman* in the summer of 2014, laying out another principle of the creed. Two years later, before the 2016 election, he wrote, "Absolutists?

You bet. When it comes to the defense of our uniquely American rights and the liberty they secure, we proudly accept that title."

A new media product called *NRA News* appeared on cable television on the Sportsman Channel and on the Patriot Network of the new subscription-based Sirius XM satellite radio, as LaPierre and McQueen went on collaborating to lead the NRA to meet people where they are. NRA publications ran story after story about the latest firearms, from "next generation" AR-15s to "combat Magnum" revolvers and other easily concealable handguns—the latter having become popular across the nation in states that allow concealed carry.

LaPierre successfully led the NRA through the storm of Sandy Hook. In the spring of 2012, a number of liberal observers predicted the NRA's demise due to the nation's undeniably changing demographics; *The New Republic* even published a piece titled "This Is How the NRA Ends." But by the next winter, LaPierre would have occasion to thank "every member for *a job well done*" (his emphasis) in the *American Rifleman*. "[D]ay after day and month after month, you stood firm. You lit up the phones of Capitol Hill. You sent truckloads of mail to Congress and filled up their email boxes. You stood up at town meetings and made your voice heard. And when the dust settled, Barack Obama wasn't able to sign his name to a single new gun control bill in 2013—not one."

It wasn't for want of trying. "I'll use whatever power this office holds to engage my fellow citizens," promised President Obama, backed by Democratic congressional leaders, "in an effort aimed at preventing more tragedies like this." Yet in a show of extraordinary resilience by the NRA, no new federal gun control laws were passed whatsoever.

The main gun bill to emerge after Sandy Hook was sponsored by Senator Joe Manchin, an often conservative-leaning Blue Dog Democrat representing West Virginia, and Senator Pat Toomey, a Republican representing Pennsylvania. These two senators from potential swing states in the mid-Atlantic bent over backward to reassure gun owners they had nothing to fear.

"I've said this, if you're a law-abiding gun owner, you'll love this bill," Senator Manchin told anchor Chris Wallace on Fox News.

The Manchin-Toomey gun bill proposed what many saw as modest goals. The bill sought to expand mandatory background checks for all commercial gun sales, including gun shows and Internet transactions—which poll after poll has shown the overwhelming majority of Americans support—but still included language to exclude transactions in which family or friends give or sell guns to each other. The same bill encouraged but did not require states to provide records to the preexisting federal Instant Criminal Background Check System by directing grant money to states that would do so and reducing funds to those that would not.

The bill further proposed reducing the waiting period for a federal background check from three days to forty-eight hours, with the goal of reducing it within four years to twenty-four hours. Moreover, in an attempted concession to gun owners, the bill included language making it illegal to "consolidate or centralize" any records of gun owners or gun transfers of any kind, with violations punishable by up to fifteen years in prison, even though such laws were already on the books and had been since the NRA helped pass the Firearms Owners' Protection Act nearly thirty years before. Finally, the bill called for a commission to study the causes of gun violence, including mental health issues and portrayals of violence in the media, and to also examine school safety.

Presented as a "gun control compromise," the Manchin-Toomey bill failed by a vote of fifty-four to forty-six, when it needed at least sixty votes to move on without the risk of being impeded by a Republican filibuster. Four Democrats and four Republicans each crossed party lines to vote against and for the bill, respectively. "Shame on you!" shouted at least two women watching from the Senate gallery, one of whose daughters had been wounded in the shooting at Virginia Tech six years before.

The EVP was right. Despite the "emotionalism" displayed by many people about Sandy Hook—led by President Obama, who teared up in a press conference and seemed to embody the nation's sadness for the painfully intimate loss—all efforts to change a single bit of the federal gun laws failed. NRA leaders attacked House Minority Leader Nancy Pelosi and Senator Chuck Schumer over their purported gun control plans—though both were overshadowed by the *American Rifleman*'s repeated outrage at former New York City mayor Michael Bloomberg.

Furthermore, only a handful of states, including New York, Connecticut, and Maryland, passed gun control laws in the wake of Sandy Hook. Once again, the NRA wall had held.

* * *

Around 2010, a group was formed in Moscow called Right to Bear Arms (RBA), a rare nongovernmental advocacy group arising in Russia—a nation tightly controlled by President Vladimir Putin, a former communist intelligence chief. As early as 2011, RBA and the NRA had begun collaborating. For five years starting in 2012, a Russian cofounder of RBA named Alexander Torshin attended NRA conventions, reported Mark Follman in *Mother Jones*. In 2013 NRA president David Keene gave a speech in Moscow at an event hosted by RBA, a video of which the Russian group later posted on YouTube. In 2014, at the NRA annual meeting in Indianapolis, NRA president James W. Porter II received an award from RBA presented to him by RBA "founder" and American University graduate student Maria Butina.

* * *

In the wake of Sandy Hook, mass shootings have become more and more a fact of American life.

In the summer of 2015, a twenty-one-year-old white supremacist armed with a Glock 41 .45-caliber pistol killed nine African American worshippers at the Emanuel African Methodist Episcopal Church in Charleston, South Carolina. He joined the Bible study group and even contributed to the collection plate before he opened fire.

In the summer of 2016, a twenty-nine-year-old security guard, a lone-wolf jihadist with a troubled past who in a 911 call before the attack expressed loyalty to the Islamic State, armed with a Sig Sauer MCX semiautomatic rifle and a Glock 17 9 mm semiautomatic pistol, killed forty-nine people and wounded over fifty more in Orlando, Florida, at the Pulse nightclub, which was popular among gay Hispanic men.

One month later, an African American U.S. army reservist who was a veteran of the Afghan War, acting in apparent retaliation for the recent police shootings of black men, killed five police officers in Dallas and wounded nine others with a Russian Saiga AK-74 semiautomatic rifle before police finally killed him using a bomb attached to a robot. This was the worst attack on American law enforcement since 9/11.

* * *

Honoring civilian law enforcement, like honoring the military, is central to the modern NRA, which finds ways to acknowledge both at every annual meeting. In 2019 in Indianapolis, the NRA honored Sergeant Michael Parsons of the Tulsa, Oklahoma, Police Department. Both at the Leadership Forum and the Board of Directors meeting, the NRA showed a video of Parsons, who had been wounded in the leg by a gunman but waved off requests by his men to exfiltrate him from the scene; after a medic assessed his wounds, he led the formation of an arrest team to safely apprehend the suspect.

At the NRA Foundation Banquet and Auction, the NRA honored law enforcement and military personnel together. The honorees included the sheriff of Barron County, Wisconsin, a young veteran who had been injured by a two-hundred-pound IED while he was on deployment in Iraq; three World War II veterans; and the father of a young man who was killed in a car accident two weeks after returning from his second combat deployment. Anthony Imperato, CEO of Henry Repeating Arms and an NRA donor, presented each man with an "engraved tribute-edition" rifle.

"We know your son is looking down on all of us at this moment and I would like to present this rifle to you in his honor and memory," Imperato said to the father who lost his son. "God rest his soul, God bless these fine men behind me on stage, and God bless the United States of America."

God, and often Jesus too, is invoked at nearly every NRA function, sometimes more than once. Board member Susan Howard has often offered the opening prayer. Chris Cox and other leaders have frequently said in a genuinely welcoming tone that people of all faiths are welcome, although Christian deities are the only ones I've ever heard referenced in prayer. The frequency of prayers, with up to three supplications before a Leadership Forum meeting, for instance, has notably increased over the past few decades.

To try to diversify the Board of Directors, its Nominating Committee has recommended a few minority candidates. Antonio Hernández Jr. is a competitive sports shooter and former deputy counsel for the Republican Party in Puerto Rico. Hernández had backed Mitt Romney in the 2012 elections. The Nominating Committee recommended him twice, in 2014 and 2016, but each time he failed to garner enough votes to make the board.

The Nominating Committee also put forth Mark Robinson from Greensboro, North Carolina, for the 2019 board election. The spring before—seven weeks after the high school shooting in Parkland, Florida—Robinson spoke up at a Greensboro city council meeting. The Greensboro mayor, a Democrat named Nancy Vaughan who had been reelected in 2015 in a landslide with 88 percent of the vote, had suggested the city council cancel an upcoming gun and knife show in Greensboro because of the Parkland shooting.

"When are you all going to start standing up for the majority?" Robinson, a broad African American man, asked at a city council meeting. The "majority" he referred to, a group he identifies with, consists of "law-abiding citizen[s] who'[ve] never shot anybody, never committed a serious crime, never committed a felony." He later said that he did not yet own a gun, but that he was interested in buying one, and that he had recently joined the NRA.

"I've never done anything like that, but it seems like every time we have one of these shootings, nobody wants to put the blame where it goes, which is at the shooter's feet," Robinson went on at the meeting. "You want to put it at my feet," he said. "And guess who's gonna to be the one that suffers? It's gonna be me," he added. "Our rights are the ones that are being taken away. That's the reason why I came down here today. Gun show or no gun show, NRA or no NRA, I'm here to stand up for the law-abiding citizens of this community."

After the Republican congressman for the area, Mark Walker, put a video of Robinson's comments on Facebook, it went viral. The NRA invited Robinson to speak a month later at the annual meeting in Dallas. Soon footage of Robinson addressing the Greensboro city council appeared in an NRA television commercial. Robinson has since been profiled in more Ackerman McQueen–produced NRA commercials. By the fall of 2018, Mark Robinson had been named by the Nominating Committee as a candidate for the board.

However, the NRA's eligible voting members, demonstrating their own autonomy, failed to elect him. The matter showed that even though the board, through its Nominating Committee, still largely controls who manages to get on the ballot for board elections, getting on the ballot itself is no guarantee that even a favored candidate like Robinson will get elected. All board members are elected nationally, meaning they do not represent regions or states. NRA members eligible to vote—a privilege limited to life members or those who have paid dues for at least five consecutive years—are asked to vote instead for up to twenty-five names out of about thirty-three on the ballot. So incumbents who are already familiar to members have an advantage.

Twelve

THE CREED

One in five U.S. presidents have been NRA members: Ulysses S. Grant, Theodore Roosevelt, William Howard Taft, Dwight D. Eisenhower, John F. Kennedy, Richard Nixon, Ronald Reagan, George W. Bush, and Donald Trump. (George H. W. Bush had been a member but resigned.) All were Republicans except Kennedy.

The NRA did not endorse any candidate for president for its first 109 years. Even the post-1977 NRA endorsed no more than a handful of presidential candidates—all Republicans—from 1980 to 2012, often doing so with reservations, while declining to officially endorse other GOP candidates during the same period. And never before had the NRA given any presidential candidate such a bear hug of an endorsement as it gave Donald Trump in 2016.

The National Rifle Association of America's endorsement of Donald J. Trump for president in 2016 was a case of first impressions in four ways. For the first time, the NRA made its endorsement not on the eve of the election or even a month before, but in the spring of 2016, months before the November vote. The Association for the first time, too, announced its endorsement at the NRA annual meeting in Louisville, immediately before giving Trump the floor to address NRA members. (Trump had first spoken the prior year at the annual meeting in Nashville, before he announced his candidacy, and he has addressed NRA members at every annual meeting since.) And the NRA donated more money than ever before—$54.4 million—to support candidates in the 2016 elections. Finally, in the summer of 2016 Chris Cox became the first NRA representative ever to be given the floor at either major political party's national convention—lending the Association a mark of acceptance that it had long reached for but never before grasped. "I want to talk to you tonight about a very personal freedom: your right to protect your life. Because as much as we don't like to think about it, we live in dangerous times. We're worried, and we have reason to be. Because our government has failed to keep us safe. You have to be able to protect yourself and your family. And that's what the Second Amendment is all about," the NRA lobbying chief told delegates in Cleveland at the Republican National Convention. But he chose his words carefully, making a compelling but safe argument that made no mention of the Second Amendment affording citizens the right to freely access arms in order to fight their own government.

But Trump himself raised at least the idea of armed resistance later that summer when he said that "the Second Amendment people" might act if his challenger, Hillary Clinton, was elected President and then went on to nominate candidates for the Supreme Court who favored gun control. He seemed to be speaking then not to the NRA leadership but to his own base. "He pointed out that an armed populace is a check on lawless politicians," wrote one gun activist about Trump's remarks, adding in an ironic tone, "I wonder if anybody else ever thought of that? Or codified it in a document of some type?"

Trump was not the only Republican candidate who made remarks about armed resistance during the campaign. Ben Carson was a gifted neurosurgeon who had been head of pediatric neurosurgery at Johns Hopkins University Hospital in Baltimore for nearly thirty years. In a book he wrote about what he called America's coming constitutional crisis, he claimed that gun control had helped lead to the Holocaust as well as atrocities in a half dozen other nations "after the people had been disarmed by tyrants"—but offered no sources to back up his claims.

In an interview with CNN anchor Wolf Blitzer, Carson repeated the same notion—finally putting this view, which has roiled beneath the surface of America's gun activist community for decades, before a national television audience. "The likelihood of Hitler being able to accomplish his goals would have been greatly diminished if the people had been armed," he told Blitzer, later standing by his remarks in an address at the National Press Club. The Anti-Defamation League, the nation's largest organization aimed at combating anti-Semitism, had previously called on critics of gun control "to stop using references to Hitler and the Nazis, saying they are 'historically inaccurate and offensive,' especially to Holocaust survivors and their families."

Carson's remarks drew a response from a Holocaust historian. "To anyone who studies Nazi Germany and the Holocaust for a living, as I do, Ben Carson's statements about gun control are difficult to fathom," Alan E. Steinweis, a professor of history and Holocaust studies at the University of Vermont and author of several books on Nazi Germany, wrote in a *New York Times* op-ed.

"Mr. Carson's argument," Steinweis went on, "is strangely ahistorical, a classic instance of injecting an issue that is important in our place and time into a historical situation where it was not seen as important. I can think of no serious work of scholarship on the Nazi dictatorship or on the causes of the Holocaust in which Nazi gun control measures feature as a significant factor. Neither does gun control figure in the collective historical memory of any group that was targeted by the Nazi regime, be they Jews, Gypsies, the disabled, gay people or Poles. It is simply a nonissue."

The NRA officially said nothing about the exchange, even though it touched the very heart of the modern Association's purported worldview and creed. But the NRA-funded scholar David Kopel did address the issue the next day in a piece for *The Volokh Conspiracy*, a conservative legal blog with a tongue-in-cheek name, hosted online for years by *The Washington Post*. Wrote Kopel:

> *Professor Steinweis's assertion that fighting Jews . . . made no difference is contrary to the historical record. His speculation that Jewish disarmament was irrelevant to [the] Holocaust is belied by the intensity of Nazi efforts to disarm their intended victims. Adolf Hitler, Josef Stalin, Mao Zedong, Idi Amin, Robert Mugabe, Pol Pot and other 20th-century mass murderers did not start their genocides until* after *they had disarmed whom they planned to exterminate. Murdering an armed person is harder than murdering the defenseless. The immediate victims may end up dead regardless, but they can still kill perpetrators, so that fewer perpetrators are available to murder the next victims. More guns, less genocide.*

By then Kopel was among the nation's most-quoted experts on gun issues in the press, besides also writing his own opinion pieces in *The Washington Post*, *The New York Times*, and *The Wall Street Journal*—and he went for years without mentioning his NRA funding. After dozens of people were killed and hundreds injured in a mass shooting in Las Vegas in 2017, a *Post* news story quoted Kopel as an independent expert applauding President Trump for "undoing or moderating anti-gun policies from anti-gun administrations." The *Journal* described Kopel as "a Colorado attorney and gun-rights advocate," but still did not disclose his NRA funding. The *Times* in a news story quoted Kopel without mention of his NRA funding, either.

In 2013, Stephen P. Halbrook, the scholar who back in 2008 had filed the amicus brief in *Heller* on behalf of most members of Congress, came out with a book titled *Gun Control in the Third Reich: Disarming the Jews and "Enemies of the State."* In it, he admits that,"[f]or whatever reason, historians have paid no attention to" the case he was making in the book. "Virtually none of the many tomes on the Third Reich so much as hints at the role that Weimar-era legislation and decrees were used by the Hitler government to consolidate power by disarming political enemies, Jews, and other 'enemies of the state.'" This alleged failure in historical scholarship, he warns, poses a grave danger today. "With selective memory of the historical events, a movement currently exists in the United States and Europe that denies the existence of any right to keep and bear arms and argues that firearms should be restricted to the military and the police."

The book was endorsed by a number of academics, including Steven B. Bowman, author of *Jewish Resistance in Wartime Greece*, and Ron Paul, the former congressman and presidential candidate. The privately published book lent itself to countless memes on social media, however, suggesting that gun control had led to the Holocaust—including Facebook posts by Ted Nugent in 2016.

"Based on newly discovered secret documents from German archives, diaries and newspapers of the time," the book "presents the definitive, yet hidden history of how the Nazi regime made use of gun control to disarm and repress its enemies and consolidate power," read the *American Rifleman*'s review. "While voluminous scholarship has documented the Third Reich and the Holocaust, this is the first thorough examination of the laws restricting firearm ownership that rendered Hitler's political opponents, as well as the Jews, defenseless." The review went on to point out that the book's lessons remain "instructive" for today, and no one should "take for granted the safeguards built into [our] constitutional system to deter the rise of unchecked power." The supposedly seminal book went unreviewed by almost every major newspaper and by policy and academic journals across the country. But *The Washington Times*, the capital's smaller daily, founded and still controlled by the Unification Movement (associated with the late Sung Myung Moon), eventually reviewed it. That reviewer, Robert Ver-Bruggen, hedged his bets. "There is no way to prove it," he wrote of the book's central idea—that gun control contributed to, if not caused, the Holocaust. But he did note that the book provides an "extensive history" of the matter.

* * *

The NRA's unqualified support for Trump, combined with allegations and evidence of financial mismanagement, has raised several issues for the Association that may yet prove hard to overcome. The NRA's tax filings for 2016, 2017, and 2018 show combined losses of over $66 million. In 2017, income from membership dues dropped by about $35 million, partly because the fear that Obama might seize weapons was gone, while revenue from contributions, grants, and gifts dropped another $35 million. This left the Association with a $32 million unrestricted asset deficit—although this figure seems to be buried in the NRA financial report that was shared with members in 2019 in Indianapolis.

The NRA's unprecedented role in Trump's presidential campaign also embroiled the Association in an international espionage scandal involving Maria Butina of the Moscow-based group Right to Bear Arms, who in December 2018 pled guilty to a charge of conspiracy to act as an unregistered foreign agent on behalf of Russia. Fluent in English, Butina was one of the few foreigners most NRA leaders had ever met who seemed to completely share their point of view. They seemed so pleased to know that another group in another major country even existed that they never bothered to check whether that group had any real constituency or base in Russia beyond having plenty of funds.

"It just doesn't exist," Anders Åslund, a Russia expert and senior fellow at the Atlantic Council, told *BuzzFeed* about the group. Butina had previously worked for a Russian banker and government official close to President Vladimir Putin named Alexander Torshin. Butina founded the group with Torshin's support sometime between 2010 and 2011, but it quickly gained a much greater presence in the United States than in Russia. "It's a ridiculous front organization with the purpose of infiltrating American groups and forging cooperation with the NRA," added Åslund.

Butina reached out to NRA officials, and soon invited the Association's president, David Keene, to speak at what seemed like a lightly attended Right to Bear Arms event in Moscow in 2013. There, perhaps feeling safe addressing a Russian-speaking audience, Keene openly discussed the NRA's shift from a group focused on marksmanship to one that concentrated on gun rights, using plainer language there than any NRA official has ever employed at home.

"At the National Rifle Association, which was formed in 1871, we spent a hundred years basically providing technical information to shooters, working with hunters, running national and international competitions and the like. But when it came to the time when our rights in the United States were threatened, we shifted our focus to defending those rights," he said in a speech videotaped by his Russian hosts, who put it up on YouTube.

Keene invited Butina to attend the NRA annual meeting in Indianapolis the following year, where she posed for one photograph with EVP Wayne LaPierre and another shot in which she handed the incoming NRA president, James W. Porter II, a plaque from Right to Bear Arms.

Butina reached out to Christian evangelicals, too, emphasizing the roles of both Christianity and firearms. "My story is simple—my father is a hunter, I was born in Siberia," she told an American evangelical talk radio host in 2015, comparing Siberia with rural areas in this nation like South Dakota, and saying that in both places guns are "necessary for survival" and to defend lives and property. In 2016 Butina managed to get invited to the National Prayer Breakfast in Washington, which opened the doors for her to meet high-profile Republicans, including Wisconsin governor Scott Walker and Donald Trump. (But in the spring of 2019, on the very same day that President Trump and Vice President Pence would address NRA members at the annual meeting in Indianapolis, Butina would be sentenced in federal court to eighteen months in prison. The matter of her conviction would not be raised at the NRA annual meeting at all.)

In November 2016, six days after Trump won the presidency, the NRA released a video of Wayne LaPierre on NRATV.com. In it he proclaimed, "In the face of the bitter hatred and elitist condemnation, this is our historic moment to go on offense and defeat the forces that have allied against our freedom once and for all." Meanwhile, during its lame-duck period before President Trump's inauguration, the Obama administration expelled thirty-five Russian diplomats from Washington over evidence of their suspected involvement in Russian government hacking of social media as part of a conspiracy to influence the election.

The NRA, which had all but invented the self-romanticizing notion of an everyday American struggling in the face of "bitter hatred and elitist condemnation," found their perfect partner in Trump, with his railing against "elites." Within a span of little more than four years, the NRA has been drawn in from the right-wing edge of the GOP to the very heart of the Trump-led Republican Party.

This alliance has already borne fruit in the Supreme Court. Justice Antonin Scalia was replaced by Neal Gorsuch, a former federal appellate judge who is now among the most conservative justices ever to sit on the Court. Combined with the replacement of retired

Justice Anthony Kennedy with Brett Kavanaugh, this has shifted the Court markedly to the right, which seems all but certain to have a profound impact on any future gun cases.

* * *

In October 2017, a sixty-four-year-old man legally brought an arsenal of weapons packed inside over a dozen suitcases into a luxury hotel in Las Vegas with the help of bellhops. Sometime later he broke open a window and opened fire from the thirty-second floor, discharging more than a thousand rounds onto a crowd of country music festival-goers below. He used a crude bump-stock device to convert rifles, including AR-15s with extended magazines holding up to a hundred rounds each, into slow but still automatic-firing weapons, meaning that the rifle will keep reloading and firing after each bump from the recoil as long as the shooter keeps depressing the trigger. In the nation's worst modern gun tragedy (as of this writing), fifty-eight people died, and more than eight hundred were injured, both by the gunfire and in the ensuing panic.

Little more than a month later, in Texas, a twenty-six-year-old man with a domestic violence conviction in a military court-martial— which legally disqualified him from purchasing firearms—opened fire with an AR-15 rifle, a Ruger AR556, at the First Baptist Church in Sutherland Springs, killing twenty-six people and injuring twenty more in the nation's deadliest shooting at a house of worship. Despite his conviction, he had been able to buy weapons because the U.S. Air Force had never reported his conviction to the FBI, which manages the National Instant Criminal Background Check System for gun purchases.

In Parkland, Florida, on Valentine's Day 2018, a nineteen-year-old man armed with an AR-15 rifle, a Smith & Wesson M&P15, opened fire inside his former school, Marjory Stoneman Douglas High School, killing seventeen people, including fourteen students, and wounding seventeen more.

The shooting at Marjory Stoneman Douglas High School challenged the NRA like never before. The Parkland secondary school had been named after a Florida environmentalist and suffragette. "I would be very sad if I had not fought. I'd have a guilty conscience if I had been here and watched all this happen to the environment and not been on the right side," Marjory Stoneman Douglas once said. After the shooting, surviving students including Emma González and David Hogg spoke out, helping to galvanize a movement of "emotionalism" that soon spread nationwide—and was so powerful that companies from rental-car brands to Yeti cut ties with the NRA.

One week after the Parkland shooting, the NRA hired Dana Loesch, the gun activist and nationally syndicated conservative talk radio host, as Wayne LaPierre's new special assistant for public communication. The next day both she and LaPierre spoke in Washington before the Conservative Political Action Committee. Loesch accused the press of profiteering from Parkland, while LaPierre blamed even darker forces. It was the pressure from surviving Parkland students that seemed to compel LaPierre to deviate from his usual balancing act and heat up his message.

"The first to go will be the Second Amendment of the United States Constitution," he said. "It is all backed in this country by the social engineering and the billions of people like George Soros, Michael Bloomberg, Tom Steyer and more." Two different columnists from the liberal Israeli daily *Haaretz* noted that the three billionaires named by LaPierre all happened to be Jewish.

Eight months later, on October 27, 2018, a forty-six-year-old man who had made recent anti-Semitic and anti-immigrant remarks on social media and was armed with a Colt AR-15 rifle and three Glock .357 Sig pistols killed eleven people and injured seven more in

Pittsburgh's Tree of Life synagogue, in the deadliest attack yet on the Jewish community in the United States.

* * *

Carry Guard, an NRA-issued insurance program to pay for the legal defense of someone who uses a concealed or openly carried weapon in defense of themselves or others, was launched in the spring of 2016 and was expected to be a moneymaker for the Association. But things did not turn out as planned. The rates ranged from $13.95 a month for up to $250,000 in civil protection and $50,000 in criminal defense to a "gold plus" policy that cost $49.95 a month and provided up to $1.5 million in civil protection and $250,000 in criminal defense. Critics called it "murder insurance." The plan was marketed and administered by Lockton, the world's largest insurance brokerage firm, and was underwritten by another insurance giant, Chubb. The states of California, Washington, and New York soon launched investigations.

Carry Guard was pushed hard by the NRA on its members. To help promote it, the NRA offered members at annual meetings the opportunity to experience in virtual reality what it might be like to fire a weapon to defend themselves and others. Equipped with a virtual gun and immersion headset, one finds oneself in a three-dimensional, 360-degree panaroma of a convenience store, when a man in plain sight with a gun near an innocent woman tries to rob the store. Seeing a clean shot, shooters of all kinds end up firing and hitting the armed suspect in this virtual environment, only to soon find themselves being loaded into the back of a police car and then interrogated by two detectives all but accusing them of murder.

New York State authorities under Governor Andrew Cuomo in 2018 fined ten insurance firms up to $5 million for underwriting Carry Guard, saying they "unlawfully provided insurance coverage" for "defense coverage in a criminal proceeding that is not permitted by law" and for actions that go "beyond the use of reasonable force." By then the NRA had already sued New York State—shortly after the first fines were levied—after a number of insurers stopped underwriting Carry Guard. The NRA claimed in its lawsuit that New York's actions were a violation of free speech that had cost the NRA tens of millions of dollars and "imperiled" its financial health.

But in 2018, after the Parkland high school shooting, Chubb decided to stop underwriting the plan. Lockton agreed to pay New York $7 million for violations of state law in marketing the plan and to terminate policies held by New Yorkers. The NRA in 2019 finally admitted it was no longer offering the plan.

A more surprising lawsuit is the pending legal matter between the NRA and Ackerman McQueen. In the spring of 2019, the NRA filed a suit in Virginia against its longtime "communications wing" for an alleged "lack of transparency" in billing records. The suit occurred amid allegations that Dana Loesch and Oliver North had negotiated separate contracts of nearly $1 million a year each with Ackerman McQueen for their respective work on AM-run NRATV, according to *The New Yorker*. The combination of financial and internal troubles associated with this case led the generally measured Associated Press to describe the NRA as "weakened."

The NRA lawsuit claimed that Ackerman McQueen had failed for nearly a year to provide requested records. The request was prompted by a change in New York State laws requiring more transparency and oversight for all nonprofit groups registered in the state. What seemed like a routine accounting request to comply with new requirements surprisingly ended up rupturing the nearly forty-year relationship between Ackerman McQueen and the NRA.

"Ackerman McQueen has served the NRA and its members with great pride and dedication for the last 38 years," the company said in a statement, calling the NRA's suit against the firm "frivolous, inaccurate and intended to cause harm to the reputation of our company."

The NRA in the lawsuit is also demanding documentation about Ackerman McQueen's third-party contract with Oliver North. North had been an NRA director since 2001. In Dallas in the spring of 2018, North announced he was stepping down from his paid position as an on-air commentator on Fox News to assume his new duties as NRA president. He was the handpicked choice of LaPierre and his allies on the board. But in its lawsuit the NRA alleges that North was already negotiating a reported $1 million salary from Ackerman McQueen to appear on NRATV, in an arrangement whereby the salary would be billed along with other costs to the NRA.

"As Col. North prepared to assume the presidency of the NRA, he separately discussed a potential engagement by [Ackerman McQueen] as the host of an NRATV documentary series," reads the NRA's lawsuit. The Association claims that Ackerman McQueen's failure to provide the NRA with complete billing records makes it impossible for the leadership to determine whether Ackerman McQueen has charged the NRA "fair market value" for its services as specified in their contract.

North addressed NRA members in 2019 in Indianapolis but did not attend the board meeting afterward, saying he had learned the board would not support his reelection for the customary second one-year term. Instead, North had NRA first vice president Richard Childress, a former NASCAR racing driver, read a letter in front of board directors in support of North. The letter accused LaPierre, who was sitting in the room, of financial mismanagement and corruption, including $200,000 worth of wardrobe purchases that he allegedly billed to a vendor in order to have it paid for by the NRA. But before Childress got through more than a few paragraphs, a director motioned to move the meeting into executive session, which was seconded and then approved by a majority voice vote with many dissensions, showing the split in the room and leadership. NRA staffers and the attending members, including myself and Mark Robinson, along with many spouses, left the room. The executive session lasted more than six hours, longer than even during the Knox wars back in the 1990s.

LaPierre was soon under fire again, as he had apparently arranged for the NRA to take steps to purchase a $6 million French-chateau-style house in a tony suburb of Dallas, claiming that he and his wife, who have no children, needed the home for security reasons after the Parkland high school shooting. The NRA never went through with the purchase. In its 2019 annual meeting in Indianapolis, Childress read a prior letter by Oliver North to the floor of the Members' Meeting saying that the improprieties could threaten the nonprofit status of the NRA, which was currently under investigation in New York by the state attorney general. One of the more prominent board directors to support North and Childress's call for an internal audit was rocker Ted Nugent, who told *The Washington Times* that the NRA under LaPierre has been "less than accountable."

By then LaPierre had accused North of having used "the parlance of extortionists" in a phone call to LaPierre's longtime executive assistant, in which he demanded that LaPierre resign and that the NRA withdraw the lawsuit against Ackerman McQueen. LaPierre further said that some of North's allies warned him that if he did not resign he would "be smeared." Meanwhile, a number of prominent members backing North, including large individual donors, demanded independent oversight (by someone other than board members) of LaPierre and the board's finances. But board members including former NRA presidents Marion Hammer—who flew up from her home in Tallahassee to support LaPierre in her first attendance at any NRA annual meeting in over a decade, as she has been caring for her grandchildren since her daughter's death—and James W. Porter II defended LaPierre. Porter, in particular, pointed to the unprecedented success the Association had enjoyed over just the past few years because of the NRA's historic alliance with President Trump.

Since at least the late 1990s, former NRA officials and others have been accusing Ackerman McQueen of overcharging the Association. Calling today's allegations "exactly the same," Jeff Knox said, "It's not clear what we're paying for, it's not clear what we're accountable to, we don't have standards, and this needs to change."

Dana Loesch's contract was also reportedly under review, although she was not named in the lawsuit. One of NRATV's biggest stars for over a year until it folded, Loesch has used the platform to attack critics of both the NRA and President Trump. Two months after President Trump's inauguration, Loesch launched a broadside attack against NRA critics, including members of the press, using language not too far from possibly inciting violence:

> To every lying member of the media, to every Hollywood phony, to the role-model athletes who use their free speech to alter and undermine what our flag represents. To the politicians who would rather watch America burn than lose one ounce of their own personal power. To the late-night hosts who think their opinions are the only opinions that matter. To the Joy-Ann Reids, the Morning Joes, the Mikas. To those who stain honest reporting with partisanship. To those who bring bias and propaganda to CNN, The Washington Post, and The New York Times. Your time is running out. The clock starts now.

More than a year before, also on NRATV, Loesch had used explicitly violent language against the press, saying, "I'm happy, frankly, to see them curb-stomped." She was using a term that the online Urban Dictionary defines as "To place someone's mouth on a cement curb, and then stomp on their head from behind to break out their teeth." Loesch went on to say the mainstream media "are the rat-bastards of the earth. They are the boil on the backside of American politics." More recently, Loesch has received death threats on Twitter from users, some of whom were later blocked by Twitter administrators. Loesch has also posted pictures on Twitter of bagged clothes and personal items piled up in her home's foyer, saying she and her family have had to temporarily leave their house due to the threats. NRATV, established in 2014, has in more recent years taken an increasingly "apocalyptic tone, warning of race wars, calling for a march on the Federal Bureau of Investigation and portraying the talking trains in the children's show 'Thomas & Friends' in Ku Klux Klan hoods."

It remains unclear whether or how the relationship between the NRA and Ackerman McQueen might recover after the lawsuit, or what the fallout may yet mean for the NRA's messaging considering that its partnership with the group has long been stable.

It also remains unclear what the future holds for Wayne LaPierre. "The Captain," as LaPierre was dubbed by Senator Orrin Hatch, still enjoys the confidence of the NRA board, including Hammer and Porter, and as of this writing he has been able to hold on to power.

The nation's gun industry itself, of course, has a key interest in the NRA's fate. Gun sales across America peaked in 2016 at 15.7 million units, out of fear that a victory by Hillary Clinton might usher in a new era of gun control. But the industry has nonetheless enjoyed strong gun sales in recent years. According to the National Shooting Sports Foundation, "The total economic impact of the firearms and ammunition industry in the United States increased from $19.1 billion in 2008 to $52.1 billion in 2018, a 171 percent increase, while the total number of full-time equivalent jobs rose from approximately 166,000 to almost 312,000, an 88 percent increase in that period."

There is a lot of money at stake for the NRA's own long-term executives, too. In 2018, the NRA slashed its hunter and field programs by more than half, while its legal fees tripled. That same year the annual salary for EVP LaPierre rose 55 percent, to $2.2 million, besides $821,000 in other compensation. The NRA presidency, on the other hand, has long been a voluntary, pulpit post. Yet President North's annualized salary that same year was about $2.1 million. In 2019, LaPierre also forced out chief lobbyist Chris Cox, who had been earning at least $1.2 million. For years Cox, who was well-liked among the board directors and the membership, had been rumored to one day succeed LaPierre as the EVP. But now if LaPierre is forced out, no one knows who will replace him. LaPierre still faces not only an ongoing investigation by New York State authorities but also board directors like Ted Nugent and Allen West who are hostile to him and popular among members. Not since the eve of the Cincinnati Revolt has the leadership looked so unstable.

* * *

"The NRA is a fellowship of average, everyday people," Dana Loesch said recently.

In many ways, Loesch is right. Many, many honorable people are members of the National Rifle Association. But the worldview and creed they support with their dues would be harder and harder for the Association's progenitors to identify with.

Today this ideology or creed has two parts: No law-abiding gun owner should ever be penalized or even inconvenienced over the misuse of firearms by others. And almost any form of gun control would require gun registration, which would inevitably lead to gun confiscation, followed by tyranny if not genocide. The dubious merits of these assertions aside, it is important to note that for more than forty years the NRA's leaders have done their best not to say this out loud very often in public. Nonetheless, as we have seen, it is a creed shared by many NRA members and other gun rights advocates, not to mention by tens of millions more Americans—including, it would seem, the president of the United States.

Nothing better illustrates the influence of the NRA and the power of its creed than President Trump's flip-flop in the summer of 2019 over background checks. Days before, over an August weekend, the nation suffered two massive back-to-back shootings, in El Paso, Texas, and Dayton, Ohio, each one leaving dozens dead and dozens more wounded. President Trump first said he was in favor of background checks. Then he spoke on the phone with the NRA EVP. Shortly afterward this tweet appeared from the NRA's official account: "I spoke to the president today. We discussed the best ways to prevent these types of tragedies. @realDonaldTrump is a strong #2A President and supports our Right to Keep and Bear Arms!—Wayne LaPierre."

"You know they call it the slippery slope, and all of a sudden everything gets taken away. We're not going to let that happen," President Trump told reporters, reversing himself on background checks and repeating the modern NRA's central creed—that even the most seemingly benign form of gun control is a slippery slope to gun registration, leading to gun confiscation and then tyranny if not genocide—even though this is only a theory and there is no actual evidence to support this claim.

Or, as LaPierre himself wrote in a 2015 column, "Don't Buy Their Lies: 'Universal Background Checks' Mean Gun Registration, Gun Bans and Confiscation":

Around the world and throughout history, gun registration schemes have one thing in common: registration virtually always precedes mandatory and compulsory gun surrender or confiscation. Yet too many Americans say, "It can't happen here" or "You don't have anything to worry about." But it can happen here. It has happened here. And it is happening here.

It is the consequences of this very same belief in the horror of gun registration—a belief that arose within the NRA as early as the 1930s, and that was put on the books in 1986, signed into law by President Reagan—that make America truly exceptional, distinguishing the United States from every other advanced nation. Every other developed nation in the world has gun control based on the licensing of gun owners and registering of guns, to the degree that private gun ownership is permitted at all, and every one of these same nations has exponentially less gun violence and fewer police shootings than the United States does. Even more staggering, more Americans have died from gun violence since 1968—the same year, ironically, that a compromise gun control law, later weakened, passed with NRA support—than have died in all the nation's wars since the Revolutionary War.

Nor is gun control responsible for the recent rise of authoritarian governments in many other nations. All this may help explain why the NRA could never find a like-minded counterpart in Canada, the countries of Western Europe, Japan, or most other places. The National Rifle Association of the United Kingdom, the progenitor of the NRA as we know it, continues to promote marksmanship and competitions without challenging its nations' strict gun laws, much like other gun clubs do around the world. Meanwhile, one of the first foreign gun groups to advocate for gun rights like the NRA does, the Moscow-based Right to Bear Arms, has still not demonstrated any measurable following in its own country.

In October 2019—on the eve of the 2020 NRA board elections for 25 of the 76 directors who control his fate—LaPierre, noting the uprising against him, brandished his own early ties to the legendary leader of the Cincinnati Revolt for the first time in decades. "I learned from great leaders, such as Harlon B. Carter, and was part of a team you funded to protect your freedom," he wrote in his "Standing Guard" column.

It was Harlon Carter, the founding father of the modern NRA

and nearly the only past NRA leader of any era whose legacy is still quietly honored, who said that "he would rather let convicted violent felons and the mentally deranged buy guns than endorse a screening process for gun sales. . . . That's the 'price we pay for freedom.'"

"This is the price of freedom," former Fox News anchor Bill O'Reilly wrote on his own blog in 2017 after the gun tragedy at the country music festival in Las Vegas. "Violent nuts are allowed to roam free until they do damage, no matter how threatening they are. The 2nd Amendment is clear that Americans have a right to arm themselves for protection. Even the loons."

* * *

Everyone in America knows another mass shooter looms around the corner, close to home, ready to strike without warning, targeting innocent people (including if not especially women and children) who for whatever reason have drawn his ire.

That first weekend in August 2019 sent a jolt to a country already numb from seemingly countless prior attacks. One Saturday morning, as shoppers of largely Hispanic descent were buying clothes and other items before the end of summer and the start of a new school year, a man opened fire in a Walmart parking lot in El Paso, Texas, near the Mexican border, with a Romanian-made semiautomatic version of a Kalashnikov rifle; then he entered the store and continued shooting. He killed twenty-two people and injured twenty-seven more before police apprehended him. Among the dead were thirteen Americans, eight Mexicans, and one German; the youngest was fifteen years old. A manifesto the shooter appears to have posted less than a half hour before the attack praised the March 15, 2019, mosque shooting in Christchurch, New Zealand, in a white power screed that echoed both neo-Nazi and so-called alt-right language, not to mention some of the language used by President Trump; it said the shooter was targeting immigrants as a way of "defending my country from cultural and ethnic replacement brought on by an invasion."

Thirteen hours later, a gunman armed with an AM-15 version of an AR-15 firing mechanism with a shortened barrel and equipped with a 100-round double-drum magazine killed nine people in Dayton, Ohio, including his sister, with whom he had just had a drink, and wounded at least seventeen more in a span of no more than thirty-two seconds before he was shot dead by police already on patrol in the area. His motivations seem less clear. Former high school classmates said he had a "hit list" of people whom he said he wanted to kill. The same shooter used his Twitter account to retweet left-wing and anti-police posts, and to tweet in support of "Antifa" or anti-fascist militants. Authorities were investigating whether the El Paso attack meets the threshold for a federal hate crime. The Dayton shooting at this point at least does not.

Both the El Paso and Dayton shooters, like the perpetrators in most other such mass shootings, bought their weapons, accessories, and ammunition legally. While these two shootings together prompted national attention, many other mass shootings with smaller death tolls—albeit no less deadly for the victims and traumatic for surviving loved ones—do not.

And by the time you're reading this there will have been others.

* * *

The National Rifle Association is a quintessentially American group, unlike any other of its size or influence in the nation or around the world. The NRA is the strongest vanguard of America's gun rights movement, which has light and dark sides, including white power groups. The NRA since its shift in 1977 has rewritten several aspects of history, including its own, to support its goals. The NRA is perhaps the only organization to have an archive of priceless documents and videos that it still refuses to share with its own members, let alone the world.

Looking back over the NRA's rich, exhumed history, one stands in awe of an organization rooted in patriotism, steeped in service, long dedicated to the promotion of safe and better riflery for soldiers and citizens alike. An organization that was once an early pioneer of environmental awareness and which established the very practice of hunter conservation. An organization that has heralded tradition and the passing on of firearms and their proper use down through families across the generations.

One stands in awe, too, of the long, shifted arc of the same Association. One can only wonder what William Conant Church and George Wood Wingate might think of the NRA they founded nearly a century and half ago. They were grand men who always acted beyond themselves, who promoted common good and civic virtue at every turn. Church, a veritable Renaissance man, and Wingate, the public schools athletic pioneer, would no doubt agree that if this is the price of freedom, it is a steep price to pay.

ACKNOWLEDGMENTS

I am grateful to a world of people. Jake Bernstein and Candace Nicole provided invaluable input early on. Peter Bergen generously lent his support. Mel Berger at William Morris Endeavor took a chance on a guy without a single trade book to his name. Noah Eaker at Flatiron Books guided the manuscript, shaping and sharpening it at every turn. David Hinds at WME and Lauren Bittrich at Flatiron were each selfless. Karyn-Siobhán Robinson unearthed rare materials. Janet Hawkins backstopped my research. Laura Zornosa dug up more facts. Tony Speranza shared insight. Flatiron's Alan Bradshaw polished the prose.

Archivists at the University of Maryland Hornbake Library, the University of West Georgia Ingram Library, the New York Public Library, The Civil War Research Engine at Dickinson College, and the Gerald R. Ford Presidential Library at Texas A&M University opened documents for this book.

The Carey Institute for Global Good generously included me among the fall 2019 Logan Nonfiction Fellows. I am grateful to each of my Fellows colleagues along with the Jonathan Logan Family Foundation for their support.

Many more people have lent me their kindness or gone to bat for me over the years, and they include family, friends, colleagues, editors, mentors, and others. However, rather than list them here, I am reaching out to thank each one personally.

There is a story behind the dedication. Peter L. Mazzarella was a founding charter member of the Rotary Club of Fair Lawn, New Jersey, and a lifelong Republican, besides being my grandfather who helped raise me. In the summer of 1973, as we were watching officials testify in the Watergate hearings, he turned to me, then still a tween, and said, "Watch this one, Frankie. He's lying."

"How do you know, Grandpa? How do you know?"

"Just keep watching, Frankie. You'll see."

On another personal note, neither my mother, Dolores, nor my dad, Jim, nor my father who died young, Frank, are still with us. But I remain grateful for them and for countless more blessings.

NOTES

INTRODUCTION

1 "Major League" baseball: The National Association of Professional Base Ball Players was the nation's first "Major League," and their first game fielded the Cleveland Forest Citys against the hometown Fort Wayne Kekiongas on May 4, 1871, noted *The Civil War Era and Reconstruction: An Encyclopedia of Social, Political, Cultural and Economic History*, by Mary Ellen Snodgrass (London and New York: Routledge, 2015), 565. The National League of Professional Baseball Clubs with one of the same clubs, the New York Mutuals, was formed in 1876, and this league in 1903 merged into MLB.

1 "shifted [its] focus": Mark Follman, "NRA President Offered to Work with Accused Russian Spy's Group in Moscow: Video from the 2013 Event with Maria Butina Sheds Further Light on NRA-Russia Ties," *Mother Jones*, July 20, 2018, online at https://www.motherjones.com/politics/2018/07/nra-russia-maria-butina-alexander -torshin-republicans-trump. Original event: David Keene, ex-president, current board member of the US National Rifle Association, at the 2nd Congress of the Right to Arms public movement in Moscow, October 31–November 1, 2013, https://www .youtube.com/watch?v=1tj-ceQb9Ao&feature=youtu.be.

3 the Association's helm: James B. Trefethen, comp., *Americans and Their Guns: The National Rifle Association Story—Through Nearly a Century of Service to the Nation*, ed. James E. Serven (Harrisburg, PA: Stackpole, 1967), 255–256, 260.

3 NRA oral history: NRA oral history interview with Lieutenant General Milton A. Reckord, conducted by Elwood Maunder, accompanied by NRA official Louis F. Lucas, in Reckord's home in Towson, Maryland, March 14, 1974, on file under "Oral History, National Rifle Association," in the Milton Reckord Papers, archived at Hornbake Library at the University of Maryland, 561-C-24.

3 "The Dope Bag": "The Dope Bag," *Arms and the Man: The Official Organ of the National Rifle Association of America*, January 15, 1922, 27.

3 "The Fox gun you mention": "The Dope Bag: A 'Super' Duck Gun, Answer by Captain Askins," *Arms and the Man*, October 15, 1922, 27.

4 "There is no difference": Wayne LaPierre, "Standing Guard: In Today's Democratic Party, Democrat Equals Socialist," NRA, America's 1st Freedom, March 6, 2018, online at https://www.americas1stfreedom.org/articles/2018/3/6/standing-guard-in-todays-democratic-party-democrat-equals-socialist/.

4 "the bedrock values of our society": Wayne LaPierre, "Standing Guard: Reclaiming America," American Rifleman, August 2014, 12–13.

7 prospective members were required to affirm: "NRA Membership Pledge," sidebar to "NRA Disavows Connections with Groups Advocating Violence," American Rifleman, October 1964, 72–73.

8 Hammer remains as pivotal: Mike Spies, "The Unchecked Influence of NRA Lobbyist Marion Hammer," The Trace, February 23, 2018, online at https://www.thetrace.org/features/nra-influence-florida-marion-hammer-gun-laws/.

10 "climate controlled room with restricted access": "Report by the NRA Secretary Edward L. Land, Jr., to NRA Board of Directors and Executive Council," Arlington, Virginia, November 3–4, 2001, archived in the Bob Barr Papers, Ingram Library, University of West Georgia.

ONE: WITH AN EYE TOWARD FUTURE WARS

15 an economic boom would transform the nation: See Richard White, The Republic for Which It Stands: The United States During Reconstruction and the Gilded Age, 1865–1896 (New York: Oxford University Press, 2017).

16 At least 360,000 Union: Thomas L. Livermore, Numbers and Losses in the Civil War in America 1861–1865 (Boston: Houghton, Mifflin, 1900). See also Guy Gugliotta, "New Estimate Raises Civil War Death Toll," New York Times, April 3, 2012.

16 No other war since has claimed: Jeremy Bender, "This Chart Shows the Astounding Devastation of World War II," Business Insider, May 29, 2014.

16 "Each day has been an era": Pierrepont, "A Day of Rest—A Review of the Week's Work—Gen. Stoneman Within Fifteen Miles of Richmond—Skirmishes on the Way," New York Times, May 11, 1862; and Donald Nevius Bigelow, William Conant Church and the Army and Navy Journal (New York: Columbia University Press, 1952), 83.

16 "At times it seemed doubtful": George W. Wingate, The Last Campaign of the Twenty-Second Regiment N.G.S.N.Y. (New York: C. S. Wescott, 1864), 21–22, cited in "Recollection in 1864 of the Shelling of Carlisle, July 1, 1863 by George Wood Wingate," in House Divided: The Civil War Research Engine at Dickinson College, online at housedivided.dickinson.edu.

17 William Church was a lifetime member: Society of Colonial Wars in the State of New York, Year Book for 1920–1921, no. 29, May 1921, 107–108.

17 "In addition to the muscular development": George W. Wingate, "The Public Schools Athletic League," Outing Magazine, May 1908, 169.

17 the best shot in his company: "Life Sketches, Colonel George W. Wingate," National Guardsman, April 1978, 146, cited in Jeffrey A. Marlin, "The National Guard, the National Board for the Promotion of Rifle Practice, and the National Rifle Association: Public Institutions and the Rise of a Lobby for Private Gun Ownership," PhD diss., Georgia State University, 2013, 62, online at https://pdfs.semanticscholar.org/d733/582660311b553174751cf7dc37de8810b149.pdf.

18 He would eventually author: George W. Wingate, "Theoretical Instruction" [excerpt from *Manual for Rifle Practice: Including Suggestions for Practice at Long Range and for the Formation and Management of Rifle Associations*, 5th ed.], *United States Army and Navy Journal, and Gazette of the Regular and Volunteer Forces*, 1876, 58–59.

18 "I jumped off my horse": George Wood Wingate, *Through the Yellowstone Park on Horseback* (New York: O. Judd, 1886), 161–162.

19 "In leaving us": Bigelow, *William Conant Church*, 35.

19 "He was as much at home": Bigelow, *William Conant Church*, 243.

20 The *Galaxy*'s contributors: Bigelow, *William Conant Church*, 232–234.

20 Both were supportive of an active role: Frederick Whitaker, "The Story of Creedmoor," *Galaxy*, August 1876, 258–266; Marlin, "The National Guard," 84–172.

20 But the unexpected deaths of three: Russell L. Gilmore, "Another Branch of Manly Sport: American Rifle Games 1840–1900," in *Guns in America: A Reader*, vol. 1, ed. Jon E. Dizard, Robert Merrill Muth, and Stephen P. Andrews Jr. (New York: New York University Press, 1999), 108.

21 But in the Prussian campaigns against first Austria: David Gates, *Warfare in the Nineteenth Century* (Houndmills, UK: Palgrave, 2001), 3–5, 150–165.

21 "An association should be organized": *Army and Navy Journal*, August 1871; Trefethen, *Americans and Their Guns*, 34.

21 Wingate and Church convened a group of sixteen men: "The National Rifle Association: What It Was Organized For, Who Compose It, What It Proposes to Do, and What It Has Done," January 14, 1873, in *The National Rifle Association 1873. Address, Annual Reports, and Regulations for Rifle Practice* (New York: Reynolds & Whelpley, 1877), 7.

21 They packed themselves: Trefethen, *Americans and Their Guns*, 34–35.

22 The Fifteenth Amendment: Eric Foner, *A Short History of Reconstruction 1863–1877* (New York: HarperCollins, 2014), 191–193.

22 The 1871 Indian Appropriation Act: "Enrolled Acts and Resolutions of Congress, 1789–2011," General Records of the United States Government, Record Group 11, National Archives, Washington, D.C. The act was passed on March 3, 1871.

22 Major General Alexander Shaler: Trefethen, *Americans and Their Guns*, 38–39.

22 Major John N. Partridge: Edgar L. Murlin, *The New York Red Book: An Illustrated Legislative Manual* (Albany, NY: James B. Lyon, 1901), 49.

22 General Franz Sigel: "Franz Sigel (1824–1902)," Profiles of Historic Missourians, State Historical Society of Missouri, online at https://historicmissourians.shsmo.org/historicmissourians/name/s/sigel/.

22 Colonel Watson C. Squire: "Sharpshooter to Senator," in "Washington Gossip: This Week's Doings at the National Capital," *National Tribune*, December 5, 1889, 5.

22 A man "of medium height, rather stout": H. H. Boone and Theodore P. Cook, *Life Sketches of Executive Officers and Members of the Legislature of the State of New York* (Albany, NY: Weed, Parsons, 1870), 3, 194–196.

23 "I had engaged a *valet de place*": "Impetuous Mr. Blaine; How Mr. Cullen Enjoyed That Overcoat Incident," *New York Times*, November 13, 1887, 9.

23 Alfred W. Craven: Board of Water Commissioners, *The Brooklyn Water Works and Sewers. A Descriptive Memoir.* (New York: P. Van Nostrand, 1867); and "Site of the Founding Meeting of ASCE on Nov. 5, 1852," American Society of Civil Engineers, online at https://www.asce.org/project/site-of-the-founding-meeting-of-asce-on-nov-5,-1852/.

23 Its mission was documented: "The National Rifle Association: What It Was Organized For," edited and reprinted in part in "The Creedmoor Rifle Range," *Harper's Weekly*, June 28, 1873, 557–558.

24 "[T]he Civil War had demonstrated with bloody clarity": George W. Wingate, "Early Days of the NRA: Recollections of the National Rifle Association," *American Rifleman*, May 1951, 32.

TWO: THE "ROYAL" NRA

25 Established in 1859: Barrie Rose, "The Volunteers of 1859," *Journal of the Society for Army Historical Research* 37, no. 151 (September 1959): 97–110.

25 Alfred Tennyson: Alfred Tennyson, "Rifleman Form!," *Times* of London, May 9, 1859.

25 Queen Victoria herself: David Minshall, "Wimbledon and the Volunteers," 30–37, and Christopher C. Bunch, "The First Wimbledon Meeting," 38–47, both in the *British National Rifle Association Journal*, September 2010.

26 to prevent "any international confusion": James B. Trefethen, comp., *Americans and Their Guns: The National Rifle Association Story—Through Nearly a Century of Service to the Nation*, ed. James E. Serven (Harrisburg, PA: Stackpole, 1967), 77.

26 "Fortunately, David W. Judd": George W. Wingate, "Early Days of the NRA: Recollections of the National Rifle Association," *American Rifleman*, May 1951, 33.

26 Upon seeing the marshland: Trefethen, *Americans and Their Guns*, 42.

26 "while Gen. John B. Woodward": Trefethen, *Americans and Their Guns*, 47.

26 The NRA adopted the range distances: Wingate, "Early Days of the NRA," 32–35. Wingate also said that he took "ideas from the French and German systems" too.

27 "Finding that there were no American establishments": "Proceedings of Annual Meeting, January 14, 1873," report to NRA Board by Geo. W. Wingate, Secretary, New York, January 14, 1873; *The National Rifle Association 1873. Address, Annual Reports, and Regulations for Rifle Practice* (New York: Reynolds & Whelpley, 1877), 15.

27 "The fact is that the shooters": Trefethen, *Americans and Their Guns*, 74–75.

27 the NRA's second official history, *NRA: An American Legend*: Jeffrey A. Rodengen, *NRA: An American Legend* (Fort Lauderdale, FL: Write Stuff, 2002).

28 "The NRA Archives": Edward L. Land Jr. to NRA Board and Executive Council, National Rifle Association of America Report of the Secretary, Arlington, Virginia, November 3–4, 2001, archived in the Bob Barr Papers, Ingram Library, University of West Georgia.

29 Lieutenant Colonel West was fined: Deborah Sontag, "The Struggle for Iraq Interrogations; How Colonel Risked His Career by Menacing Detainee and Lost," *New York Times*, May 27, 2004.

29 "From this time forth": Donald N. Bigelow, *William Conant Church and the Army and Navy Journal* (New York: Columbia University Press, 1952), 200.

29 "We should never forget": Gen. Geo. W. Wingate, *Why Should Boys Be Taught to Shoot?* (Boston: Sub-Target Gun Co., 1907), 1.

30 "He asked that 'nigger' and 'dago'": Bigelow, *William Conant Church*, 194–195.

30 "We cannot have 20,000": *Army and Navy Journal*, March 27, 1869, in Bigelow, *William Conant Church*, 191. See also Richard White, *The Republic for Which It Stands: The United States During Reconstruction and the Gilded Age, 1865–1896* (New York: Oxford University Press, 2017), 202–208; and, among others, G. J. A. O'Toole, *The Spanish War: An American Epic 1898* (New York: W. W. Norton, 1986); and "Maine Blown Up" and "We Must Keep What We Want" in Michael Beschloss, *Presidents of War* (New York: Crown, 2018), 240–292.

30 "classical realist": See Robert D. Kaplan, "Kissinger, Metternich, and Realism," *Atlantic*, June 1999.

30 "To devour or to be devoured": Bigelow, *William Conant Church*, 188.

30 "into inaction by unwise reliance": Bigelow, *William Conant Church*, 189–190.

31 did not feel "kindly toward the trolley companies": Jerry Cooper, *The Rise of the National Guard: The Evolution of the American Militia, 1865–1920* (Lincoln: University of Nebraska Press, 1997), 57.

31 seeing their "contempt for authority": Bigelow, *William Conant Church*, 228.

31 Wingate, by now promoted: Trefethen, *Americans and Their Guns*, 56–58.

31 "the cool climate of the Emerald Isle": Trefethen, *Americans and Their Guns*, 63.

31 "The regular and special trains": Trefethen, *Americans and Their Guns*, 62.

32 "A roar of applause": Trefethen, *Americans and Their Guns*, 62.

32 The Irish won the coin toss: Trefethen, *Americans and Their Guns*, 62–63.

32 "Only Dr. J. B. Hamilton": Trefethen, *Americans and Their Guns*, 63. These two shooters each outshot the others.

32 "Wingate had arranged": Trefethen, *Americans and Their Guns*, 65–66.

33 Dr. Hamilton approached: Trefethen, *Americans and Their Guns*, 66.

33 "Every one of the thousands": George W. Wingate, "Early Days," *American Rifleman*, May 1951, 35.

33 Church—who had already presided: Frederick Whitaker, "The Story of Creedmoor," *Galaxy*, August 1876, 260.

34 Burnside is popularly known: See Andrew Marvel, *Burnside* (Chapel Hill: University of North Carolina Press, 1991), 9–16; C. Meade Patterson and Cuddy DeMarco Jr., "Civil War Carbines," in *Civil War Small Arms* (Washington, D.C.: National Rifle Association of America, reprinted from the *American Rifleman*, February 1948–June 1959), 14–21; and Harold L. Peterson, "Famous Firearms: Burnside Carbine," *American Rifleman*, June 1967, 8.

34 Senator Burnside became an ally: Bigelow, *William Conant Church*, 205.

34 "very diplomatically worded": Trefethen, *Americans and Their Guns*, 77.

34 In the spring of 1877: Trefethen, *Americans and Their Guns*, 77–78.

35 "It was a full-size replica": Trefethen, *Americans and Their Guns*, 76.

35 Church began complaining: Trefethen, *Americans and Their Guns*, 79–80.

35 "The National Rifle Association of Creedmoor": "The National Guard," *Army and Navy Journal*, November 10, 1877, 220.

36 "The National Rifle Association was formed": "The International Military Match," *Army and Navy Journal*, March 9, 1878, 492.

36 The winner was awarded the Hilton Trophy: Trefethen, *Americans and Their Guns*, 82–83.

36 The pace of competition: Geo. S. Schermerhorn Jr., "Seventh Annual Report of the Secretary of the National Rifle Association of America," January 14, 1878, in *Annual Report, 1873–78*.

37 Lookouts should be placed on the range: Geo. W. Wingate, *Manual of Rifle Practice: Including a Complete Guide to Instruction in the Use and Care of the Modern Breech-Loader* (New York: W. C. & F. P. Church, 1872), 128, 130, 215.

37 "systematic instruction in rifle practice": Bigelow, *William Conant Church*, 185.

37 "There will be no war": Trefethen, *Americans and Their Guns*, 88–89.

37 The group was in trouble: Trefethen, *Americans and Their Guns*, 99–100.

38 "I enclose a formal obituary of the NRA": George W. Wingate, letter to the editor, *Shooting and Fishing*, July 1892, 13, and quoted in Jeffrey A. Marlin, "The National Guard, the National Board for the Promotion of Rifle Practice, and the National Rifle Association: Public Institutions and the Rise of a Lobby for Private Gun Ownership," PhD diss., Georgia State University, May 2013, 126, online at https://pdfs .semanticscholar.org/d733/582660311b553174751cf7dc37de8810b149.pdf.

39 one on the role of Ulysses S. Grant: William Conant Church, *Ulysses S. Grant and the Period of National Preservation and Reconstruction* (New York: G. P. Putnam's Sons, 1897).

39 journeyed west with his wife and daughter: George W. Wingate, *Through the Yellowstone Park on Horseback* (New York: O. Judd, 1886).

39 "to include the Secretary of War": Trefethen, *Americans and Their Guns*, 115.

39 "finally issued his call to arms": Bigelow, *William Conant Church*, 245.

40 "Prophet and patriot": *Army and Navy Journal*, June 2, 1917, cited in Bigelow, *William Conant Church*, 248.

THREE: THE PROMISCUOUS TOTING OF GUNS

41 Take James A. Drain: John Zent, "NRA Hunters' Leadership Forum," *American Hunter*, January 15, 2015, and "James A. Drain, All-American: The Career of the New National Commander," *American Legion Weekly*, October 10, 1924, 6.

41 Drain served as a lieutenant colonel: James Andrew Drain Sr., *Single Handed* (Cambridge, WI: Mark L. Bardenwerper Sr., 2013); Raymond E. Carlson, "Tanks," *Army Ordnance: The Journal of the Army Ordnance Association* 1 (September–October 1920): 115.

41 He "was a youthful, bustling": James B. Trefethen, comp., *Americans and Their Guns: The National Rifle Association Story—Through Nearly a Century of Service to the Nation*, ed. James E. Serven (Harrisburg, PA: Stackpole, 1967), 137.

41 But in 1906 Drain: Trefethen, *Americans and Their Guns*, 138.

42 "Sporting Goods Row": Trefethen, *Americans and Their Guns*, 141.

42 This display became a familiar feature: Trefethen, *Americans and Their Guns*, 144–145.

43 "commissioned Frederic Remington": Trefethen, *Americans and Their Guns*, 160.

43 "there were few other restrictions": Trefethen, *Americans and Their Guns*, 290.

43 This law is still on the books: "Bar Hidden Weapons on Sullivan's Plea," *New York Times*, May 11, 1911. Also cited in "The Birth of Modern Gun Control: The Sullivan Act (1911)," in *Gun Politics in America: Historical and Modern Documents in Context*, Volume 1, ed. Harry L. Wilson (Santa Barbara, CA: ABC-CLIO, 2016), 105–107.

43 Its sponsor, Timothy D. Sullivan: Sewell Chan, "Big Tim Sullivan, Tammany Kingmaker," *New York Times*, December 18, 2009.

43 The new NRA president: Trefethen, *Americans and Their Guns*, 159–160.

44 They paid a visit to Senator Henry du Pont: Trefethen, *Americans and Their Guns*, 167–168.

44 "In addition to providing the needed funds": Trefethen, *Americans and Their Guns*, 167–168.

44 "The great matches of 1913": Trefethen, *Americans and Their Guns*, 170.

44 "Under the increasingly tense international situation": Trefethen, *Americans and Their Guns*, 181–182.

45 he ended up selling *Arms and the Man*: Trefethen, *Americans and Their Guns*, 180.

45 "Long experience with conditions in France": Trefethen, *Americans and Their Guns*, 184–185.

45 Starting in 1903, the government contributed $2,500: Fifty-Seventh Congress, Sess. II, Ch. 975, 1903, 941–942, online at https://www.loc.gov/law/help/statutes-at-large/57th-congress/session-2/c57s2ch975.pdf.

46 "to establish and maintain indoor and outdoor": Sixty-Eighth Congress, Sess. I, Ch. 291, 1924, 509–510, online at https://www.loc.gov/law/help/statutes-at-large/68th-congress/session-1/c68s1ch291.pdf.

46 the "sale to members of the National Rifle Association": Sixty-Eighth Congress, Sess. I, Ch. 291, 1924, 510.

46 "placed the United States solidly on the top": Trefethen, *Americans and Their Guns*, 198.

46 By 1920, "the Association had 766": Trefethen, *Americans and Their Guns*, 198.

46 "After a major outbreak": Trefethen, *Americans and Their Guns*, 208; "Mail Clerks and Banditry," *Arms and the Man*, March 1, 1922, 10.

47 "Our readers are the kind of men": "Anti-Firearms Laws," *Arms and the Man*, October 1, 1922, 50; and Stephen Trask, "The Bolshevik Fusee," *Arms and the Man*, July 27, 1918, 343.

48 Distinguished Service Medal: Decorations and Citations—W.W. I, Milton A. Reckord: Service Record and Military History, Milton Reckord Papers, Hornbake Library, University of Maryland.

48 "It is felt that the N.R.A. has a vital interest": C. B. Lister, "The Annual Report of the Acting Secretary of the National Rifle Association of America for the Calendar Year Ending December 31, 1925 to the Board of Directors," *American Rifleman*, January 15, 1926, 3.

49 "Under the conditions that prevailed in the 1920s": Trefethen, *Americans and Their Guns*, 291.

49 Chicago White Sox: See Charles Fountain, *The Betrayal: How the 1919 Black Sox Scandal Changed Baseball* (New York: Oxford University Press, 2015).

49 New York Commission on Uniform Laws: Karl T. Frederick, "Pistol Regulations, Its Principles and History," *American Rifleman*, July 1931, 20–21, 41.

49 St. Valentine's Day Massacre: Associated Press, "Major Silloway Advances Theory in Gang Killings," *Lincoln Star*, February 15, 1929, 1; John O'Brien, "The St. Valentine's Day Massacre," *Chicago Tribune*, February 14, 2014.

50 "so that police in recovering a weapon": "Editorial: Merry Christmas—and Gun Laws," *American Rifleman*, December 1929, 6.

50 "I do object to being singled out": "Document 36: The NRA President Testifies in Favor of State Gun Regulations (1934)," in *Gun Politics in American Culture: Historical and Modern Documents in Context*, Volume 1, ed. Harry L. Wilson (Santa Barbara, CA: ABC-CLIO, 2016), 127–142. The full transcript is in National Firearms Act: Hearings before the Committee on Ways and Means, House of Representatives, Seventy-Third Congress, Second Session on H.R. 9066, April 16, 18, and May 14, 15, and 16, 1934. The link is: https://books.google.com/books?id=8AsvAAAAMAAJ&pg=PA59&lpg=PA59&dq=%E2%80%9CI+do+not+believe+in+the+general+promiscuous+toting+of+guns.+I+think+it+should+be+sharply+restricted+and+only+under+licenses.%E2%80%9D&source=bl&ots=OTEbGWu4SB&sig=ACfU3U2zGlZa8TX51IDwI7YS_Fe_w26ZcQ&hl=en&sa=X&ved=2ahUKEwjw2NLzpq7lAhXokOAKHTFHDd0Q6AEwD3oECA8QAQ#v=onepage&q=%E2%80%9CI%20do%20not%20believe%20in%20the%20general%20promiscuous%20toting%20of%20guns.%20I%20think%20it%20should%20be%20sharply%20restricted%20and%20only%20under%20licenses.%E2%80%9D&f=false.

51 "I have never believed in the general practice of carrying weapons": National Firearms Act: Hearings, 59.

51 The National Rifle Association hailed: NRA oral history, 561-C-24, among the Bob Barr Papers, Ingram Library, University of West Georgia.

52 The act established a national tax and regulatory regime: Franklin E. Zimring, "Firearms and Federal Law: The Gun Control Act of 1968," *Journal of Legal Studies* 4, no. 1 (January 1975): 143.

FOUR: A HIGH PLANE OF HONEST, FRANK DISCUSSION

53 "This is a political year": "Powder Smoke: The Campaigns Get Under Way," *American Rifleman*, July 1936, 2.

54 During Roosevelt's second term: Alfred M. Ascione, "The Federal Firearms Act," *St. John's Law Review*, 13, no. 2 (April 1939): Article 27, 4.

54 The NRA still awards a trophy in his name: "C. B. Lister Memorial Trophy," online at https://competitions.nra.org/documents/pdf/compete/nat-trophy/tro-038.pdf.

54 "In view of the fact that the Magnum": C. B. Lister, "Problems as Well as Progress Expected in 1937," *American Rifleman*, January 1937, 5–6.

54 "especially trained *in the use of these weapons*": Lister, "Problems as Well as Progress," 6.

55 "Inasmuch as the gun performs": "Powder Smoke: Legislation in 1937," *American Rifleman*, January 1937, 4.

55 "one of the 'daddies' of the S. & W. Magnum": "Powder Smoke: More on Legislation," *American Rifleman*, March 1937, 6.

55 "We believe a murderer should be tried": C. B. Lister, "Federal Firearms Registration," *American Rifleman*, January 1938, 27.

56 This act required licensing all manufacturers: Ascione, "The Federal Firearms Act."

56 But unlike the 1934 law, this second law: Franklin E. Zimring, "Firearms and Federal Law: The Gun Control Act of 1968," *Journal of Legal Studies* 4, no. 1 (January 1975): 140–143.

56 The 1938 law prohibited licensed firearms dealers: Federal Firearms Act, Public Law No. 785, Ch. 850, June 30, 1938, 1251 (d).

56 "miracle of deliverance": See Walter Lord, *The Miracle of Dunkirk: The True Story of Operation Dynamo* (New York: Open Road Media, 2017).

57 Their goal was to "rearm the police and Home Guard": James B. Trefethen, comp., *Americans and Their Guns: The National Rifle Association Story—Through Nearly a Century of Service to the Nation*, ed. James E. Serven (Harrisburg, PA: Stackpole, 1967), 244–245.

57 Churchill later praised: Winston Churchill, *The Collected Works of Winston Churchill*, Volume VIII, *Home Defense*, Prime Minister to First Lord, September 27, 1940.

57 After Pearl Harbor, Reckord took a leave: Milton A. Reckord, Service Record and Military History, Reckord Papers, Hornbake Library, University of Maryland.

57 C. B. Lister "worked unceasingly": Trefethen, *Americans and Their Guns*, 237, 247.

57 "At least three prominent members": Trefethen, *Americans and Their Guns*, 250.

57 Distinguished Service Medal: Milton A. Reckord, Service Record and Military History, Reckord Papers.

57 Among his duties as the U.S. military police commander: "Milton Reckord, Top M.P., 95, Dead," *New York Times*, September 10, 1975, 48.

58 "The tradition of the citizen soldiery": Trefethen, *Americans and Their Guns*, 250.

58 "Listen, America!" wrote Lister: C.B.L., "Listen America!," *American Rifleman*, March 1944, 15.

58 "Think! *Decide*": C. B. Lister, "Registration—Confiscation," *American Rifleman*, March 1946, 9.

59 Lister replied not with evidence but with a series: C.B.L., "The History of Liberty," *American Rifleman*, May 1946, 9.

59 "they [would] resort to every form of trickery": C.B.L., "War and Peace," *American Rifleman*, June 1947, 6.

59 "it was the *police* state which set Mussolini and Hitler": C. B. Lister, "Pattern in Red," *American Rifleman*, April 1948, 10.

59 "carefully planted and skillfully nurtured communist propaganda": C. B. Lister, "First Things First," *American Rifleman*, March 1951, 10.

60 Also in 1949, the National Rifle Association: See the National Press Club's history page at www.press.org; and David F. Larcker and Brian Tayan, "Pioneering Women on Boards: Pathways of the First Female Directors," Stanford Closer Look Series,

Stanford University, September 3, 2013, 2, 7–8, online at https://www.gsb.stanford.edu/sites/gsb/files/publication-pdf/cgri-closer-look-35-women-boards.pdf.

60 Alice H. Bull: "Alice Bull, 88, Set Her Sights on Marksmanship," *Seattle Times*, December 3, 1998; Trefethen, *Americans and Their Guns*, 265.

61 "[t]he sportsman-hunter will always take great care": *NRA Hunter Safety Handbook*, NRA Safety Series (Washington, D.C.: National Rifle Association of America, 1957), 21.

61 "Not a day passes": Merritt A. Edson, "Executive Director's Report, Annual Members' Meeting," *American Rifleman*, May 1954, 35–36.

61 It was there that Edson: Jon T. Hoffman, *Once a Legend: "Red Mike" Edson of the Marine Raiders* (Novato, CA: Presidio Press, 1994), 52.

62 "all over the place, encouraging, cajoling": "The Marine Corps Medal of Honor Recipients, Featuring Marine Medal of Honor Recipients from WWII–Korea–Viet Nam and Iraqi Freedom, MERRITT A. EDSON, Colonel, United States Marine Corps"; and "The Hall of Valor Project," Merritt Austin Edson, *Military Times*, at https://valor.militarytimes.com/advanced-search?first_name=merritt&last_name=Edson&conflict=&award=.

62 "the seemingly eternal struggle between Communism and Democracy": Merritt A. Edson, ". . . Keep Your Powder Dry!," *American Rifleman*, July 1954, 14.

62 The requested budget for the National Board: Merritt A. Edson, "What Price National Security?," *American Rifleman*, November 1951, 16.

62 "If that small group of men who had banded together": Merritt A. Edson, "To Keep and Bear Arms," *American Rifleman*, August 1952, 16.

63 "Certain controls such as those which exist": Merritt A. Edson, "The Right to Bear Arms," *American Rifleman*, July 1955, 14.

63 General Edson committed suicide: UPI, "Edson Is Dead from Inhaling Carbon Fumes," *Bennington Evening Banner*, August 15, 1955, 1.

63 Not just observers but NRA board members: Osha Gray Davidson, *Under Fire: The NRA and the Battle for Gun Control* (New York: Henry Holt, 1993), 180.

FIVE: PUBLIC OPINION DEMANDS SOME CONTROL

65 The NRA went from 84,000 members in 1945: Merritt A. Edson, "In Unity There Is Strength," *American Rifleman*, March 1952, 12; Alan C. Webber, "NRA Had Banner Year in Membership—Orth," *American Rifleman*, February 1969, 13; "From the Staff Officers," Special Bicentennial Issue, *American Rifleman*, January 1971, 29.

65 By the late sixties the NRA had evolved: Merritt A. Edson, "An Open Letter to the Membership," *American Rifleman*, September 1951, 12; and "Why a Hunting Magazine," *American Rifleman*, June 1973, 18.

65 The increase in dues from members and advertising: "Executive Order: Withdrawing Public Land for Use of the War Department for Military Purposes," *Federal Register*, December 30, 1911, 6787–6788.

65 Articles regularly covered matters from hand-loading ammunition: James E. Serven, "The Sharps Sporting Rifle," *American Rifleman*, April 1962, 43.

66 choosing a first rifle for one's son: "A Most Important Gift" (editorial), *American Rifleman*, December 1956, 14.

66 Every now and then a piece concentrated: Roger Marsh, "Arms of the Chinese Communist Forces," *American Rifleman*, January 1952, 13; Merritt A. Edson, "A Bastion of Strength" (editorial), *American Rifleman*, January 1955, 14.

66 "Unless indiscriminate shooting is stopped": Michael J. Walker, "Hawks, Too, Need Peace," *American Rifleman*, December 1967, 20–21.

66 As early as 1966, the NRA stopped listing: "In Danger of Extinction," *American Rifleman*, July 1966, 16.

66 *American Rifleman* editorials in the early 1960s: "Public Hunting, American Style," *American Rifleman*, August 1962, 14.

66 In 1956, an all-women team: James B. Trefethen, comp., *Americans and Their Guns: The National Rifle Association Story—Through Nearly a Century of Service to the Nation*, ed. James E. Serven (Harrisburg, PA: Stackpole, 1967), 278.

66 In 1957, in the President's Match: Trefethen, *Americans and Their Guns*, 282–283. The Marine was T/Sgt. V. D. Mitchell.

67 Orth "had graduated from the School of Economics": Trefethen, *Americans and Their Guns*, 285.

67 Schooley was "one of America's leading pistol shots": Trefethen, *Americans and Their Guns*, 285.

67 His background was as a special investigator: Trefethen, *Americans and Their Guns*, 285.

68 "Hotter than a pistol these days": Sheldon M. Gallagher, "Fast-Draw Fad Brings Boom to Handguns," *Popular Science*, October 1959, 136.

68 "Today Western-style sixguns are selling": Gallagher, "Fast-Draw Fad Brings Boom to Handguns," 137.

68 By then the NRA itself was lamenting: "The Quick-Draw Craze," *American Rifleman*, February 1959, 14.

68 the women's magazine *McCall's* ran an article: Carl Bakal, "This Very Day a Gun May Kill You!," *McCall's*, July 1959, 50. See also Wolfgang Saxon, "Carl Bakal, 86, Offered a Warning on Firearms," *New York Times*, April 3, 2004.

68 The NRA responded: Louis F. Lucas, "This Very Day," *American Rifleman*, August 1959, 16.

69 American Institute of Public Opinion: "Gallup Poll Hits Gun Owners," *American Rifleman*, October 1959, 12. See also Tom W. Smith, "The 75% Solution: An Analysis of the Structure of Attitudes on Gun Control, 1959–1977," *Journal of Criminal Law and Criminology* 71, no. 3 (Fall 1980): 300.

69 "foundation stone of American liberty": "A Man and His Gun" (editorial), *American Rifleman*, March 1959, 14.

69 the *American Rifleman* changed its masthead: *American Rifleman*, March 1963, 4.

69 "Certainly law-abiding, God-fearing men and women": Trefethen, *Americans and Their Guns*, 299.

70 the NRA identified four red lines: Trefethen, *Americans and Their Guns*, 300–301.

70 Harry Belafonte: Harry Belafonte with Michael Shnayerson, *My Song: A Memoir of Art, Race, and Defiance* (New York: Vintage Books, 2012), 271–278; and Carl M. Cannon, "Hollywood's Who's Who Marched with King in '63," Real Clear Politics,

August 29, 2013, online at https://www.realclearpolitics.com/articles/2013/08/29 /hollywood_whos_who_marched_with_king_in_63__119762.html.

71 Charlton Heston, best known at that time: Charlton Heston, *In the Arena: An Autobiography* (New York: Boulevard, 1995), 260; Emilie Raymond, *From My Cold Dead Hands: Charton Heston and American Politics* (Lexington: University Press of Kentucky, 2006), 5.

71 Lee Harvey Oswald had ordered a cheap surplus: Advertisement, Klein's Sporting Goods, *American Rifleman*, February 1963, 65.

72 There were also fears that arms were being diverted: Warren Berry, "Is U.S. Arming Race Fanatics," *Salina Journal*, May 24, 1964, 20.

72 Three men who belonged to such a group: "No Place in U.S. for Private Armies" (editorial), *Daily Review* (Hayward, CA), November 20, 1964, 8.

72 New York police later seized: "The Definition of Madness: From the Washington Post," *Madison Capital Times*, November 15, 1966, 34.

72 "private armies": Inez Robb, "Inez Robb Reports," *Arkansas City* (Kan.) *Daily Traveler*, April 3, 1965, 4. See also Alfred E. Clark, "Inez Robb, an Ex-Columnist, Dies; Was a World War II Correspondent," *New York Times*, April 6, 1979.

73 "The NRA vehemently disavows": "NRA Disavows Connection with Groups Advocating Violence," *American Rifleman*, October 1964, 72–73.

74 In California in the spring of 1967: Adam Winkler, *Gunfight: The Battle over the Right to Bear Arms in America* (New York: W. W. Norton, 2013), 225–262.

74 "It was a noon-hour session": Associated Press, "Sacramento Investigates Security Precautions After Spree," *Kingston Daily Freeman*, May 3, 1967, 7.

74 The same month the *American Rifleman* ran: "Who Guards America's Homes?" (editorial), *American Rifleman*, May 1967, 16.

74 More riots broke out that summer: See Robert Shellow, ed., *The Harvest of American Racism: The Political Meaning of Violence in the Summer of 1967* (Ann Arbor: University of Michigan Press, 2018).

74 The "dramatic incident" inside the Sacramento: Ken Green, "Reagan Crime War Gains Listed," *Bakersfield Californian*, August 12, 1967, 3.

74 The NRA supported the new California restriction: "Congress Faced with Clearcut Choice on Gun Control Legislation," *American Rifleman*, June 1967, 23. The bill in question was California: Assembly Bill 1591.

75 "imposing and effective array of firearms laws": Trefethen, *Americans and Their Guns*, 297–299.

75 Orth was at times critical of Dodd's first two bills: "Federal Firearms Legislation: Public Hearings Are Terminated in the U.S. Senate and House of Representatives," *American Rifleman*, September 1965, 21.

75 "It is a fact that known felons": Franklin L. Orth, "Federal Gun Legislation: An Open Letter from the NRA Executive Vice President," *American Rifleman*, December 1965, 18.

75 Orth fired back: Alan C. Weber, "Where the NRA Stands on Gun Legislation: 97-Year Record Shows Positive Approach to Workable Gun Laws," *American Rifleman*, March 1968, 22.

76 "I think it is a terrible indictment" and "a smear of a great American organization": Alan C. Webber, associate editor, "Where the NRA Stands on Gun Legislation," *American Rifleman*, March 1968, 22.

76 "The duty of Congress is clear": Weber, "Where the NRA Stands on Gun Legislation."

76 "The NRA does not advocate:": "NRA Submits 4-Point Gun Control Plan in Testimony Before House Subcommittee, NRA Office of Public Relations, For P.M. Release, Monday, April 10, 1967," Reckord Papers, Hornbake Library, University of Maryland.

77 betraying "every sportsman" (editorial): *Fishing and Hunting News*, quoting in Richard Harris, "If You Love Your Guns," *New Yorker*, April 12, 1968, 82.

77 Others demanded that Orth resign: Richard Harris, "If You Love Your Guns," *New Yorker*, April 20, 1968, 57.

77 At the same time, President Johnson: "Remarks upon Signing the Gun Control Act of 1968, October 22, 1968," Document 49: The Gun Control Act of 1968, in *Gun Politics in America: Historical and Modern Documents in Context*, Volume 1, ed. Harry L. Wilson (Santa Barbara, CA: ABC-CLIO, 2016), 216.

77 Herblock: A.H., "Cartooning as Gangsterized by Herblock," *American Rifleman*, February 1969, 39.

78 "the Second Article of the Bill of Rights": Merritt A. Edson, "To Keep and Bear Arms," *American Rifleman*, August 1952, 16.

78 "disavow[ed] any connection with, or tacit": "NRA Disavows Connection with Groups Advocating Violence," *American Rifleman*, October 1964, 72–73.

SIX: THE AWAKENING

83 Born Harlan B. Carter in Granbury: John M. Crewdson, "Hard-Line Opponent of Gun Laws Wins New Term at Helm of Rifle," *New York Times*, May 4, 1981.

83 He was seventeen years old on the day: "Carter Murder Trial Gets Underway: Mother of Dead Boy Takes Stand," *Laredo Times*, April 14, 1931, 1.

84 After graduating from the University of Texas: "Carter Ready to Tackle NRA's Foes," *American Rifleman*, June 1975, 17.

85 "is one of a handful of civilian shooters": Sidebar to "Carter Ready to Tackle NRA's Foes," *American Rifleman*, June 1975, 17.

85 "We were hundreds of miles deep in Mexico": Harlon B. Carter, "A Rifleman Goes Shotgunning," *American Rifleman*, April 1955, 28.

85 He denied the allegations, and no charges: Crewdson, "Hard-Line Opponent of Gun Laws."

86 "When he was 5 years old": Michael Powell, "The NRA's Call to Arms," *Washington Post Magazine*, August 6, 2000, SMB8.

86 "the only girl on . . . campus": Chris Knox, comp., *Neal Knox: The Gun Rights War* (Phoenix: McFarlane Press, 2009), 10.

86 Knox was "a gun buff" above all else: Knox, *Neal Knox*, 19.

86 "A modified choke is about right": Neal Knox, "Chukar Partridge," *Handloader Magazine*, January 1970, cited in in Knox, *Neal Knox*, 21.

86 "the only source of real information": "Foreword by Tanya K. Metaksa," in Knox, *Neal Knox*, 13.

86 "At the time he was shooting a lot": Knox, *Neal Knox*, 19.

87 "The anti-gun clan has based its arguments": Neal Knox, "The Dodd Bill Both Fact: and Fantasy 2," July 1966, cited in Knox, *Neal Knox*, 58; and Stephen Budiansky, *The Bloody Shirt: Terror After Appomattox* (New York: Viking, 2008), 1–5.

87 Knox was at the time perhaps the loudest: See, for instance, Neal Knox letter to Max L. Friedersdorf, July 11, 1975, and response, Box 18, Folder "Gun Control (2)," Philip Buchen Files, Gerald R. Ford Presidential Library, Grand Rapids, Michigan.

87 "Suddenly one of the interviewers": "Whose Right to Be Biased? Gun Owners Ask TV Network," *American Rifleman*, May 1967, 38–39.

88 "After I had finished my work on the documentary": Robert MacNeil, *Looking for My Country: Finding Myself in America* (Boston: Houghton Mifflin, 2004), 129.

88 But, in fact, a point was made: See, for instance, Joan Crosby, "Television Examines a Loaded Question," *Dominion Post* (Morgantown, WV), March 26, 1967, 1-C.

88 "In all the ads in hunting and gun magazines": See, for instance, "Genuine Luger Pistols: Available Again for the First Time Since 1914, in 9 M/M" (advertisement), Stronger Arms Corporation, 507 Fifth Avenue, New York, NY, online at https://www.pinterest.com/pin/384213411952888802, and "1919–20 Luger, regimental markings. Beautiful reblue. XIntl shooter. 1944 Walther P-38, perfect condition. Nazi markings" (advertisement), *The News* (Van Nuys, CA), May 21, 1972, 37, col. 6.

89 After Orth died of a heart attack: "Franklin L. Orth, Gun Control Foe: N.R.A. Executive, Olympic Committee Head, Dies," *New York Times*, January 5, 1970, 37. See also "Franklin L. Orth, 1907–1970," *American Rifleman*, February 1970, 34.

89 Rich was awarded: "The Rich Years," Salt Lake Chamber of Commerce, at slchamber.com.

89 Maxwell backed a plan to move NRA: "New Mexico May Be Site of NRA National Center," *American Rifleman*, May 1973, 8; also "Report of the Executive Vice President Maxwell E. Rich," January 11, 1975, Reckord Papers, Hornbake Library, University of Maryland.

90 "This means that a father who lives in Virginia": NRA Legislative Information Service, "The NRA's Principal Objections to the 1968 Federal Gun Control Act," *American Rifleman*, March 1971, 20.

90 more than 560 policemen had been slain: Ralph Blumenthal, "Lindsay Appeals for Gun Control," *New York Times*, August 26, 1971, 1.

90 "Saturday night special": See an early reference to a "Saturday night special" in "Police Run into Wall in Killing: Press Search for Porter's Slayer," *News-Palladium* (Benton Harbor, MI), July 19, 1961, 16, as an apparent appropriation of the era's "Saturday night specials"—retailers' sales—as in Advertisement, "Everybody's Excited About These Outstanding Saturday Night Specials," *Dixon (IL) Evening Telegraph*, May 27, 1955, 15.

90 "Notoriously inaccurate": Blumenthal, "Lindsay Appeals for Gun Control." See also Robert Sherrill, "The Saturday Night Special and Other Hardware," *New York Times*, October 10, 1971, 15.

91 "There is already afoot a movement": "In Fairness to Hunting," *American Rifleman*, April 1971, 16.

91 "Never before has the need for conservation": "From the Staff Officers," *American Rifleman*, Special Bicentennial Issue, January 1971, 29.

91 the term "hunter-conservationist": "Give Thanks for Hunter Conservationists," *American Rifleman*, November 1970, 16. See also Lowell E. Baier, *Inside the Equal Access to Justice Act: Environmental Litigation and the Crippling Battle over America's Lands, Endangered Species, and Critical Habitats* (Lanham, MD: Rowman & Littlefield, 2016), 20.

91 "trail blazer among hunter-conservationists": Ashley Halsey Jr., "Theodore Roosevelt Trail Blazer Among Hunter-Conservationists," *American Rifleman*, June 1972, 14–19.

91 The magazine also returned its gaze: Ashley Halsey Jr., "Hunter Conservationists Curb Arctic Sea Chases," *American Rifleman*, February 1973, 36.

92 "What to do or not to do about hunting": *American Rifleman*, April 1971, 16.

92 "to promote good sportsmanship and to foster": "NRA Information," *American Rifleman*, March 1974, 7.

92 elephant grounds in Kenya: "The Ecological Dilemma over the Pachyderms (Or, What to Do About Elephants?)," *American Rifleman*, January 1972, 19.

92 "Joint teams will be formed": "Wildlife Cooperation Planned," *American Rifleman*, January 1976, 16.

92 "More and more American hunters": Leslie E. Lahr Sr., "How You Can Help Foil Game Thieves," *American Rifleman*, July 1974, 17.

92 The NRA . . . launched a national program: "NRA Plans Drive for 'Eyes' for Game Law Enforcement," *American Rifleman*, July 1974, 20.

93 In 1975, the Association announced: "NRA Will Sponsor Conservation Camp," *American Rifleman*, March 1975, 35.

93 "On the evening of Nov. 1, millions": "How Anti-Gun Propaganda Is Twisted into 'News,'" *American Rifleman*, December 1971, 47.

93 "Ann Landers, the syndicated sexpert": "Some Advice for Ann Landers" (editorial), *American Rifleman*, May 1974, 16.

94 Senator Edward M. Kennedy challenged: "The NRA Accepts a Kennedy Challenge," *American Rifleman*, October 1972, 20.

94 discussed . . . whether to boycott: "Boycott Nearly Everybody?" (editorial), *American Rifleman*, July 1975, 16; and "Would a Blackout by You the Viewer, Cure Network TV?" (editorial), *American Rifleman*, November 1975, 20.

94 referring to a set of "rules": Ashley Halsey Jr., "Ending the Mystery of the 'Rules,'" *American Rifleman*, January 1973, 15–16.

94 "Nearly all the clamor": "Communism, Assassinations and Anti-Gun Attitudes" (editorial), *American Rifleman*, October 1974, 22.

95 "For the first time in its 103 years": John M. Snyder, "NRA Registers as Lobby to Uphold Gun Ownership," *American Rifleman*, April 1974, 16.

95 They "were disarming new faces who destroyed stereotypes": Jeffrey A. Rodengen, *NRA: An American Legend* (Fort Lauderdale, FL: Write Stuff, 2002), 175.

95 Peter S. Ridley: "Peter S. Ridley Jr. Dies, D.C. Attorney Since '70," *Washington Post*, July 3, 1980, B6; and Restricted Scholarships, Peter S. Ridley, Jr. Memorial Endowed Scholarship, online at https://www.wcl.american.edu/school/admissions/finaid/grants-scholarships/restricted/.

96 "activities like camping": Osha Gray Davidson, *Under Fire: The NRA and the Battle for Gun Control* (New York: Henry Holt, 1993), 35.

96 "Weekend Massacre": National Rifle Association, Appellant, v. John C. Ailes et al., Appellees, No. 79-342, District of Columbia Court of Appeals, argued March 20, 1980, decided March 5, 1981.

96 Carter himself . . . was too powerful to fire: Davidson, *Under Fire*, 35.

96 "There will be an awakening": "NRA Institute for Legislative Action," excerpts from speech by Harlon B. Carter, *American Rifleman*, June 1976, 20.

96 In his last point, Carter was picking up: Donald N. Bigelow, *William Conant Church and the Army and Navy Journal* (New York: Columbia University Press, 1952), 182.

97 Kenyon Ballew: See "Arms Raid in Maryland Leaves Collector Paralyzed," *New York Times*, September 26, 1971, 38; Gary W. Hansen, "The History of Gun Control," M.A. thesis, Portland State University, History Department, 1976, 78–79, online at https://pdxscholar.library.pdx.edu/open_access_etds/2281/; and E. B. Mann, "Our Endangered Tradition: Here We Go Again!," *Field & Stream*, April 1978, 20.

97 "Treasury Gestapo at Work": William Loeb, "Treasury Gestapo at Work," *Manchester* (NH) *Union Leader*, July 8, 1971, entered in the U.S. Congressional Record by Rep. Luis C. Wyman of New Hampshire on July 19, 1971. See also "Official Report Defends Raids, Admits Errors," *American Rifleman*, September 1971, 26–27.

97 Ballew, who had fired upon: See "Ballews Suing over ATFD Raid," *American Rifleman*, September 1971, 24.

97 By then the NRA was already crafting: Harold W. Glassen, "Right to Keep Arms Is Older Than the Second Amendment," *American Rifleman*, April 1973, 22–23.

97 "God-given right": Ashley Halsey Jr., "Can the Second Amendment Survive?," *American Rifleman*, March 1973, 17.

97 "There have been charges": "Our Strength Is in Unity," *American Rifleman*, May 1977, 18–19.

98 "The event took on a Watergate-like atmosphere": Reginald Stuart, "Rifle Group Ousts Most Leaders in Move to Bolster Stand on Guns," *New York Times*, May 23, 1977.

98 "The effects were stunning": NRA staff, "Concerned NRA Members Redirect Their Association," *American Rifleman*, July 1977, 18.

99 "He had a shaved head": Joel Achenbach, Scott Higham, and Sari Horwitz, "How NRA's True Believers Converted a Marksmanship Group into Mighty Gun Lobby," *Washington Post*, January 12, 2013.

99 "The sweeping changes voted today": Stuart, "Rifle Group Ousts Most Leaders."

99 "a crowd of well over 2,000": "Concerned NRA Members Redirect Their Association," *American Rifleman*, July 1977, 16–17.

99 "When it was all over": "Concerned NRA Members Redirect," 16.

99 "I have the distinct honor": "Official Journal: President's Column, by James W. Porter II, President: Outgoing President Reflects on the Past, Looks to the Future," *American Rifleman*, May 2015, 14.

100 The changes made at the meeting: "Bylaw Changes a Testament to Strength of NRA Members," *American Rifleman*, July 1977, 23–25; Stuart, "Rifle Group Ousts Most Leaders."

100 "I'm going to tell you one thing": "Concerned NRA Members Redirect," 16–17.

SEVEN: A GREAT RELIGION

103 For a few years one might still see stories: Joel Vance, "Turkey Restoration," *American Hunter*, March 1978, 17–19; Rod Cochran, "Killing Deer with Kindness," *American Hunter*, September 1978, 64–65.

103 the shooting of crows: Byron Dalrymple, "Where Crow Shooting Is Alive and Well," *American Hunter*, January 1978, 40–44.

103 a .357 or .44 Magnum revolver: Clair Rees, "Handguns for Deer?," *American Hunter*, June 1978, 21–23.

103 Articles like "Horsebackpack Hunting": Fred and Dora Burris, "Horsebackpack Hunting," *American Hunter*, June 1975, 12–15; Pete Nelson, "Four-Wheel Drive— The Hunters' Bargain," *American Hunter*, May 1978, 52–55.

103 In order to grow its membership: "NRA-Sponsored Insurance Services for You" (advertisement), *American Rifleman*, December 1978, 79.

103 And the NRA lobbied Congress to sell surplus: See, for instance, Gary L. Anderson, "NRA, Civilian Marksmanship: Partners in Nation's Defense," *American Rifleman*, December 1979, Official Journal section, 1–2.

105 Under his tutelage, membership rose: "Never Before in History Has the NRA Offered More Benefits, Programs and Services. Be Sure You Know," *American Rifleman*, April 1981, 42.

105 "That nominee was, of course, Harlon B. Carter": "Crowded Members Meeting Acclaims Carter's NRA Team," *American Rifleman*, June 1978, 52–53.

106 "I continue to regret the incident deeply": UPI, "Leader of Rifle Group Affirms That He Shot Boy to Death in 1931," *New York Times*, May 6, 1981.

106 "Knox pointed out that bombs can be rigged": "NRA Official Journal: Critics Pulverize Powder Tagging Scheme," *American Rifleman*, April 1979, 8.

107 "[S]even key pro-gun legislators": "General Sessions Offer the Knowledge of Experts," *American Rifleman*, June 1978, 57.

108 endorse Ronald Reagan for president: Reagan drew the NRA's support in the 1980 election by campaigning on a vow to merge the Bureau of Alcohol, Tobacco, and Firearms into the Secret Service, both of which were part of the Treasury Department. But the NRA later had a change of heart, fearing the Secret Service could make for a more formidable agency, and lobbied Congress to change language in legislation to stop the planned merger. Tim Murphy, "Flashback: How Republicans and the NRA Kneecapped the ATF," *Mother Jones*, January 17, 2013, https://www.motherjones.com/politics/2013/01/atf-obama-gun-reform-control-alcohol-tobacco-firearms/.

108 "In every instance in which we find such a terrible act": "Washington Boasts Tough Gun Law," *Nashua* (NH) *Telegraph*, March 31, 1981, 22.

109 "bitterly-partisan, campaign-type" of infighting: "A Message from Harlon Carter," *American Rifleman*, September 1981, 54.

109 After the 1982 annual meeting: "Resolution," sidebar to "Executive Vice President Carter Honored at Members Meeting," *American Rifleman*, June 1982, 45; "Neal Knox and the NRA," in *Neal Knox: The Gun Rights War*, comp. Chris Knox (Phoenix: MacFarlane Press, 2009), 301.

109 his supporters changed the NRA bylaws: Dan E. Moldea, "The NRA Goes to War with Itself," *Regardie's*, April 1987, online at https://www.moldea.com/NRA-1987.html.

109 The Association's claimed membership grew threefold: Harlon Carter, "Here We Stand," *American Rifleman*, May 1984, 7.

109 President Ronald Reagan, who became the first: *American Rifleman*, July 1983.

109 J. Warren Cassidy: Moldea, "The NRA Goes to War with Itself."

109 Another beneficiary was Wayne LaPierre: "NRA Headquarters Staff," *American Rifleman*, July 1982, 47.

109 Marion P. Hammer: See Glen Rubin, "Do You Know Who the NRA's Marion Hammer Really Is?," AmmoLand: Shooting Sports News, January 18, 2018, online at https://www.ammoland.com/2018/01/do-you-know-who-the-nras-marion-hammer-really-is/#axzz63bABxfIh; Mike Spies, "The Unchecked Influence of NRA Lobbyist Marion Hammer," The Trace, February 23, 2018, online at https://www.thetrace.org/features/nra-influence-florida-marion-hammer-gun-laws/.

110 eventually named the NRA Civil Rights Defense Fund: "NRA Official Journal: Will Using Your Gun in Self-Defense Put You Behind Bars?," *American Rifleman*, December 1988, 49.

110 Just one year after being fired: "NRA Official Journal: NRA Leadership Is Supported by Overwhelming Member Vote," *American Rifleman*, July 1983, 42–44; "NRA Official Journal: Recommend Your Directors," *American Rifleman*, July 1983, 56–57.

110 the first NRA director ousted: "NRA Official Journal: NRA Board Votes 45 to 24 to Expel Director Knox," *American Rifleman*, March 1984, 50–51.

111 Representative John Dingell: Reuters, "Dingell Quits NRA Board, Votes for Crime Bill," *Los Angeles Times*, August 22, 1994.

111 LaPierre was born in Schenectady: Gregg Zoroya, "The Sunday Profile: On the Defensive," *Los Angeles Times*, June 25, 1995.

111 Although eligible for the draft: David Emery, "Did NRA Leader Wayne LaPierre Receive a Draft Deferment for a 'Nervous Disorder'?," February 21, 2018, updated April 22, 2018, online at https://www.snopes.com/fact-check/nra-leader-wayne-lapierre-receive-draft-deferment-nervous-disorder/.

111 LaPierre volunteered for the ill-fated: Sheryl Gay Stolberg and Jodi Kantor, "Shy No More, N.R.A.'s Top Gun Sticks to Cause," *New York Times*, April 13, 2013.

112 LaPierre then attended Boston College: Email from Jack Dunn, Boston College News & Public Affairs Director, to author, January 26, 2013.

112 "I concluded that a lot needs to be done": Zoroya, "The Sunday Profile"; "NRA

Official Journal: Veteran Staffers Assume New Posts at Headquarters," *American Rifleman*, November 1986, 46.

112 In 1977 LaPierre became a legislative aide: Associated Press, "NRA's LaPierre: 'Policy Wonk' with a Megaphone," *USA Today*, February 9, 2013.

113 Arnett won his five-year term by a landslide: "NRA Official Journal: An Unprecedented Vote Is Cast at Seattle Annual Meeting of Members," *American Rifleman*, June 1985, 43.

113 Arnett had served two terms as president: Office of the Secretary, Department of the Interior, "G. Ray Arnett, Nationally Known Conservationist, to Be Nominated as Assistant Interior Secretary," News release, February 18, 1981.

114 "Arnett was known in hunting circles as a 'slob hunter'": Josh Sugarmann, *National Rifle Association: Money, Firepower and Fear* (Washington, D.C.: National Press Books, 1992), 69–70.

114 Game wardens observed him fire at clapper rails: Moldea, "The NRA Goes to War with Itself."

114 a $125 fine: Sugarmann, *National Rifle Association*, 75.

114 "I know of no judicial district in which these defendants": Sugarmann, *National Rifle Association*, 75.

115 "You have been on board this ship": Jeffrey L. Rodengen, *NRA: An American Legend* (Fort Lauderdale, FL: Write Stuff, 2002), 219.

115 Firearms Owners' Protection Act: S. 49—Firearms Owners' Protection Act, Summary: S. 49, 99th Congress (1985–1986); Brad Plumer, "Just How Easy Is It to Buy a Gun over the Internet?," *Washington Post*, August 5, 2013.

116 "the establishment of any system of registration": S. 49—Firearms Owners' Protection Act, Summary: S. 49, 99th Congress (1985–1986), passed House amended (April 10, 1986), online at https://www.congress.gov/bill/99th-congress/senate-bill/49.

116 controls in place today in every other developed nation: Jonathan Masters, "U.S. Gun Policy: Global Comparisons," Backgrounder, Council on Foreign Relations, November 14, 2017, online at https://www.cfr.org/backgrounder/us-gun-policy-global-comparisons.

116 banned the production and sale of new machine guns: "A Brief History of Firearms Law," Violence Policy Center, online at http://vpc.org/publications/cease-fire-a-comprehensive-strategy-to-reduce-firearms-violence/a-brief-history-of-firearms-law/; S. 49—Firearms Owners' Protection Act, 99th Congress.

116 This measure was the result of a last-minute amendment: David Welna, "The Decades-Old Gun Ban That's Still on the Books," *All Things Considered*, National Public Radio, January 16, 2013, online at https://www.npr.org/sections/itsallpolitics/2013/01/18/169526687/the-decades-old-gun-ban-thats-still-on-the-books.

116 This provision, too, is still on the books: Dan Zimmerman, "ATF Reveals the Number of Registered Machine Guns," *The Truth About Guns*, March 7, 2016, online at https://www.thetruthaboutguns.com/atf-reveals-the-number-of-registered-machine-guns/.

116 "The National Rifle Association supports the right": Stephen P. Halbrook, "NRA Official Journal: Federal Machine Gun: A Threatening Precedent," *American Rifleman*, December 1986, 49; Sugarmann, *National Rifle Association*, 222–223.

117 Arnett fired the entire staff: Sugarmann, *National Rifle Association*, 79–80.

117 "Both . . . denied rumors": Sugarmann, *National Rifle Association*, 80.

117 By then Arnett had made other enemies: Moldea, "The NRA Goes to War with Itself."

118 Arnett was suspended without pay: Moldea, "The NRA Goes to War with Itself."

118 "best wishes for continued success": G. Ray Arnett, "NRA Official Journal: Former EVP's Final Message," *American Rifleman*, July 1986, 53.

118 Four months after that, the board nominated: J. E. Reinke, "A Note from the President," sidebar to J. Warren Cassidy, "Here We Stand," *American Rifleman*, October 1986, 7.

118 In 1987 the organization managed to pass: "NRA Official Journal: Bylaw Amendments Decided by Large Voting Margins," *American Rifleman*, June 1987, 53.

119 The Association ended up settling with the employee: Jay Mathews, "Amid Tough Times, NRA to Convene," *Washington Post,* June 8, 1990. https://www.washingtonpost.com/archive/politics/1990/06/08/amid-tough-times-nra-to-convene/bbdf1fbd-ff50-4ec4-b060-28cf3840794f/?utm_term=.2473a29275ec.

119 "a host of unprecedented legislative, financial, and program fiascos": Mathews, "Amid Tough Times, NRA to Convene."

119 The NRA lost a quarter million members: Mathews, "Amid Tough Times, NRA to Convene."

119 "the NRA spent about $60 million more": Charles M. Madigan and David Jackson, "NRA in the Crosshairs," *Chicago Tribune*, August 3, 1995.

119 "Weaklings will consider it tough": Harlon Carter, "Winning the War on Drugs," *American Rifleman*, September 1989, 14–18. See also "A War Game from the NRA" (editorial), *Washington Post*, September 10, 1989.

120 "A lot of these people take it very seriously": Associated Press, "One-Issue Politics Make Gun Control Tough to Enact," *Appeal-Democrat* (Marysville–Yuba City, CA), February 25, 1989.

121 "We share the grief of the tragedy in Stockton": Associated Press, "Drive to Ban Assault Weapons Losing Steam," *Daily News-Record* (Harrisonburg, VA), March 6, 1989.

121 "I want to hear it again": Stephanie Salter, "NRA Stand Is Like Saying Everyone Has a Right to Die," *Examiner* (Independence, MO), January 28, 1989.

121 California banned about sixty different types: Sherry Bebitch Jeffe, "How the NRA Got Shot Down in California," *Los Angeles Times*, July 30, 1989.

121 "I do not believe in taking away the right of the citizen": Jeff Wilson, "Reagan's 78th Birthday Includes Posh Party, Campus Speech, Courtesy Call," Associated Press, February 7, 1989, online at https://www.apnews.com/2792a3c920c27eaebb4109a1a1dfddec.

122 Reagan broke with the NRA again: Ronald Reagan, "Why I'm for the Brady Bill," *New York Times*, March 29, 1991.

122 "You would get a far better understanding": Richard Lacayo, Jonathan Beaty, Michael Riley, and Richard Woodbury, "Under Fire: The N.R.A. Is More Than Just Another Special Interest Group," *Time*, January 29, 1990.

122 At forty-one, Wayne LaPierre was realizing his dream: Wayne LaPierre, "Standing Guard," *American Rifleman*, June 1991, 7.

122 Wayne LaPierre was realizing his dream: While LaPierre said upon becoming the EVP in his first "Standing Guard" column above that he was realizing his "dream," twenty-eight years later, in a rare interview with an independent journalist, he suggested something else. "I never set out for any of it to happen," he said. "This identity that I end up getting—it just kind of happened." Danny Hakim, "Inside Wayne LaPierre's Battle for the N.R.A.," *New York Times Magazine*, December 18, 2019.

EIGHT: THE POLITBURO

125 "You Loot—We Shoot": Marion P. Hammer, "You Loot—We Shoot," *American Rifleman*, November 1992, 61.

125 "Weaver invited the informant to his home": U.S. Department of Justice, "Report of the Ruby Ridge Task Force to the Office of Professional Responsibility of Investigation of Allegations of Improper Governmental Conduct in the Investigation, Apprehension and Prosecution of Randall C. Weaver and Kevin L. Harris," June 10, 1994, 13, 2–3, online at https://www.justice.gov/sites/default/files/opr/legacy/2006/11/09/rubyreportcover_39 .pdf.

126 Weaver and his family, along with a friend: U.S. Department of Justice, "Report of the Ruby Ridge Task Force," 14.

126 "'Here you had federal agents come'": *American Rifleman*, November 1993.

127 Four federal agents and six Branch Davidians were killed: "What Really Happened at Waco: Six Years Later Controversy Continues," *60 Minutes*, CBS, January 25, 2000.

127 Autopsies later showed: "Autopsies: Children at Waco Were Shot," *Washington Post*, July 14, 2000; PBS, "Waco: The Inside Story: Frequently Asked Questions," *Frontline*, October 17, 1995.

129 The same legislative package permanently barred: Jerry Gray, "Republicans Weaken House Bill on Combating Terrorism," *New York Times*, August 3, 1996; Congressional Office of Technology Assessment, *Taggants in Explosives* (Washington, D.C.: U.S. Government Printing Office, April 1980); National Research Council, *Black and Smokeless Powders: Technologies for Finding Bombs and the Bomb Makers* (Washington, D.C.: National Academies Press, 1998).

129 As a result, when trying to trace: Dan Friedman, "The ATF's Nonsensical Non-Searchable Gun Databases, Explained," The Trace, August 24, 2016, online at https://www.thetrace.org/2016/08/atf-non-searchable-databases/.

129 Out of 224 militias identified: Neil A. Hamilton, *Militias in America* (Santa Barbara, CA: ABC-CLIO, 1996), 73. See also David Levitas, *The Terrorist Next Door: The Militia Movement and the Radical Right* (Nashville: Thomas Dunne Books, 2002), 301–334; Carolyn Gallaher, *On the Fault Line: Race, Class, and the American Patriot Movement* (Lanham, MD: Rowman & Littlefield, 2003), 69–96.

129 up to 5 million strong: Kathleen Belew, *Bring the War Home: The White Power Movement and Paramilitary America* (Cambridge, MA: Harvard University Press, 2018), 5.

129 Timothy McVeigh, a decorated former soldier: John Kifner, "McVeigh's Mind," *New York Times*, December 31, 1995.

129 While initial speculation focused: Walter Goodman, "Terror in Oklahoma City: TV Critics's Notebook; Wary Network Anchors Battle Dubious Scoops," *New York Times*, April 20, 1995.

130 The number of inmates in federal prisons: Allen J. Beck and Paige M. Harrison, "Prisoners in 2000," *Bureau of Justice Statistics Bulletin*, Office of Justice Programs, U.S. Department of Justice, August 2001, online at https://www.bjs.gov/content/pub/pdf/p00.pdf.

131 "The Second Amendment is not about duck hunting": See YouTube video of her testimony: https://www.youtube.com/watch?v=FgrIsuO5PLc.

131 13,827 hunting and shooting clubs: Advertisement with Charlton Heston, Life Member, *American Rifleman*, August 1991, back cover.

132 "Let Armed Criminals Be Warned": *American Rifleman*, February 1992, glossy insert.

132 concentrating on finding new and innovative ways to be heard: "NRA's TV Show Is Viewed by Millions," unsigned, ILA Report, *American Rifleman*, July 1995, 24.

132 Ernestine Stodelle: "Ernestine Stodelle, 95, Modern Dancer, Dies," *New York Times*, January 9, 2008.

133 "I remained on good personal terms with Jim Baker": Richard Feldman, *Ricochet: Confessions of a Gun Lobbyist* (Hoboken, NJ: John Wiley & Sons, 2007), 201.

133 "This is the fight of the decade": Southern Legal Resource Center, "Defending the Rights of All Americans, Advocating for the Confederate Community," Facebook page, post dated April 23, 2012.

133 "This is the crucible": Leonard Zeskind, "Armed and Dangerous: The NRA, Militias and White Supremacists Are Fostering a Network of Right Wing Warriors," *Rolling Stone*, November 2, 1995.

133 "The NRA is an organization": Zeskind, "Armed and Dangerous."

134 "like a current that spans centuries": Wayne LaPierre, "Standing Guard," *American Rifleman*, January 1993, 7.

134 "Today," Kopel went on: Dave Kopel, "Defend Your Rights," *American Rifleman*, January 1993, 18.

134 Knox had begun saying: Dan E. Moldea, "The NRA Goes to War with Itself," *Regardie's*, April 1987, online at https://www.moldea.com/NRA-1987.html.

135 "If you want to understand the NRA Board": Osha Gray Davidson, *Under Fire: The NRA and the Battle for Gun Control* (New York: Henry Holt, 1993), 180.

135 "The Leon Trotsky, if you will": Michael Powell, "The NRA's Call to Arms," *Washington Post Magazine*, August 6, 2000, SMB8.

135 Rumors had grown so loud: Dennis Cauchon, "NRA Regroups, with Double-Barrelled Agenda: Gun Backers Planning New Tactics," *USA Today*, May 20, 1994, 9A.

136 Johnston founded a militia: David Whiting, "NRA Instructor Teaches Shooting, Battles Gun Control," *Orange County* (CA) *Register*, February 16, 2013, online at https://www.ocregister.com/2013/02/16/whiting-nra-instructor-teaches-shooting-battles-gun-control/.

136 Florida gun rights activist Marion P. Hammer: Recently reached at the phone number of Unified Sportsmen of Florida, the gun rights group she has long run from her home, Hammer, now eighty, said she would have the NRA's chief spokesman, Andrew Arulanandam, determine if her cooperation for this book would receive a "fair and honest presentation." Both Arulanandam and Hammer declined further comment.

138 (I myself was in the room: Frank Smyth, "Crossfire: The War Behind the Closed Doors of the NRA," *Village Voice*, June 3, 1994.

138 "Words alone can't express": Joe Foss, "The President's Column," *American Rifleman*, January 1989, 52.

139 "That's always a bad situation": Frank Smyth, "In the Line of Fire: Under Attack the NRA Hard-Line Makes a Stand," *Village Voice*, June 6, 1995.

139 A motion was soon made: The National Rifle Association of America Bylaws, as Amended February 3 and May 21, 2001, Article V, Sec. 3 (h), 22, Bob Barr Papers, Ingram Library, University of West Georgia.

139 "I spoke with directors who attended": David Brock, "Wayne's World," *American Spectator*, May 1997, 42.

140 Timothy McVeigh, motivated by: See Belew, *Bring the War Home*, 188.

140 *The Turner Diaries*: Andrew Macdonald, *The Turner Diaries*, 2nd ed. (Hillsboro, WV: National Vanguard Books, 1999), chapter 23, online at e-reading.club/bookreader .php/133469/The_Turner_Diaries.pdf.

141 "the number 88 represents": Brian Palmer, "White Supremacists by the Numbers: What's Up with 14 and 88? And What About the Shaved Heads and White Tuxedos?," *Slate*, October 29, 2008.

142 Three days later, Pratt attended: Alexander Zaitchik, "The Zealot: Larry Pratt Is the Gun Lobby's Secret Weapon," *Rolling Stone*, July 14, 2014.

142 "gives jackbooted Government thugs": Wayne LaPierre, fundraising letter.

142 president George H. W. Bush: "Letter of Resignation Sent by Bush to Rifle Association," *New York Times*, May 11, 1995.

142 Lapierre, after initially defending his words, apologized: Twenty-four years later, however, in a rare interview with an independent reporter, LaPierre said that it was the NRA board director and Democratic representative from Michigan, John Dingell, who had referred to ATF agents as "a jackbooted group of fascists" in an NRA promotional film back in 1981, while suggesting that NRA staffers had used the term again in the 1995 letter under his name without his knowledge. "I remember calling down, going, 'We couldn't possibly have a letter out there saying that A.T.F. were a bunch of jackbooted thugs, could we?'" Danny Hakim, "Inside Wayne LaPierre's Battle for the N.R.A.," *New York Times Magazine*, December 18, 2019.

142 "I really feel bad": Associated Press, "NRA Official Issues Apology for Controversial Fund-Raising Letter," *Los Angeles Times*, May 18, 1995.

143 "maggots": Neal Knox, "Bombing Gun Law Reform," Report to the Firearms Coalition, Washington, D.C., April 22, 1995, online at http://rkba.org/knox/2may95.

143 "Unless those people have committed": Kim Masters, "Recoil from the NRA's Two Top Guns," *Washington Post*, April 29, 1995.

143 speaking to anyone here in the room "who supports—or even fantasizes about": Wayne LaPierre speech.

143 "Keep your firearms out of sight": Smyth, "In the Line of Fire."

144 "People have passed out literature": Smyth, "In the Line of Fire."

144 "I do not want to kill this motion": Smyth, "In the Line of Fire."

144 "Gun owners—all gun owners": David E. Petzal, "Endangered Tradition" column, *Field & Stream*, June 1994.

145 As Petzal later acknowledged in an interview with the *Village Voice*: Smyth, "Crossfire."

145 Petzal's pieces later sometimes criticized: David E. Petzal, "Shot Show 2016, Part I," *Field & Stream*, January 25, 2016, online at https://www.fieldandstream.com/blogs /the-gun-nuts/shot-show-2016-part-i/.

145 "tell the truth": David E. Petzal, "Media Mysteries Explained," *American Rifleman*, June 29, 2017, online at https://www.americanrifleman.org/articles/2017/6/29/media -mysteries-explained/.

145 The Association's cash and investment portfolio: Brock, "Wayne's World," 44.

146 Knox went on using his newsletters: Wayne LaPierre, "Standing Guard," *American Rifleman*, December 1995, 7.

146 "legacy of good works": Marion P. Hammer, "The President's Column," *American Rifleman*, February 1996, 22.

146 over alleged overbilling: Jeff Knox, "NRA's Future: Only Two Options, Can the BOD Save Us?," *Ammoland: Shooting Sports News*, April 22, 2019, online at https:// www.ammoland.com/2019/04/nras-future-only-two-options-can-the-bod-save-us /#axzz63TDoBRTj.

147 "a Zen anarchist": Michael Powell, "The NRA's Call to Arms," *Washington Post Magazine*, August 6, 2000, SMB8.

147 "We used our best techniques": Powell, "The NRA's Call to Arms."

147 As Hammer later told *The Washington Post*: Powell, "The NRA's Call to Arms."

148 "Good morning, gun lobby": "National Rifle Association Report of the First Vice President to the NRA Annual Meeting of Members," May 3, 1977, Seattle, WA, Bob Barr Papers, Ingram Library, University of West Georgia, 8–11.

148 "It is Americans who have proven": "National Rifle Association of America Report of the Executive Vice President to the Annual Meeting of Members," Barr Papers, 24.

148 The year before, in Dallas, he had given: "1996 Annual Meetings in Dallas: NRA Celebrates 125 Years of Service to America," *American Rifleman*, July 1996, 42.

149 a photo of LaPierre, Hammer, Metaksa, Heston: *American Rifleman*, July 1997.

149 "Are Gun Rights Lost on Our Kids?": *American Rifleman*, September 1997.

150 "Heaven help the God-fearing": Charlton Heston, "The Second Amendment: America's First Freedom," speech at the National Press Club, Washington, D.C., September 11, 1997, in *Guns in America: A Reader*, ed. Jan E. Dizard, Robert Merrill Muth, and Stephen P. Andrews Jr. (New York: New York University Press, 1999), 201.

150 Then the board changed the Association's bylaws: Article V, Officers, Section I, Number and Election, National Rifle Association of America Bylaws, as Amended February 3 and May 21, 2001, Barr Papers, 19. See also Gina M. Schmidt, "'Do Your Best, Keep Your Promises,'" *America's 1st Freedom*, October 10, 2003, online at https://www.nraila.org/articles/20031010/do-your-best-keep-your-promises.

150 Membership dipped again: Dave Gilson, "The NRA Says It Has 5 Million Members. Its Magazines Tell Another Story," *Mother Jones*, March 7, 2018, online at https:// www.motherjones.com/politics/2018/03/nra-membership-magazine-numbers-1/.

150 "freedom's insurance policy": Charlton Heston, "The President's Column," *American Rifleman*, July 1999, 13.

150 Near the end, LaPierre's camp smeared: Katharine Q. Seelye, "Close Votes in N.R.A. Elections Quash Hope for Internal Unity," *New York Times*, May 6, 1997.

152 "When loss of liberty is looming": Charlton Heston, speech at the 2000 NRA annual meeting in Charlotte, NC.

NINE: THE BUSINESS MODEL

153 none other than Charlton Heston: Charlton Heston, "The President's Column," *American Rifleman*, February 2000, 12.

154 "recreational use of firearms": "Report of the Executive Vice President to the Board of Directors, National Rifle Association of America," Arlington, VA, September 2000, Bob Barr Papers, Ingram Library, University of West Georgia.

154 "where public affairs used to be": Richard Feldman, *Ricochet: Confessions of a Gun Lobbyist* (Hoboken, NJ: John Wiley & Sons, 2007), 197.

154 "powered by pride, love of country, respect for the military": nracountry.com/about.

154 "blatant conflict of interest": Feldman, *Ricochet*, 129, 197.

155 "paid media": Deposition of Angus McQueen, Taken on behalf of the Intervenors in Oklahoma City, Oklahoma, on September 24, 2002, *McConnell et al. v. Federal Election Committee*, U.S. District Court, Washington, D.C., online at https://campaignlegal .org/sites/default/files/823.pdf.

155 "during the summer, Public Affairs staff": "Report of the Executive Vice President to the Board of Directors, National Rifle Association," Arlington, VA, November 3–4, 2001, Barr Papers.

155 "the language currently being used": "Report of the Special Committee on Language to the Public Affairs Committee," submitted September 14, 2001, Barr Papers.

156 its website: http://www.nramuseum.org/museums/national-firearms-museum.aspx.

156 "there was a run on the Model 29 revolvers": Dan Gagliasso, "Hollywood History at the National Firearms Museum," *American Rifleman*, May 2002, 80–84.

156 guns in history: Recent features include Bill Vanderpool, "'Bring Enough Gun: A History of the FBI's Long Arms," *American Rifleman*, October 2013, 80; Kenneth L. Smith-Christmas, "Guns of the Battle of Blair Mountain," *American Rifleman*, March 2014, 64; Martin K. A. Morgan, "The Men and Guns of the Battle of the Bulge," *American Rifleman*, January 2015, 72.

156 "Panther Across the Sky": Mark Sage, "Panther Across The Sky: Tecumseh's Northwest Trade Gun," *American Rifleman*, July 2015, 56.

157 Winchester Model 70: Bryce M. Towsley, "Not Your Daddy's Model 70," *American Rifleman*, October 2004, cover, 60–65.

157 access over conservation: J. R. Robbins, "NRA Launches New Website Devoted to Hunters' Rights," *American Rifleman*, March 2008, 52–53.

157 four million members: "Report of the Executive Vice President," November 3–4, 2001.

158 "Each horrible act can't become": Knight-Ridder, "Still-Grieving Colorado Turns Out to Protest NRA Meeting," *Baltimore Sun*, May 2, 1999.

159 "We think it's reasonable": Testimony of Wayne LaPierre, House Judiciary Committee, Subcommittee on Crime, May 27, 1999; see also Louis Jacobson, "Barack Obama says, 'The NRA used to support expanded background checks,'" PolitiFact, April 18, 2013, online at https://www.politifact.com/truth-o-meter/statements/2013/apr/18/barack-obama/barack-obama-says-nra-used-support-expanded-backgr/; and "1998 NRA Board Election Results, Inside NRA," *American Rifleman*, August 1998, 16. In his first run for the board, Congressman Barr received more votes, 144,392, than every other candidate except Charlton Heston, with 161,172.

160 Oliver North: Awarded two Purple Hearts, a Bronze Star with valor, and a Silver Star during the Vietnam War, North is best known for having masterminded the selling of arms to Iran in the 1980s in violation of a U.S.-backed arms embargo on Iran in a scheme to divert the proceeds of the arms sale to support Nicaraguan right-wing counterrevolutionaries, known by their nickname in Spanish as the "Contras," in a way that circumvented the need for congressional approval of such support. North later claimed the purpose was to trade the arms for the release of seven American hostages being held by Iranian-backed Hezbollah in Lebanon, but a congressional investigation showed the arms sales had begun before any of the hostages had been taken. North was convicted on three felony counts but later had all charges dismissed on appeal.

160 A keynote speaker at the NRA's annual Women's Leadership Forum: Mike Spies, "Tom Selleck Quits NRA Board," The Trace, September 18, 2018, online at https://www.thetrace.org/2018/09/tom-selleck-quits-nra-board/; L. A. Luebbert, "Tom Selleck, Kellyanne Conway Featured Guests at Women's Leadership Forum," NRA Family, May 9, 2017, online at https://www.nrafamily.org/articles/2017/5/9/tom-selleck-kellyanne-conway-featured-guests-at-women-s-leadership-forum/.

161 "EVCs work with the various pro-gun campaigns": Glen A. Caroline, "Memorandum 2002 Election Volunteer Coordinator (EVC) Program," Grassroots Division, NRA-ILA, to NRA Board of Directors, NRA Field Representatives, NRA State Association Presidents, February 11, 2002, Barr Papers.

162 "very strategic with its war chest": Liz Plank, "The NRA Doesn't Buy Politicians. It Swings Elections," Vox, July 13, 2016, online at https://www.vox.com/2016/7/13/12111322/nra-elections.

162 When a colleague interviewed Watson: Frank Smyth, "Behind the Badge: Meet the NRA's Law Enforcement Front Group," *Texas Observer*, July 30, 2004.

163 NRA tax filings: Billy Corriher, "NRA Working to Elect Pro-Gun Judges and Prosecutors in Michigan," Center for American Progress, February 14, 2013, online at https://www.americanprogress.org/issues/courts/news/2013/02/14/53076/nra-working-to-elect-pro-gun-judges-and-prosecutors/.

163 "It's absurd to suggest": Smyth, "Behind the Badge."

164 "useful safety devices": Corriher, "NRA Working to Elect Pro-Gun Judges."

164 only six states . . . allowed concealed carry: See David Yamane, "The History of Concealed Weapons Laws in the United States, Part 3: The Rise of the Shall-Issue (Right-to-Carry) Era of Concealed Carry," Gun Culture 2.0 (blog), June 19, 2014, online at https://gunculture2point0.wordpress.com/2014/06/19/the-history-of-concealed-weapons-laws-in-the-united-states-part-3-the-rise-of-the-shall-issue-right-to-carry-era-of-concealed-carry/; Clayton E. Cramer and David B. Kopel, "'Shall Issue': The

New Wave of Concealed Handgun Permit Laws," *Tennessee Law Review* 62, no. 3 (Spring 1995): 679–757.

164 Close to a quarter of that number: Christopher Ingraham, "3 Million Americans Carry Loaded Handguns with Them Every Single Day, Study Finds," *Washington Post*, October 19, 2017, https://www.washingtonpost.com/news/wonk/wp/2017/10/19/3-million -americans-carry-loaded-handguns-with-them-every-single-day-study-finds/.

165 "No one else has accomplished": Speech by NRA-ILA Executive Director Chris Cox at the Members' Meeting in Indianapolis, April 27, 2019, online at home.nra.org.

165 Jeff Cooper: "1988 Director Nominations," *American Rifleman*, February 1988, 58–64.

165 Influenced by rising crime: Evan Osnos, "Making a Killing: The Business and Politics of Selling Guns," *New Yorker*, June 20, 2016.

165 "It doesn't make me feel a whole lot warmer": Michael Warren, "Packing Guns No Problem: Frontier-Justice Visions Simply Not the Reality," *News Herald* (Panama City, FL), November 4, 1990.

166 "After four or five years of filibustering": J. L. Griffin, "Missouri to Vote on Amendment April 6," *Joplin* (MO) *Globe*, March 21, 1999.

166 "The gun industry should send me a basket of fruit": Alix M. Freedman, "Tinier, Deadlier Pocket Pistols Are in Vogue," *Wall Street Journal*, September 12, 1996.

167 according to the Johns Hopkins Bloomberg School of Public Health: Daniel W. Webster, Cassandra K. Crifasi, Jon S. Vernick, and Alexander McCourt, "Concealed Carry of Firearms: Facts vs. Fiction," Center for Gun Policy and Research Bloomberg American Health Initiative, November 16, 2017, 5, online at https://www .jhsph.edu/research/centers-and-institutes/johns-hopkins-center-for-gun-policy -and-research/_archive-2019/_pdfs/concealed-carry-of-firearms.pdf.

167 Other scholars disagree: See Cramer and Kopel, "'Shall Issue'"; John R. Lott, *More Guns, Less Crime: Understanding Crime and Gun Control Laws* (Chicago: University of Chicago Press, 2010).

167 "Whenever a state legislature first considers": David Kopel, "The Untold Triumph of Concealed Carry Permits," *Policy Review*, July/August 1996, quoted in "Concealed Carry | Right-to-Carry," NRA-ILA, 2019.

167 violent crime has showed an increasing upward trend: John J. Donohue, Abhay Aneja, and Kyle D. Weber, "Right-to-Carry Laws and Violent Crime: A Comprehensive Assessment Using Panel Data and a State-Level Synthetic Control Analysis," National Bureau of Economic Research Working Paper No. 23510, Issued June 2017, revised November 2018; M. Siegel, Z. Xuan, C. S. Ross, S. Galea, B. Kalesan, E. Fleegler, and K. A. Goss, "Easiness of Legal Access to Concealed Firearm Permits and Homicide Rates in the United States," *American Journal of Public Health*, October 19, 2017, both cited in Webster et al., "Concealed Carry of Firearms: Facts vs. Fiction," 6.

167 This rise in gun violence in concealed-carry states: John Gramlich, "5 Facts About Crime in the U.S.," Fact Tank, Pew Research Center, October 17, 2019, online at https://www.pewresearch.org/fact-tank/2019/10/17/facts-about-crime-in-the-u-s/.

167 one recent study of thirty-three states: John J. Donohue, Abhay Aneja, and Kyle D. Weber, "Right-to-Carry Laws and Violent Crime: A Comprehensive Assessment Using Panel Data and a State-Level Synthetic Control Analysis," *Journal of Empirical Legal Studies* 16, no. 2 (2019).

168 NRA's "dream" goal: "NRA Applauds Hudson's Concealed Carry Reciprocity Act to Eliminate Confusing Patchwork of State Laws," NRA-ILA, January 4, 2019, online at https://www.nraila.org/articles/20190104/nra-applauds-hudsons-concealed-carry -reciprocity-act-to-eliminate-confusing-patchwork-of-state-laws.

168 "It's a lot easier to play a leading man": Wayne LaPierre, "Standing Guard," *American Rifleman*, June 2003, 12.

168 one U.S. Department of Justice–funded study: Christopher S. Koper with Daniel J. Woods and Jeffrey A. Roth, "An Updated Assessment of the Federal Assault Weapons Ban: Impacts on Gun Markets and Gun Violence, 1994–2003," Report to the National Institute of Justice, United States Department of Justice, Jerry Lee Center of Criminology, University of Pennsylvania, June 2004, 1–3.

168 "inconclusive evidence": "Effects of Bans on the Sale of Assault Weapons and High-Capacity Magazines on Violent Crime," RAND Corporation, March 2, 2018, online at https://www.rand.org/research/gun-policy/analysis/ban-assault-weapons/violent -crime.html.

169 "the 'Black Rifle'": "National Matches at Camp Perry," *American Rifleman*, December 2001, 68–69.

169 This program was deplored by critics: See "Guns in the Home Proving Deadly for Kids," *USAToday*, May 11, 2013.

169 Children from five to fourteen: David Hemenway, "Risks and Benefits of a Gun in the Home," *American Journal of Lifestyle Medicine*, February 2, 2011.

169 The act limited issue advocacy ads: Wayne LaPierre, "Standing Guard," *American Rifleman*, June 2001, 12.

170 Rehnquist Supreme Court: Warren Richy, "Court Upholds 'Soft Money' Ban," *Christian Science Monitor*, December 11, 2003.

170 "stop the tyranny": Wayne LaPierre, "Standing Guard," *American Rifleman*, April 2003, 12.

170 "I freaked out": Kevin Cool, "Top Gun," *Stanford Magazine*, March/April 2006.

170 "stop the Schumer-Emanuel gun-ban": Wayne LaPierre, "Standing Guard," *American Rifleman*, October 2006, 10.

170 "If we lose control of the Senate": Sandra S. Froman, "President's Column," *American Rifleman*, October 2006, 12.

171 federal background check system: Michael Luo, "Cho's Mental Illness Should Have Blocked Gun Sale," *New York Times*, April 20, 2007.

171 "Our thoughts and prayers": "NRA Joins in Day of Mourning," April 20, 2007, NRA-ILA, online at https://www.nraila.org/grassroots-alerts/grassroots-alert/?id=1892.

171 "Some Virginia Tech victims and survivors": David Burnett, "I Would Give Anything," *America's 1st Freedom*, June 4, 2015, online at https://www.americas1stfreedom.org /articles/2015/6/4/i-would-give-anything/.

TEN: HIDDEN HANDS

173 "NRA Endorses Reagan": Associated Press, "NRA Endorses Reagan," *Framington* (NM) *Daily Times*, October 30, 1980. A reprint of the same *American Hunter* editorial first appeared in a paid political advertisement with permission of the National Rifle

Association Institute for Legislative Action in the *Daily Gazette* (Xenia, OH), October 10, 1980, 10, attributed to a local resident who may have been an NRA member.

174 columns in both the *American Rifleman* and the *American Hunter*: J. Warren Cassidy, "Here We Stand," *American Rifleman*, October 1988, 7; Joe Foss, "The President's Column," *American Rifleman*, October 1988, 58.

174 NRA withheld its support: Dave Kopel, "George Bush and the NRA," *Gun World*, 1996, online at http://www.davekopel.org/2A/Mags/George-Bush-and-the-NRA.htm.

174 NRA declined to endorse anyone: Katharine Q. Seelye, "Staying on Sidelines in Presidential Race, N.R.A. Snubs Dole," *New York Times*, September 18, 1996.

174 Although Wayne LaPierre early on: James Dao, "The 2000 Campaign: The Gun Lobby; N.R.A. Tightens Its Embrace of Republicans with Donations," *New York Times,* April 26, 2000.

174 "Polls suggest that the NRA": James Dao, "The 2000 Campaign: The Endorsements; To Help Bush, N.R.A. Withholds Backing," *New York Times*, September 12, 2000.

174 "President Bush and Vice President Dick Cheney": "NRA Endorses George W. Bush for President," NRA-ILA, October 13, 2004, online at https://www.nraila.org/articles/20041013/nra-endorses-george-w-bush-for-preside.

174 Despite the Association's differences with McCain: "NRA-PVF Endorses John McCain for U.S. Senate," NRA-ILA, June 3, 2010, online at https://www.nraila.org/articles/20100603/nra-pvf-endorses-john-mccain-for-us-s.

175 "From 1970 to 1989": "The History and Politics of Second Amendment Scholarship: A Primer," in *The Second Amendment in Law and History: Law and Constitutional Scholars on the Right to Bear Arms*, ed. Carl Bogus (New York: New Press, 2002), 4, quoted in Michael Waldman, *The Second Amendment: A Biography* (New York: Simon & Schuster, 2014), 97–98.

176 "It's hard to convey fully": Waldman, *The Second Amendment: A Biography*, 98.

177 The institute reveals not a single one of its donors: Michael Wyland, "Treasury Weakens Donor Disclosure Requirements for Some Nonprofits," *Nonprofit Quarterly*, July 18, 2018, online at https://nonprofitquarterly.org/2018/07/18/treasury-weakens-donor-disclosure-requirements-for-some-nonprofits.

177 "We do not name our donors": Telephone interview by the author with Josh Williams, Donor Relations Manager, Independence Institute, April 10, 2019.

177 "Writers and editors make": Frank Smyth, "Five Years After Sandy Hook, Major U.S. Papers Still Have a Serious Gun Problem," *The Progressive*, December 21, 2017.

178 Kopel began testifying before Congress: James J. Kilpatrick, "Very Little to Gun Legislation," *Daily Independent* (Kannapolis, NC), August 15, 1988.

179 amicus brief filed to the Supreme Court: Supreme Court of the United States, *District of Columbia et al. v. Dick Heller*, No. 07–290, online at https://www.nraila.org/heller/proamicusbriefs/07-290_amicus_ileeta.pdf.

179 This brief by Kopel: Supreme Court of the United States, Syllabus, *District of Columbia et al. v. Heller*, No. 07–290, argued March 18, 2008, decided June 26, 2008, 21.

179 Kopel's brief in the *McDonald* case: Supreme Court of the United States, Syllabus, *Otis P. McDonald, et al., v. City of Chicago, et al.*, No. 08–1521, argued March 2, 2010, decided June 28, 2010, online at https://www.supremecourt.gov/opinions/09pdf/08-1521.pdf.

179 Supreme Court rule 29.6: Rules of the Supreme Court of the United States, Adopted April 19, 2013, Effective July 1, 2013, i.

180 "the nation's leading expert": Adam Winkler, *Gun Fight: The Battle over the Right to Bear Arms in America* (New York: W. W. Norton, 2013), 54.

180 *The Founders' Second Amendment: Origins of the Right to Bear Arms*: "Supported Research (Previous Years)," NRA Civil Rights Defense Fund, n.d., online at www .nradefensefund.org; Stephen P. Halbrook, *The Founders' Second Amendment: Origins of the Right to Bear Arms* (Oakland, CA: Ivan R. Dee/Independent Institute, 2008).

180 Halbrook filed an amicus brief: Supreme Court of the United States, *District of Columbia, et al., Petitioners v. Dick Anthony Heller*, No. 07–290.

180 Justice Scalia's decision: Supreme Court of the United States, Syllabus, *District of Columbia et al. v. Heller*.

180 And in 2010 Halbrook was one of the attorneys: 130 S. Ct. 3020 (2010), *Otis McDonald, et al., Petitioners, v. City of Chicago, Illinois, et al.*, No. 08–1521, argued March 2, 2010, decided June 28, 2010.

181 "[A]fter engaging in hyper-literal reading": Waldman, *The Second Amendment: A Biography*, 125.

181 "Only two pages out of his 64-page opinion": Rachel Brody, "Decoding the Gun Debate," *U.S. News & World Report*, July 24, 2014; Michael Kammen, ed., *Documents on the First Congress Debate on Arms and Militia, Extracted from The Origins of the American Constitution, A Documentary History* (New York: Penguin Books, 1986); Helen E. Veit et al., eds., *Creating the Bill of Rights: The Documentary Record from the First Federal Congress* (Baltimore: Johns Hopkins University Press, 1991).

181 A narrative that had been proffered: Tom Kertscher, "NRA Founded to Fight KKK, Black Leader Says," PolitiFact, June 5, 2013, online at https://www.politifact.com /wisconsin/statements/2013/jun/05/harry-alford/nra-founded-fight-kkk-black -leader-says/.

181 But more recently he had seen: Mary Katharine Ham, "Meet Otis McDonald: The Man Behind the SCOTUS Chicago Gun Case," *Washington Examiner*, March 2, 2010.

181 "Mr. McDonald felt strongly": Dahleen Glanton, "Otis McDonald, 1933–2014: Fought Chicago's Gun Ban," *Chicago Tribune*, April 6, 2014, quoted in Wayne La-Pierre, "Those Who Call the NRA Racist Don't Know Our History," *America's 1st Freedom*, September 27, 2017.

182 "As an American black man": Allen West, "The Tale of Two Organizations, from the Perspective of an American Black Man," CNSNews.com, September 10, 2018, online at https://www.cnsnews.com/commentary/allen-west/allen-west-tale-two-organiza tions-perspective-american-black-man.

182 "Tickling Sambo's fancy": William Conant Church, *Army and Navy Journal*, July 22, 1865, cited in Donald N. Bigelow, *William Conant Church and the Army and Navy Journal* (New York: Columbia University Press, 1952), 167.

183 "The negroes had ceased to be slaves": William Conant Church, *Ulysses S. Grant and the Period of National Preservation and Reconstruction* (New York: G. P. Putnam's Sons, 1897), 344–350.

184 "a National Convention of coloured men": Church, *Ulysses S. Grant*, 395.

184 "partisan courts and judges": Church, *Ulysses S. Grant*, 350.

184 Although he did mention the Union Army's decision: Church, *Ulysses S. Grant*, 186.

184 The local KKK: Robert F. Williams, *Negroes with Guns* (Mansfield Center, CT: Martino Publishing, 2013), 52–58.

185 "Williams and the black men of Monroe": Nicholas Johnson, *Negroes and the Gun: The Black Tradition of Arms* (Amherst, NY: Prometheus Books, 2014), 21–22.

185 "Citizens Fire Back at Klan": "Citizens Fire Back at Klan: Ku Kluxers Use Guns at Monroe, NC: Shots Exchanged Near Residence of NAACP Head," *Journal and Guide*, October 12, 1957.

185 simply not on the NRA's agenda: The NRA did sell ammunition at bulk discount prices to at least one armed black group, however (Deacons for Defense and Justice, formed in 1964 in Jonesboro, Louisiana), doing so as part of the NRA's collaboration with the Civilian Marksmanship Program, then nearing its end, to sell surplus government ammunition to hundreds of affiliated gun clubs across the nation. But the Deacons for Defense and Justice in Louisiana, unlike Monroe's Black Armed Guard in North Carolina, does not appear to have been affiliated with the NRA. Moreover, their "members provided their own guns," according to Christopher B. Strain, "We Walked Like Men: Deacons for Defense and Justice," *Louisiana History: The Journal of the Louisiana Historical Association* 38, no. 1, Winter, 1997, 49. Yet, David Kopel, citing this piece and one other scholarly source, somehow claimed "the NRA was the Deacons' arsenal" in *American Rifleman* in 2013, later reposted online in America's 1st Freedom as "Deacons for Defense and Justice," August 5, 2015. His other scholarly source was Lance E. Hill, *The Deacons for Defense: Armed Self-Defense and the Civil Rights Movement* (Chapel Hill: University of North Carolina Press, 2004), which makes no mention of the NRA at all.

185 "U.N. global gun-ban movement": Sandy Froman, "President's Column," Official Journal Special Report, *American Rifleman*, September 2006, 10.

185 "protect[ing] our firearm freedoms": David Keene, "President's Column: We Must Protect Our Firearm Freedoms from Foreign and Domestic Threats," *American Rifleman*, September 2011, 14.

186 "Obama's Secret Plan to Destroy the Second Amendment": Wayne LaPierre, "Obama's Secret Plan to Destroy the Second Amendment by 2016," *American Rifleman*, December 2011, 40–45.

186 the riots began after the British police shot: David Rooney, "It Will Never Happen Here," *American Rifleman*, December 2011, 16–18.

187 *The Dark Knight Rises*: Jennifer Brown, "12 Shot Dead, 58 Wounded in Aurora Movie Theater During Batman Premiere," *Denver Post*, July 20, 2012.

188 "lorem ipsum" text: Christina Wilkie, "Law Enforcement Alliance of America, NRA Front-Group, Spends Millions to Elect Pro-Gun Judges," *Huffington Post*, February 14, 2013, online at https://www.huffpost.com/entry/law-enforcement-alliance-of-america_n_2689591.

188 These wars fueled demand: Ali Watkins, John Ismay, and Thomas Gibbons-Neff, "Once Banned, Now Loved and Loathed: How the AR-15 Became 'America's Rifle,'" *New York Times*, March 3, 2018.

188 "The injury along the path of the bullet": Heather Sher, "What I Saw Treating the

Victims from Parkland Should Change the Debate on Guns," *Atlantic*, February 22, 2018.

189 In the spring of 2019: Associated Press, "2 Men Arrested After Shooting Each Other While Wearing Bulletproof Vest," ABC 13, April 4, 2019, online at https://abc13.com /men-shoot-each-other-while-wearing-bulletproof-vest-/5233769/.

189 Had the men attempted the same stunt: See Leana Wen, "What Bullets Do to Bodies," *New York Times*, June 17, 2017.

189 a "make-believe unicorn term": Dana Loesch, *Hands Off My Gun: Defeating the Plot to Disarm America* (New York: Center Street, 2014), 42–43.

190 "AR-15-style rifles are NOT 'assault weapons'": "Modern Sporting Rifle: Introduction, Understanding America's Rifle," National Shooting Sports Foundation, online at https://www.nssf.org/msr/.

191 While these rifles accounted for 3 percent: Nick Clossman and Chris Long, "A Business Case Analysis of the M4/AR-15 Market," Joint Applied Project, Naval Postgraduate School, September 2015, 19, online at https://apps.dtic.mil/dtic/tr/fulltext/u2 /1008889.pdf.

191 estimated revenues generated: Clossman and Long, "A Business Case Analysis," 21.

191 total economic impact of the firearms and ammunition industry: "Firearms and Ammunition Industry Economic Impact Report 2013," National Shooting Sports Foundation, April 2014, online at www.trbas.com.

192 greater than the annual sales of major individual companies: "Fortune 500 2013," *Fortune,* online at fortune.com/fortune500/2013.

192 "a material adverse effect": "Annual Report for the Fiscal Year Ended December 31, 2012," Remington Outdoor Company, 4, online at www.remingtonoutdoorcompany .com.

192 Companies in the firearms industry: "Blood Money II: How Gun Industry Dollars Fund the NRA," Violence Police Center, September 2013, online at http://vpc.org /studies/bloodmoney2.pdf; John Crook, "NRA Membership Dues Tumbled Last Year," The Trace, September 20, 2018.

192 LaPierre gave a speech at the United Nations: "Wayne LaPierre Fights for the Second Amendment Before the United Nations," NRA-ILA, July 11, 2012, online at https:// www.nraila.org/articles/20120711/wayne-lapierre-defends-the-second-amendment -before-the-united-nations.

193 treaty, which ultimately passed: Arms Trade Treaty, at https://unoda-web.s3-accelerate .amazonaws.com/wp-content/uploads/2013/06/English7.pdf.

ELEVEN: A FAMILY SPORT

194 "The physical things are difficult": Tara Parker-Pope, "How to Manage Stress Like an Olympic Biathlete," *New York Times*, February 21, 2018.

195 "When preparing to fire a single shot": Woody, "Becoming One with the Gun: 'Zen, Meditation & the Art of Shooting'" (review), Cheaper Than Dirt!, January 9, 2015, online at https://blog.cheaperthandirt.com/gun-zen-meditation-art-shooting/.

195 But the nation's Civilian Marksmanship Program: Ashley Brugnone, "CMP Sees Unexpected Numbers at Inaugural National Smallbore Matches at Camp Perry," Civilian

Marksmanship Program, n.d., online at http://thecmp.org/cmp-sees-unexpected
-numbers-at-inaugural-national-smallbore-matches-at-camp-perry/.

195 Southern Connecticut has produced: Hap Rocketto, "A History of the United States
National Outdoor Smallbore Rifle Championships 1919–2013," unpublished manuscript, August 25, 2013, online at http://pronematch.com/wp-content/uploads/2013
/10/A%20History%20of%20the%20United%20States%20National%20Outdoor%20
Smallbore%20Rifle%20Championship%201919-2013-2.pdf.

195 Emily Caruso: See "Emily Caruso," Team USA, United States Olympic Committee,
n.d., online at https://www.teamusa.org/usa-shooting/athletes/Emily-Caruso, and
"Emily Caruso," USA Shooting, n.d., at https://www.usashooting.org/12-the-team
/usashootingteam/nationalteam/nationalrifleteam/emilycaruso.

196 In 1920, two Connecticut riflemen: Rocketto, "A History of the United States National Outdoor Smallbore," 16.

196 Nine years later: Rocketto, "A History of the United States National Outdoor Smallbore," 42.

196 In 1981 two Connecticut riflemen: Rocketto, "A History of the United States National
Outdoor Smallbore," 202.

196 Lyman, second in line: "David Botsford Lyman 1955–2017" (obituary), online at
https://www.bcbailey.com/listings.

196 NRA Double Distinguished National Smallbore Rifle Champions: Remington Perry
Lyman, "USA Shooting Team Quota Hunt in Azerbaijan," n.d., online at https://
www.bluetrailrange.com/match/remington-perry-lyman-usa-shooting-team-quota
-hunt-azerbaijan/.

197 "she has developed shooters": "2005 Sybil Ludington Women's Freedom Award Winner," NRA Explore, n.d., online at https://awards.nra.org/awards/sybil-ludington
-womens-freedom-award/patricia-clark/.

197 "Both the mother and the [son]": Report of the State's Attorney for the Judicial District of Danbury on the Shootings at Sandy Hook Elementary School and 36 Yoga-
nanda Street, Newtown, Connecticut, on December 14, 2012, November 25, 2013, 31,
online at https://portal.ct.gov/-/media/DCJ/SandyHookFinalReportpdf.pdf?la=en.

197 "Guns require a lot of respect": Mark Memmott, "Nancy Lanza, Gunman's Mother:
From 'Charmed Upbringing' to First Victim," NPR, December 18, 2012, online at
https://www.npr.org/sections/thetwo-way/2012/12/18/167527771/nancy-lanza
-gunmans-mother-from-charmed-upbringing-to-first-victim.

197 "was described as presenting" : Report of the State's Attorney, 34–35.

198 His educators identified him: Report of the State's Attorney, 35.

198 Dana Loesch . . . has accused law enforcement authorities: Sophie Tatum, "NRA
Spokesperson: 'Insane Monster' Shouldn't Have Been Able to Get a Firearm," CNN
Politics, February 22, 2018, online at https://www.cnn.com/2018/02/21/politics/dana
-loesch-nra-town-hall/index.html.

198 "Over the years his mother": Report of the State's Attorney, 35.

199 He told one of his video game companions: Report of the State's Attorney, 32.

199 In target shooting: Deceased Name: Nancy J. Lanza, Autopsy Observation Report,
Eastern District Major Crime Squad, Connecticut State Police, December 16, 2012.

200 "What was happening?": Peter Applebome and Michael Wilson, "'Who Would Do This to Our Poor Little Babies,'" *New York Times*, December 15, 2012.

202 The irony of the NRA EVP: "The NRA Board of Directors," *American Rifleman*, July 2014, 76.

203 Hardy's NRA funding: Hearing on the Assault Weapons Ban of 2013, Full Committee Hearing, February 27, 2013, and Testimony of David T. Hardy Before the Senate Committee on the Judiciary Regarding the Assault Weapons Ban of 2013, S. 150.

203 "They did not ask": Frank Smyth, "Senate Witness on Weapons Ban Funded by Gun Lobby," MSNBC, February 27, 2013, online at http://www.msnbc.com/msnbc/senate -witness-weapons-ban-funded-gun-l.

204 "balanced witness panel": Smyth, "Senate Witness on Weapons Ban Funded by Gun Lobby."

204 The first witness to testify: "What Should America Do About Gun Violence," Full Committee Hearing, Senate Judiciary Committee, January 30, 2013.

204 supported the Second Amendment: Testimony of Capt. Mark E. Kelly USN (Ret.), Senate Judiciary Committee, January 30, 2013.

204 "Today police and law-abiding citizens": Testimony of David B. Kopel, Senate Judiciary Committee, January 30, 2013.

205 Kopel led the Independence Institute: Eli Stokols, "Majority of Colorado Sheriffs Join Lawsuit Against Gun Control Laws," Fox 31 Denver, May 16, 2013, online at https:// kdvr.com/2013/05/16/majority-of-colorado-sheriffs-bringing-lawsuit-against-gun -control-laws/.

205 "require background checks": Testimony of Chief Jim Johnson, Baltimore County, Maryland, Chair, National Law Enforcement Partnership to Prevent Gun Violence, Senate Judiciary Committee, January 30, 2013.

206 "a right-wing policy group": "Dangerous Gun Myths" (editorial), *New York Times*, February 2, 2013.

209 "elitist without peer": James W. Porter II, "Bloomberg's All-Consuming Agenda," *American Rifleman*, December 2013, 14.

209 "Bloomberg and his billionaire buddies": Wayne LaPierre, "Bloomberg Banking on the 'Stupidity' of Gun Owners," *American Rifleman*, February 2015, 12.

209 "Michael Bloomberg is using his billions": Chris W. Cox, "The Wizard of Deception: Michael Bloomberg Is Using His Billions to Fund Bogus Research with the Goal of Deceiving the American People and Advancing His Gun-Ban Agenda," *American Rifleman*, September 2015, 18–20.

209 "Are you as sick and tired": Wayne LaPierre, "The Blame Flame," *American Rifleman*, August 2014, 45.

209 "Absolutists? You bet": See Wayne LaPierre, "Standing Guard: Hillary's War on Liberty, the NRA and the Second Amendment," *American Rifleman*, April 2016, 12.

210 NRA publications ran story after story: See, e.g., Michael O. Humphries, "Expect the Unexpected: SIG Sauer's SIG516," *American Rifleman*, January 2010, 44; Wiley Clapp, "Combat Mangum Resurgence," *American Rifleman*, December 2014, 42; Wiley Clapp, "Concealed Carry: 21st Century Style," *American Rifleman*, February 2010, 46–53.

210 "This Is How the NRA Ends": Alec MacGillis, "This Is How the NRA Ends," *New Republic*, May 28, 2013.

210 "every member for *a job well done*": Wayne LaPierre, "Halfway Home," *American Rifleman*, January 2014, 12.

211 Four Democrats and four Republicans: Aaron Blake, "Manchin-Toomey Gun Amendment Fails," *Washington Post*, April 17, 2013.

212 *American Rifleman*'s repeated outrage: See Chris W. Cox, "Michael Bloomberg Will Haunt You in the Afterlife," *American Rifleman*, June 2014, 18–20.

212 For five years starting in 2012: Denise Clifton and Mark Follman, "The Very Strange Case of Two Russian Gun Lovers, the NRA, and Donald Trump," *Mother Jones*, May/June 2018 (updated September 13, 2018), 45, online at https://www.motherjones.com /politics/2018/03/trump-russia-nra-connection-maria-butina-alexander-torshin-guns/.

212 In 2013 NRA president: Mark Follman, "NRA President Offered to Work with Accused Russian Spy's Group in Moscow," *Mother Jones*, July 20, 2018, online at https://www.motherjones.com/politics/2018/07/nra-russia-maria-butina-alexander -torshin-republicans-trump/.

212 In 2014, at the NRA annual meeting: "Accused Russian Spy Says NRA Involvement Helped Her Secure Visa to U.S.," The Trace, July 20, 2018, online at https://www .thetrace.org/rounds/maria-butina-nra-russia-visa-convention/; Sarah N. Lynch, "Butina Admits Being Russian Agent, Pleads Guilty in U.S. to Conspiracy," Reuters, December 13, 2018, online at https://www.reuters.com/article/us-usa-russia-butina /accused-russian-agent-butina-pleads-guilty-in-us-to-conspiracy-idUSKBN1OC1AI.

213 Sergeant Michael Parsons: Press release, "NRA Honors Sergeant Michael Parsons as 2018 NRA Law Enforcement Officer of the Year," April 23, 2019, online at https:// www.nrablog.com/articles/2019/4/pr-2018-nra-law-enforcement-officer-of-the-year/.

214 At the NRA Foundation Banquet: Guy Sagi, "Henry Repeating Arms Honors Military Veterans, Law Enforcement," NRA, *American Rifleman*, May 1, 2019, online at https://www.americanrifleman.org/articles/2019/5/1/henry-repeating-arms-honors -military-veterans-law-enforcement/.

215 "When are you all going to start standing up": "'Come Hell or High Water,' Citizens Will Keep Gun Rights, Greensboro Man Vows in Viral Video," Fox 8 (High Point, NC), April 8, 2018, online at https://myfox8.com/2018/04/07/come-hell-or-high-water -citizens-will-keep-gun-rights-greensboro-man-vows-in-viral-video/.

215 He later said: "Mark Robinson: Hard Working Citizens Are Being Overlooked by Politicians," Fox News Radio, April 6, 2018, online at https://radio.foxnews.com/2018/04 /06/mark-robinson-hard-working-citizens-are-being-overlooked-by-politicians/.

215 video of Robinson's comments: "'Come Hell or High Water,' Citizens Will Keep Gun Rights, Greensboro Man Vows in Viral Video."

215 By the fall of 2018: NRA Staff, "2019 NRA Director Nominations Announced," NRA, *American Rifleman*, October 30, 2018, online at https://www.americanrifleman.org /articles/2018/10/30/2019-nra-director-nominations-announced/.

TWELVE: THE CREED

217 The Association for the first time: John Santucci and Meghan Keneally, "NRA Endorses Donald Trump for President," ABC News, May 20, 2016, online at https:// abcnews.go.com/Politics/nra-endorse-donald-trump-president/story?id=39253893.

217 Trump had first spoken: See "Donald Trump: 2015 NRA-ILA Leadership Forum," NRA-ILA, April 10, 2015, online at https://tr-plus.net/nra/u7IDo_1a39w; and Jose A. DelReal, "Donald Trump Announces Presidential Bid," *Washington Post*, June 16, 2015.

218 And the NRA donated more money: Robert Maguire, "Audit Shows NRA Spending Surged $100 Million Amidst Pro-Trump Push in 2016," Center for Responsive Politics, November 15, 2017, online at https://www.opensecrets.org/news/2017/11/audit -shows-nra-spending-surged-100-million-amidst-pro-trump-push-in-2016/.

218 "I want to talk to you tonight": Daniel Terrill, "NRA'S Chris Cox at RNC 2016 (Video + Transcript)," Guns.com News, July 20, 2016, online at https://www.guns.com/news /2016/07/20/nras-chris-cox-at-rnc-2016.

218 But Trump himself raised at least the idea: Nick Corasanti and Maggie Haberman, "Donald Trump Suggests 'Second Amendment People' Could Act Against Hillary Clinton," *New York Times*, August 9, 2016.

218 "He pointed out that an armed populace": "[Archived Thread]—Hillary Clinton Campaign Condemns Donald Trump's 'Second Amendment' Remark at Rally," posted by rossgott on August 9, 2016, 6:51:02 PM EDT, ar15.com.

219 "after the people had been disarmed by tyrants": Ben Carson with Candy Carson, *A More Perfect Union: What We the People Can Do to Reclaim Our Constitutional Liberties* (New York: Sentinel, 2015), 61.

219 "The likelihood of Hitler": "Ben Carson Defends Linking Gun Control to the Holocaust," BBC News, October 9, 2015, online at https://www.bbc.com/news/world-us -canada-34485358.

219 The Anti-Defamation League: "Holocaust Imagery Taints Gun Control Debate," Anti-Defamation League, January 24, 2013, online at https://www.adl.org/blog/holocaust -imagery-taints-gun-control-debate; and "ADL Says Nazi Analogies Have No Place in Gun Control Debate," Anti-Defamation League, January 24, 2013, online at https:// www.adl.org/news/press-releases/adl-says-nazi-analogies-have-no-place-in-gun -control-debate.

219 "To anyone who studies Nazi Germany": Alan E. Steinweis, "Ben Carson Is Wrong on Guns and the Holocaust," *New York Times*, October 14, 2015.

220 "Professor Steinweis's assertion": David Kopel, "Alan Steinweis's Bad History," *Washington Post*, October 16, 2015.

220 By then Kopel was among the nation's most-quoted experts: Frank Smyth, "Five Years After Sandy Hook, Major U.S. Papers Still Have a Serious Gun Problem," *The Progressive*, December 21, 2017, online at https://progressive.org/dispatches/five-years -after-sandy-hook-newspapers-still-have-gun-problem-171221/.

220 "undoing or moderating anti-gun policies": Beth Reinhard and Sari Horwitz, "The Trump Administration Has Already Been Rolling Back Gun Regulations," *Washington Post*, October 4, 2017.

220 "a Colorado attorney": Joe Palazzolo and Zusha Elinson, "Las Vegas Gunman Had Arsenal in Hotel Room," *Wall Street Journal*, October 3, 2017.

220 The *Times* in a news story: Christina Caron, "'Ghost Guns,' Homemade and Untraceable, Face Growing Scrutiny," *New York Times*, November 27, 2017.

221 "Virtually none of the many tomes": Stephen P. Halbrook, *Gun Control in the Third Reich: Disarming the Jews and "Enemies of the State"* (Oakland, CA: Independent Institute, 2013), xv–xx.

221 Facebook posts by Ted Nugent: Lindsey Bever, "Ted Nugent Digs in Amid Anti-Semitic Accusations—and Calls for His NRA Ouster," *Washington Post*, February 10, 2016.

221 "Based on newly discovered secret documents": "Gun Control in the Third Reich: Disarming the Jews and 'Enemies of the State'" (review), *American Rifleman*, March 2015, 37.

222 "There is no way to prove it": Robert VerBruggen, "Gun Control in the Third Reich: Disarming the Jews and 'Enemies of the State'" (review), *Washington Times*, December 29, 2013.

222 The NRA's tax filings: Jill Colvin and Lisa Marie Pane, "Trump to Speak to a Weakened National Rifle Association," *U.S. News & World Report*, April 16, 2019.

222 combined losses of over $66 million: Mark Maremont and James V. Gimaldi, "NRA Paid Wayne LaPierre $2.2 Million in 2018, a 55% Increase," *Wall Street Journal*, November 15, 2019.

222 This left the Association: Russ McQuaid, "Indianapolis Convention Key to NRA Finances," Fox 59 (Indianapolis), April 23, 2019, online at https://fox59.com/2019 /04/23/indianapolis-convention-key-to-nra-finances/; National Rifle Association of America, "Financial Statements in 2018 Annual Report to Members: A Show of Strength for Second Amendment Freedom," released in hard copy only to members in Indianapolis, April 27, 2019, 15–26.

222 "It just doesn't exist": Vera Bergengruen, "Guns, God, and Trump: How an Accused Russian Agent Wooed US Conservatives," BuzzFeed News, July 18, 2018, online at https://www.buzzfeednews.com/article/verabergengruen/maria-butina-spent-years -wooing-us-conservatives-heres-how.

223 "At the National Rifle Association": Mark Follman, "NRA President Offered to Work with Accused Russian Spy's Group in Moscow: Video from the 2013 Event with Maria Butina Sheds Further Light on NRA-Russia Ties," *Mother Jones*, July 20, 2018, online at https://www.motherjones.com/politics/2018/07/nra-russia-maria-butina-alexander -torshin-republicans-trump. Original event: David Keene (USA), ex-president, current board member of the US National Rifle Association (NRA), at the 2nd Congress of the Right to Arms public movement in Moscow, October 31–November 1, 2013, https://www.youtube.com/watch?v=1tj-ceQb9Ao&feature=youtu.be.

224 "My story is simple": "Maria Butina," *The Eric Metaxas Show*, SoundCloud, cited in Bergengruen, "Guns, God, and Trump."

226 "I would be very sad": Marjory Stoneman Douglas, *Everglades: River of Grass* (Sarasota, FL: Pineapple Press, 2007).

226 After the shooting: Josh Hafner, "Yeti Cuts Ties with NRA Foundation, Lobbyist Says, Sparking Boycott Cries for Cooler Company," *USA Today*, April 23, 2018.

226 "The first to go will be the Second Amendment": "Conservative Political Action Committee, Wayne LaPierre Remarks," C-SPAN, February 22, 2018.

226 Two different columnists: Avraham Bronstein, "Opinion: The NRA's Wayne La-Pierre's Chilling Christian Nationalist Call to Arms," *Haaretz*, February 25, 2018; Bradley Burston, "Analysis: In NRA's Response to School Massacre: Dog-Whistle Anti-Semitism, a Star-Spangled Protocols of Zion," *Haaretz*, February 26, 2018.

227 The rates ranged from $13.95 a month: Associated Press, "NRA's Carry Guard Comes Under Fire as 'Murder Insurance,'" CBS News, October 19, 2017, online

at https://www.cbsnews.com/news/nras-carry-guard-comes-under-fire-as-murder-insurance/.

227 "unlawfully provided insurance coverage": See Steve Almasy, Jason Hanna, and Laura Ly, "NRA Lawsuit Says It's in Financial Trouble Because of Actions by New York Regulators," CNN, August 4, 2018, online at https://www.cnn.com/2018/08/04/us/nra-new-york-lawsuit/index.html; "New York Hits 10 More Insurers with Millions in Fines for Underwriting NRA Policies," The Trace, December 21, 2018, online at https://www.thetrace.org/rounds/new-york-hits-ten-more-insurers-with-millions-in-fines-for-underwriting-nra-policies/.

228 The NRA claimed in its lawsuit: "Without Insurance, Lawful Self-Defense Can Cost You a Fortune," n.d., online at www.nracarryguard.com.

228 But in 2018, after the Parkland high school shooting: Miles Kohrman and Alex Yablon, "The NRA Ends Its Carry Guard Insurance Program," The Trace, July 19, 2019, online at https://www.thetrace.org/rounds/the-nra-ends-its-carry-guard-insurance-program/.

228 In the spring of 2019: *National Rifle Association of America, Plaintiff, v. Ackerman McQueen, Inc., and Mercury Group, Inc., Defendants*, Complaint, Civil Case No. 0219001757, in the Circuit Court for the City of Alexandria, Virginia, posted by *Wall Street Journal*, April 15, 2019.

228 allegations that Dana Loesch and Oliver North: Mike Spies, "Secrecy, Self-Dealing, and Greed at the N.R.A.," *New Yorker*, April 17, 2019.

228 combination of financial and internal troubles: Colvin and Pane, "Trump to Speak to a Weakened National Rifle Association."

228 "Ackerman McQueen has served": "NRA Sues Ackerman McQueen and Mercury Group," *Capitol Communicator*, April 16, 2019.

229 But in its lawsuit: Spies, "Secrecy, Self-Dealing, and Greed at the N.R.A."

229 The letter accused LaPierre: Mark Maremont, "NRA's Wayne LaPierre Says He Is Being Extorted, Pressured to Resign," *Wall Street Journal*, April 26, 2019.

230 LaPierre was soon under fire again: Carol D. Leonnig and Beth Reinhard, "NRA Chief Sought Purchase of $6 Million Mansion in Wake of Parkland Shooting," *Washington Post*, August 8, 2019.

230 In its 2019 annual meeting in Indianapolis: Mark Maremont, "New York Attorney General Probes NRA as Oliver North Exits as President," *Wall Street Journal*, April 27, 2019.

230 "less than accountable": David Sherfinski, "Ted Nugent: NRA Has Been 'Less Than Accountable,'" *Washington Times*, April 29, 2019.

230 "the parlance of extortionists": Letter by Wayne LaPierre, NRA Executive Vice President, to the Members of the Board, April 25, 2019, obtained and posted online by *Wall Street Journal*.

231 "exactly the same": Josh Kovensky, "History Repeats Itself: How Corruption Nearly Killed the NRA Twice," Talking Points Memo, Muckraker, April 26, 2019, online at https://talkingpointsmemo.com/muckraker/nra-lawsuit-new-financial-troubles-wayne-lapierre.

231 "To every lying member of the media": Nicole Gaudiano, "NRA Spokeswoman Warns Media, Hollywood and Athletes 'Time Is Running Out,'" *USA Today*, March 5, 2018.

231 "curb-stomped": "Top Definition: Curb Stomp," *Urban Dictionary*, online at https:// www.urbandictionary.com/define.php?term=curb+stomp.

232 "are the rat-bastards of the earth": "Dana Loesch Happy to See Mainstream Media 'Curb-Stomped,'" *America's 1st Freedom*, November 23, 2016.

232 In 2018: Beth Reinhard, "NRA Boosted Executive Pay While Cutting Funding for Key Programs, Filing Shows," *Washington Post*, November 26, 2019.

232 annual salary of LaPierre: Mark Maremont and James V. Gimaldi, "NRA Paid Wayne LaPierre $2.2 Million in 2018, *a 55% Increase*," *Wall Street Journal*, November 15, 2019.

232 More recently, Loesch has received death threats: Peter Hasson, "Twitter: Saying Dana Loesch's Kids Need to Be Murdered Does Not Violate Rules," Daily Caller, August 27, 2018, online at https://dailycaller.com/2018/08/27/dana-loesch-twitter -death-threats/.

232 Loesch has also posted pictures: "Dana Loesch Forced to Move Due to 'Repeated Threats from Gun Control Advocates,'" Fox News, October 16, 2017, online at https://www.foxnews.com/us/dana-loesch-forced-to-move-due-to-repeated-threats -from-gun-control-advocates.

232 "apocalyptic tone, warning of race wars": Danny Hakim, "N.R.A. Sues Contractor Behind NRATV," *New York Times*, April 15, 2019.

232 Gun sales across America: Daniel Trotta, "U.S. Gun Sales Down 6.1 Percent in 2018, Extending 'Trump Slump,'" Reuters, January 29, 2019, online at https://www.reuters .com/article/us-usa-guns-sales/u-s-gun-sales-down-6-1-percent-in-2018-extending -trump-slump-idUSKCN1PN346.

232 "The total economic impact": *Firearms and Ammunition Industry Economic Impact Report 2019*, NSSF, The Firearms Industry Trade Association, February 2019, online at https://www.nssf.org/government-relations/impact/.

234 Wayne LaPierre, "Standing Guard," *American Rifleman*, March 2015, 12.

234 more Americans have died from gun violence: Chelsea Bailey, "More Americans Killed by Guns Since 1968 than in All U.S. Wars—Combined," NBC News, October 4, 2017, online at https://www.nbcnews.com/storyline/las-vegas-shooting/more -americans-killed-guns-1968-all-u-s-wars-combined-n807156.

235 Wayne LaPierre, "Standing Guard," America's 1st Freedom, October 22, 2019.

235 "he would rather let convicted violent felons": John M. Crewdson, "Hard-Line Opponent of Gun Laws Wins New Term at Helm of Rifle," *New York Times*, May 4, 1981.

235 "This is the price of freedom": Jessica Roy, "Bill O'Reilly Calls Mass Shootings 'The Price of Freedom,'" *Chicago Tribune*, October 2, 2017.

236 said he had a "hit list": Paul P. Murphy, Konstantin Toropin, Drew Griffin, Scott Bronstein, and Eric Levenson, "Dayton Shooter Had an Obsession with Violence and Mass Shootings, Police Say," CNN, August 7, 2019, online at https://flipboard .com/@CNN/dayton-shooter-appeared-to-have-leftist-twitter-feed/a-qiIClZVFS2C sdkWrnsBoLw%3Aa%3A33803748-fff7ebaaeb/cnn.com.

INDEX

Abbott, Greg, 162–163

abolitionists, 29

Ackerman McQueen (consulting firm), 113, 117, 118, 146–148, 154–155, 206, 215, 228–232

Afghanistan War, 188, 213

AK-47 rifle, 102, 121–122. *See* also Kalashnikov rifles

Alcohol and Tobacco Tax Division, Internal Revenue Service, 67–68

Alito, Samuel, 179

American Civil War, 119

  and Bates, John Coalter, 43

  Battle of Gettysburg, 16, 17

  and Burnside, Ambrose, 33–34

  and founding of Ku Klux Klan, 28

  and founding of NRA, 15–16, 19–21, 24, 28, 29

  Gettysburg Address (Lincoln), 188

  and Grant, Ulysses S., 39

  recollections by Sgt. Geo. W. Wingate from Carlisle, 16

  reporting by William Conant Church, 16

American Hunter, 102, 103, 118, 135, 154, 173, 174

American occupation of Nicaragua, 61

American Rifleman, 7, 27, 51, 118, 185

  advertised foreign military rifle ordered by Oswald, 71–72

  and American gun rights creed, 186–187, 209–210

  announcement of NRA's registration as a lobby, 95

  "Armed Citizen" column, 167

  on the AR-15 nickname, the "Black Rifle" (2001), 169. *See* also AR-15 style rifle

  on Bloomberg, Michael, 212

  Carter column on geese hunting in Mexico (1955), 85

  Carter column on "war on drugs" (1989), 119–120

  Cassidy and Foss columns favoring George H. W. Bush (1988), 173–174

  changes made by LaPierre (1990s), 131–132

  on Cincinnati Revolt and change of guards, 97–100

  coinage of "hunter-conservationist," 91

  and collectors, 3

  on communism, 58–59, 94

  Cox column on Bloomberg, Michael (2015), 209

  Cox column on Obama and presidential election (2008), 173

  on Cronkite, 93

  and culture wars, 94

  "The Dope Bag" column, 3

  editorial endorsing Reagan (1980), 173

  editorial on Magnum revolver (1937), 54–55

  editorial on measures supported by NRA (1929), 50

  editorial on need for unity of gun owners (1971), 91

  editorial on presidential election (1936), 53

  on establishing two tax-exempt structures, 110

  on first anniversary of Earth Day (1971), 92

  on first ouster of board director (Neal Knox, 1984), 110

first reference to Second Amendment (1952 column by Edson), 62–63, 78

Froman column on 2006 midterm elections, 170

and Gun Control Act of 1968, 74–75, 77, 89–90

on guns in history, 156

and Halbrook, Stephen P., 180

Hammer column praising the late Tom Washington (1995), 146

Heston column on the Second Amendment (2000), 153. *See also* Second Amendment

Heston on cover, 149

hunter-conservationist, 91–92, 103, 114, 136

"It Will Never Happen Here" (on London riots and American gun rights creed), 186–187

"Knox's Notebook" column, 135

and Kopel, David B., 176, 178

on Landers, Ann, 93

LaPierre column on 2006 midterm elections, 170

LaPierre column on Bloomberg, Michael (2014), 209

LaPierre column on Concord Bridge (1993), 134

LaPierre column on success after Sandy Hook shooting (2014), 210

Lister columns, 48, 54–55, 58–59

masthead change (1963), 69

"Media Mysteries Explained" (broadside against journalists), 145

for members only, 65

on Milius, John, 203

and national handgun debate, 93

nation's number two ad-revenue-generating magazine (2001), 154

as nondigital, 3

on NRA centennial, 79

"NRA Official Journal" section, 103, 106

on NRA's opposition to use of taggants, 106

"Obama's Secret Plan to Destroy the Second Amendment" (LaPierre), 186

post-Cincinnati makeover and reforms, 102–103

Reagan and Harlon B. Carter on cover of, 109

removal of NRA annual financial reports, 104

review of *Gun Control in the Third Reich* (Halbrook), 221

signatories to NRA statement denouncing extremist groups, 72–73

"Standing Guard" column (LaPierre), 4, 123, 127, 134, 135

"This Very Day" editorial (early reference to "right to keep and bear arms"), 68–69

typical topics in 1950s, 65–66

"Who Guards America's Homes?" (1967 response to race riots), 74

on wildlife conservation, 66, 92

Winchester Model 70 cover story (2004), 157

"You Loot—We Shoot" (Marion Hammer), 125

Americans and Their Guns (first NRA authorized history), 5, 31, 43, 49, 66, 67, 69, 70, 75

American Shooting Sports Council, 133

American Society of Civil Engineers, 23

American University

graduate student Maria Butina, 212

Peter S. Ridley Memorial Endowed Scholarship, 95

Anderson, Gary, 101, 104, 113

Apocalypse Now, 147. *See also* Milius, John

AR-15 style rifle, 125, 153, 156, 167, 169, 187–191, 204, 210, 225, 226, 236

Arms and the Man (formerly *Shooting and Fishing*), 42, 45, 47, 59. *See also American Rifleman*

Arms and the Man (Shaw), 42

Army and Navy Journal, and Gazette of the Regular and Volunteer Forces

call to form rifle practice group, 21

and Church, 18, 20, 21, 29, 38

on Native Americans, 29

and NRA founding, 21

"Prophet and patriot" elegiac poem for Church, 40

support for Grant's plan to annex Santo Domingo (Dominican Republic), 30

Arnett, G. Ray, 113–114, 117–118, 146

Åslund, Anders, 223

Associated Press, 74, 108, 121, 228

Atiyeh, Vic, 108

Attlee, Tracey, 117–118

Aurora, Colorado shooting, 187

Austro-Prussian War, 15, 21, 23–24

background checks, 5, 115, 128, 138, 159, 165, 171, 204–205, 211, 234

Backstrom, Gertrude, 66

Bakal, Carl, 68

Baker, James, 121

meetings with other gun rights leaders, 133. *See also* Feldman, Richard

Ballew, Kenyon, 97

Bates, John Coalter, 43–44

Beaux Arts Woodward Building, 42

Beck, Glenn, 10

Belafonte, Harry, 70–71
black helicopters debunked at 1995 NRA
annual meeting (Phoenix), 142
Black Panthers, 74. *See also* Newtown, Huey,
and Seale, Bobby
Blaine, James G., 23
Blair Mountain, Battle of, 156
Blitzer, Wolf, 219
Bloomberg, Michael, 170, 209, 212, 226
Bodine, John, 32–33
Bogus, Carl, 175
Bowling for Columbine (Moore documentary),
28–29, 168
Bowman, Steven B., 221
Brady, James, 108
Brady, Sarah, 108, 121, 138
Brady Handgun Violence Prevention Act, 108,
121–122, 128, 138
breech-loading rifles, 21, 23–24, 33–34
use in Austro-Prussian and Franco-Prussian
wars, 20–21, 23–24
Bronze Star, 67, 89, 95
Brown, Robert K., 139–140, 151
Bulkeley, John D., 57
Bull, Alice
background, 60
first woman elected to NRA board, 60
head of national all-women team, 66
nomination of Arnett as NRA executive vice
president, 113
signatory to NRA statement denouncing
extremist groups (1964), 72–73
Bureau of Alcohol, Tobacco, and Firearms,
Treasury Department, 97, 121, 126, 163
Burnside, Ambrose, 33–34
Burnside carbine 34
Bush, George H. W., 121, 140, 142, 173–174, 217
Bush, George W., 160, 174, 217
Bushmaster, 191, 199
Butina, Maria, 212, 222–224
Butz, Dave, 160

Camp Perry
NRA National Matches, 42–43, 44, 46–47,
60, 66, 85, 104, 169, 195–196
Small Arms Firing School, 45
Carry Guard, 227–228
Carson, Ben, 218–219
Carter, Harlan B., 83
Carter, Harlon B., 120, 145. *See also* Carter,
Harlan B.
Ackerman McQueen consulting firm
recommended by, 113, 146
American Rifleman columns, 85, 119–120
American Rifleman cover photos, 98–99, 109

American Rifleman "war on drugs" column,
119–120
background, 83–84
bronze bust on display at the NRA National
Firearms Museum, 83
and centralizing power and changing
bylaws, 112, 118
changing spelling of his first name, 83. *See
also* Harlan B. Carter
chief of U.S. Border Patrol, 84–85
chose J. Warren Cassidy as chief lobbyist,
109
and Cincinnati Revolt, 83, 85, 87, 97–100,
101–102, 108, 112, 134
efforts to repeal Gun Control Act of 1968,
107–108
elected NRA executive vice president,
97–100
elected to the NRA board of directors (1951),
85
elected to an unprecedented five-year term,
101
endorsement of Reagan, 173
fired Neal Knox as chief lobbyist (1982),
109
first reelection as Executive Vice President,
105
on gun rights and the price of freedom, 235
and his lieutenants, 102, 104–105
informed the board he wished to retire
(1984), 112
legacy of, 87, 112
lobbying wing diversified under, 95
murder trial of, 83–84, 105–106
named executive director of NRA-ILA, 95
and 1978 NRA annual meeting (Salt Lake
City), 105–106
NRA membership growth under, 105, 109
oratorical style, 104–105
photographed with Senator Dole and his
wife, 107
plotting against the old guard, 96
on "price we pay for freedom," 235
shared the stage in Phoenix with Reagan
(1983), 109
signatory to NRA statement denouncing
extremist groups (1964), 72–73
speech at 1976 NRA annual meeting
(Indianapolis), 96
support for McClure-Volkmer Bill, 110
"unyielding" view of gun rights, 104
Carter, Jimmy, 106
Casiano, Rámon, 84. *See also* Carter, Harlon B.,
murder trial of
Cassidy, Warren, 109, 118–119, 122, 173–174

Cato Institute, 176, 204
CBS News, 93–94. *See also* Cronkite, Walter
Charlton Heston Celebrity Shoot, 160
Cheney, Dick, 174, 180
Childress, Richard, 229–230
Christchurch mosque shooting, 236
Church, William Conant, 78, 79, 87, 237
  and American Civil War, 16, 19–20
  and *Army and Navy Journal*, 18, 20, 21, 29, 38
  background, 17–20
  brother of (Francis Pharcellus Church), 18, 20
  cofounded and edited *The Galaxy* (literary magazine), 20
  cofounded *New York Chronicle*, 19
  cofounding of NRA, 16–24, 184, 237–238
  on concerns during Reconstruction, 184
  and Creedmoor Rifle Range, 25–26
  differences with Wingate over labor unrest, 31
  on Douglass, 184
  editorial supporting President Grant's planned annexation of Santo Domingo, 30
  European correspondent for the New York *Sun*, 19
  "fellow in perpetuity," Metropolitan Museum of Art, 17
  first met Wingate, 20
  and initial goals of NRA, 20–21, 23–24, 25, 30–31, 36, 57, 96
  journalism and military writing career, 16, 17, 18–20, 38–39, 183
  later years and death, 38–40
  legacy of, 39–40, 87
  made brevet lieutenant colonel, organizing volunteer militia for Washington, D.C., 19
  on maintaining a standing army and civilian militia force, 30, 57, 96
  making case to form a rifle group (1871), 21
  member and director of the New York Zoological Society, 17
  met Whitman, Walt, 19
  militaristic if not imperial attitudes, 30
  on Native Americans, 29, 183
  NRA president, 33
  Pierrepont, pseudonym for Civil War dispatches, 19
  "Prophet and patriot" elegiac poem, subject of, 40
  on provincialism of NRA, 35–36, 44, 183
  as public intellectual, 18
  on race, abolitionism and violence against freed slaves, 29–30, 182–184
  recruitment of Grant as NRA president, 37–38
  on removal of racial epithets from army vocabulary, 30
  special correspondent for *The New York Times* and other northern newspapers, 16
  support for Grant's efforts to stop KKK, 183
  "To devour or to be devoured" speech in Albany (1873), 30
  Ulysses S. Grant and the Period of National Preservation and Reconstruction, 39, 183
  views on religion, 30
  and Wingate, 16, 20, 23–26, 35, 36, 37, 39, 87
Churchill, Winston, 56–57
Cincinnati Revolt (1997 NRA annual meeting), 2, 10, 83, 85, 87, 95–100, 101–102, 103, 105, 108, 112, 134, 138, 151, 160, 165, 173, 200, 233
Citizens Committee for the Right to Keep and Bear Arms, 105, 133
Citizens United v. FEC, 170, 187–188
Civilian Pistol Championship, 66
Civil War. *See* American Civil War
Clark, Patti, 9, 161, 196–197
Clinton, Bill, 127, 128–129, 142, 148, 168
Clinton, Hillary, 137, 218, 232
Columbine shooting, 157–159, 171, 200, 205
concealed carry, 50, 63, 70, 78, 161, 163–168, 210, 227
Congressional Medal of Honor, 22, 57, 62, 113, 138
Conway, Kellyanne, 161
Cooper, Jeff, 165
Copeland, Royal, 54
Cornell, Alonzo B., 37
Cors, Allan D., 110–111
Cotton, Charles, 161
Cox, Chris
  accused of conspiring against LaPierre, 9, 223
  on England riots of 2011, 187
  first NRA representative given floor at major political party convention, 218
  and LaPierre, 159–160, 164, 208, 209, 223
  on Obama, 173
  as a possible successor to LaPierre, 233
  promoted to NRA chief lobbyist, 159–160
  salary, 233
  on Sandy Hook, 208, 209
  speech at the 2019 NRA annual meeting (Indianapolis), 164–165
  on welcoming NRA members of many faiths, 214
Craig, Larry, 109
Craven, Alfred W., 23
Creedmoor Rifle Range, 38, 194
  Convention of Riflemen, 36
  creation of, 25–27

Creedmoor International Military Match of 1878, 36

Creedmoor International Rifle Match of 1874, 31–33

Hilton Trophy, 36

invitation to the British NRA, 34–35

match with the British Imperial Team (1877) modeled on Wimbledon, 25–27

Palma Trophy, 34–35

reduction of funding by the State of New York, 37

crime bill of 1994, 6, 130–131

Croix de Guerre with Palm, 48

Cronkite, Walter, 93

Cullen, Henry J., 22–23. *See also* Wingate & Cullen, and Wingate, Kearney & Cullen

Cuomo, Andrew, 227–228

Dallas (television series), 160

Dayton, Ohio, shooting, 234, 236–237

Denny, Reginald, 125

Dickey Amendment, 129

Dingell, John, 111

Dirty Harry (film), 147, 156, 189, 203

Distinguished Service Medal, 41, 48, 57

Distinguished Service Order (United Kingdom), 62

District of Columbia v. Heller, 178–181, 220

Dodd, Thomas J., 71–72, 75–77, 86, 87, 104

Dole, Elizabeth, 107

Dole, Robert, 107, 108, 115, 174

Douglas, Marjory Stoneman, 226

Douglass, Frederick, 183–184

Drain, James A., 41–44, 45

and gun industry, 42–43

and move of NRA headquarters to New York City and Washington, D.C., 42

and National Matches at Camp Perry, 42

purchase of *Shooting and Fishing* (renamed *Arms and the Man*), 42

sale of *Arms and the Man* to NRA, 45

succeeded by Bates, 43

and World War I, 41

Ducks Unlimited, 114

du Pont, Henry, 44

Durbin, Richard, 207

Earth Day, 60, 92

Edson, Merritt A., 57, 61–63

awarded Congressional Medal of Honor and other decorations, 57, 62

chief of the Vermont State Police, 62

committed suicide, 63

on controls on concealed weapons as "clearly constitutional," 63

deployments in Mexican Expedition, 61

deployments in Nicaragua, 61

deployments in Tulagi and Guadalcanal (Edson's Ridge), 61–62

on "eternal struggle between Communism and Democracy," 62

on first *American Rifleman* reference of "Second Article of the Bill of Rights" (1952), 62–63

hiring to lead the NRA (1951), 62

on National Board for the Promotion of Rifle Practice, 62

"Red Mike," nickname of, 61–62

Egan, Clare, 194–195

Eisenhower, Dwight D., 67, 217

El Paso Walmart shooting, 234, 236–237

Esquire magazine, 155

Evening Post, 19

Federal Assault Weapons Ban, 128–129, 130, 140, 142, 159–160, 168, 174, 190

Federal Firearms Act of 1938, 54–56

Feinstein, Dianne, 159, 206

Feldman, Richard, 133, 154

Field & Stream, 144–145

Fifteenth Amendment, 22

Firearms Owners' Protection Act (1986), 110, 115–117, 166, 211

Fishing and Hunting News, 77

Floyd, Pretty Boy, 49

Follman, Mark, 212

Foss, Joe, 113, 138–139, 173–174

Fox 31 (Denver), 205

Franco-Prussian War, 15, 20–21, 23–24

Frederick, Karl, 49–51

Freedom Group, 9, 191, 192. *See also* Bushmaster; Remington

freed slaves

remarks by West at the Roy Innis Memorial Award inauguration (2019), 182

Ulysses S. Grant and the Period of National Preservation and Reconstruction (Church), 183–184

Froman, Sandra, 161, 170

"Fudds" (gun owners who support gun regulations), 5–6, 8, 136, 144, 150, 160

Galaxy (literary magazine), 20

Game Conservation International, 114

Gettysburg, Battle of, 16, 17

Gettysburg Address, 188

Gianoutsos, Francoise, 117–118

Gianoutsos, Theodore, 117–118

Giffords, Gabby, 186, 204

Gingrich, Newt, 128

Glock
  Glock 17, 130, 213
  Glock 19, 5, 143, 171, 186
  Glock 20, 199
  Glock 41, 213
González, Emma, 226
Good Old Boys, The (film), 160
Gorsuch, Neal, 224
Gottlieb, Alan, 133
Grant, Ulysses S.
  Church's admiration for, 184
  efforts to stop the KKK, 183
  NRA member, 217
  NRA president, 38
  plans to annex Santo Domingo (Dominican
    Republic), 30
  *Ulysses S. Grant and the Period of National
    Preservation and Reconstruction* (Church),
    39, 183
Great Trolley Strike (Brooklyn, 1895), 31
Gulf War, 140
  and Kelly, 204
  and West, 29
Gun Control Act of 1968, 76–77, 105, 115
Gun Digest, 165, 190
Gun Digest Buyer's Guide, 190
Gun Digest Buyer's Guide to Assault Weapons
  (2008), 190
Gun Digest Buyer's Guide to Tactical Weapons
  (2010), 190
Gun Owners of America, 105, 133
Gun Week, 86, 133
Guns and Ammo, 86, 110, 165
Gutermuth, C. R. "Pink," 92

Haaretz, 226
Halbrook, Stephen P.
  amicus briefs to the Supreme Court, 178, 180
  background, 180
  *Gun Control in the Third Reich: Disarming
    the Jews and "Enemies of the State"*, 220–222
  and Kopel, 178
  NRA grants to the Independent Institute, 180
  law journal articles, 178
  *The Founders' Second Amendment: Origins of
    the Right to Bear Arms*, 180
  See also District of Columbia v. Heller;
    Independent Institute; and *McDonald v.
    Chicago*
Halsey, Ashley, Jr., 102
Hamilton, J.B., 32–33
Hammer, Marion P.
  on *American Rifleman* cover, 149
  background, 8, 109
  election to NRA board, 109, 165

first NRA woman president, 109, 146
  on Knox, 147
  and 1994 NRA presidential election, 109,
    136–140, 149
  and NRA Eddie Eagle gun safety program, 169
  NRA second vice president, 136
  significance of, 8, 109, 165
  support for LaPierre, 230, 232
  and Unified Sportsmen of Florida, 165
  "You Loot—We Shoot" (*American Rifleman*),
    109
Handloader magazine, 99
Hardy, David T., 203
Harper's Weekly, 23
Hatch, Orrin, 107, 111, 115, 232
Henry Repeating Arms, 214
Herblock, 77, 132
Hernández, Antonio, 214
Heston, Charlton
  American Rifleman column on Second
    Amendment guarantees, 153
  on *American Rifleman* cover, 149
  appearance in *Bowling for Columbine*
    (documentary), 168
  cochair of March on Washington's
    Hollywood delegation (1963), 71, 148
  death of, 168
  elected NRA president, 150
  keynote speaker at NRA's 125th anniversary
    celebration, 148
  lesson of celebrity status within the NRA, 160
  National Press Club speech (1997), 149–150
  1999 NRA annual meeting speech (Denver),
    150, 158
  NRA Public Affairs coordination of media
    interviews, 155
  recruited for and elected to NRA board,
    148–149
  recruited for NRA president, 7, 148–149
  resignation from NRA, 168
  2000 NRA annual meeting speech
    (Charlotte), 151–152
Hilton Trophy, 36
Hogg, David, 226
Holocaust, 10, 219–222
Home Guard (United Kingdom), 25, 56–57
Howard, Susan, 160, 214
Hunt, Helen, 20
hunter-conservationists, 91–92, 103, 114, 136,
  157
Hupp, Suzanna Gratia, 131

Imperato, Anthony, 214
Independence Institute (Denver), 177, 179, 180,
  203–205

Independent Institute (California), 180
Independent Women's Forum, 206. *See also* Trotter, Gayle
Indian Appropriation Act (1871), 22
Innis, Roy, 179. *See also* Roy Innis Memorial Award
Institute for Legislative Action (NRA-ILA; lobbying wing of NRA)
    Baker, Jim (chief lobbyist), 121, 133
    Carter, Harlon B., named executive director, 95
    Cassidy, Warren (chief lobbyist), 109, 118
    Cox, Chris (chief lobbyist), 159–160, 164–165
    creation of, 95
    endorsements of presidential candidates, 173
    expansion of, 8
    Feldman, Richard (chief lobbyist), 133, 154
    Grassroots Division, 161–162
    Knox, Neal (chief lobbyist), 101–102, 104–109, 111, 130, 132, 166
    LaPierre, Wayne (chief lobbyist), 115
    LaPierre, Wayne (lobbyist), 109, 111, 114–115
    on machine guns, 116–117
    Metaksa, Tanya, as chief lobbyist, 111, 130, 132, 166
    Metaksa, Tanya, as Knox's assistant, 102
    salary of lobbying chief Cox, 233
    and 2016 Republican National Convention, 218
    See also individual chief lobbyists
Iraq War, 29, 188, 214
Izhmash Saiga 12-gauge shotgun, 199

Jackson, Joaquin, 160
James, Henry 20
Johns Hopkins Bloomberg School of Public Health, 167
Johnson, Eric, 196
Johnson, James, 205–206
Johnson, Lyndon B., 72, 76, 77
Johnson, Nicholas, 185
Johnston, T. J., 136–137
Jones, Tommy Lee, 160
Judd, David W., 23, 26

Kalashnikov rifles, 236
    AK-47, 102, 121–122
    AK-74, 213
    of Chinese manufacture, 120
    of Romanian manufacture, 236
Kavanaugh, Brett, 225
KCOP (Los Angeles), 125
Keene, David
    elected NRA president, 185

    invitation for Maria Butina to attend NRA annual meeting, 223
    on proposed UN Arms Treaty, 185–186
    reaction to calls for gun regulation after Sandy Hook shooting, 209
    on shift in NRA focus from marksmanship to gun rights, 1–2, 81, 223
    speech at Right to Bear Arms event (Moscow, 2013), 1–2, 81, 212, 223
Kelly, Mark, 204, 205
Kennedy, Anthony, 225
Kennedy Democrats, 71
Kennedy, Edward M., 94
Kennedy, John F., 104
    assassination of, 71, 87, 135, 151
    NRA member, 217
Kennedy, Robert F.
    assassination of, 76, 135, 151
    and NRA, 75–76
Kilgore, Jerry, 163
King, Martin Luther, Jr.
    assassination of, 76, 135, 151
    March on Washington, 70–71
King, Rodney, 125, 136
Knox, Chris, 86, 150
Knox, Jeff, 150–151, 231
Knox, Neal, 122, 145, 151
    Ackerman McQueen dispute, 146–148, 154–155, 206, 215, 228–232
    background, 85–87
    and Carter, 85, 87, 104, 108–109, 134, 142–143
    and Cincinnati Revolt (1977 NRA annual meeting), 97–99, 101–102, 134–135
    clash with Carter and dismissal, 108–109
    Congressional testimony against use of taggants, 106–107
    columns in *Guns and Ammo* and other glossies, 110
    death of, 150
    editor of *The Rifle* magazine and *Handloader* magazine, 99
    elected to NRA board, 110
    endorsement of Ronald Reagan (1980), 173
    and factionalism, 104
    goal of repealing Gun Control Act of 1968, 107–108
    grand theory of gun control, 135
    and Hammer, 109
    "Knox's Notebook" column, 135
    and LaPierre, 116–117, 127, 135–140, 145–150
    on the larger militia movement, 143
    legacy of, 87, 151
    loss of election for executive vice president to G. Ray Arnett (1997), 113

meetings with other gun rights leaders, 133.
  See also Feldman, Richard
and Metaksa, 102, 130, 132, 147
named executive director of NRA-ILA, 101
and 1994 NRA annual meeting
  (Minneapolis), 135–140
and 1995 NRA annual meeting (Phoenix),
  144
and 1997 NRA annual meeting (Seattle),
  148–149
and 1999 NRA annual meeting (Denver),
  150
and NRA-ILA's endorsement of Reagan, 108
on Oklahoma City bombing, 142–143
removed from NRA board, 110–111
speech at 1978 NRA annual meeting (Salt
  Lake City), 105
succeeded by Warren Cassidy, 118
tabling motion on machine guns, 144. *See
  also* NRA 1995 annual meeting (Phoenix)
on waving the bloody shirt of emotionalism,
  209
Kollitides, George K., II, 9
Kopel, David B.
  amicus briefs to state and federal courts
    including the Supreme Court, 178–179
  background, 176–177
  column on Concord Bridge (*American
    Rifleman*), 134
  on concealed carry and gun violence, 167
  Congressional testimony on gun violence,
    178, 204–205
  contributor to *National Review*, 177
  contributor to The Volokh Conspiracy, 176.
    See also The Volokh Conspiracy, and *The
    Washington Post*
  Denver Fox31 television station disclosing
    receipt of NRA funding, 205
  grants from NRA foundations to the
    Independence Institute, 176, 203
  law journal articles, 177–178
  law review articles with Halbrook,
    Stephen P., 178. *See also* Halbrook,
    Stephen P.
  lawsuit challenging Colorado gun control
    laws, 205
  New York Times disclosing receipt of NRA
    funding, 177. *See also The New York Times*
  part-time institutional affiliations, 176
  post and salary at the Independence
    Institute, 177, 203. *See also* Independence
    Institute
  response to Steinweis on gun control and
    the Holocaust, 220. *See also* Steinweis,
    Alan E.

*The Samurai, The Mountie, and The Cowboy:
  Should America Adopt the Gun Controls of
  Other Democracies?* (1992), 177–178
writing opinion pieces and being quoted in
  news stories in the press, 176–177, 220
Korean War
  and Arnett, 114
  Defense Advisory Committee on Prisoners
    of War (Korea), 63
  and Edson, 63
Ku Klux Klan, 87
  anathema to early NRA leaders, 29
  early NRA leaders' support for Grant's
    efforts to stop the KKK, 183
  filmmaker's claim of alleged NRA ties,
    28–29. *See also* Moore, Michael, and
    Bowling for Columbine
  founding of, 28–29
  Knox on, 87
  and Monroe's Black Armed Guard, 185
  NRA claim of alleged NRA support for freed
    slaves, 29, 182. *See also* West, Alan, and
    NRA 2019 annual meeting (Indianapolis)
  portrayal on children's show "Thomas &
    Friends," 232. *See also* NRATV
  and Williams, Robert, 184–185

Land, Edward L., Jr., 28
Landers, Ann, 93
Lanza, Adam, 197–198, 201
Lanza, Nancy, 197–199, 201
LaPierre, Wayne, 175
  and "absolutist" views on gun rights, 5,
    192–193, 210
  Ackerman McQueen disputes, 146–148,
    154–155, 206, 215, 228–232
  allegedly lavish spending, 9, 230
  apology for "jackbooted Government thugs"
    reference in fund-raising letter, 142. *See
    also* Oklahoma City bombing
  and Assault Weapons Ban, 128
  background, 102, 111–112
  on background checks, 123, 159, 234
  balancing act of, 127, 128, 151
  became second-in-command of lobbying
    wing, 109
  on Bloomberg, 209
  on Bloomberg, Soros, Steyer, 226. *See*
    Conservative Political Action Committee,
    and *Haaratz*
  business model of, 131, 153–157, 169
  and Butina, 223
  and Carter, 109–110, 235
  and changes to the *American Rifleman* and
    other official journals, 131–132

LaPierre, Wayne (*continued*)
  and Childress, 230
  cochaired fundraiser for presidential
    campaign of George W. Bush, 174
  conversation on background checks with
    President Trump, 234
  and Cox, 9, 159–160, 164, 208, 233
  denouncing extremists, 143, 148. *See also*
    Oklahoma City bombing
  on early NRA's alleged opening of doors for
    minorities and defense of our common
    rights, 182
  elected NRA executive vice president, 122
  and Firearms Owners' Protection Act,
    110–111, 115–116
  former educator, 102
  going on "the offensive" after 2016 elections,
    224. *See also* NRATV
  grassroots networks under, 161, 164
  on gun registration, 123
  hiring Cox as chief lobbyist, 159
  hiring Loesch as special assistant for public
    communication, 226
  hiring by Metaksa as a lobbyist, 102, 111–112
  hiring Metaksa as chief lobbyist, 132
  and Knox, 116–117, 127, 135–140, 151,
    145–151
  legislative aide to Virginia State Rep. Vic
    Thomas, 112. *See also* Thomas, Vic
  legislative legacy of, 114–117
  1985 letter from Sen. Orrin Hatch, 115, 232.
    See also Firearms Owners Protection Act,
    and Hatch, Orrin
  on machine guns, 116. *See also* Firearms
    Owners Protection Act
  and Makris, Anthony, 147. *See also*
    Ackerman McQueeen, and Heston,
    Charlton
  marketing and media legacy of, 131–132,
    153–157
  on McCain-Feingold Act, 169–170
  media appearances with Heston, 155
  meetings with other gun rights leaders,
    132–133. *See also* Feldman, Richard
  on the Migratory Bird Treaty Reform Act,
    157
  and Milius, 146–147. *See also* Ackerman
    McQueen, and Heston, Charlton
  navigating between competing sides, 6
  and North, 9, 229–230
  and NRA finances, 145–146
  Nugent on, 230
  on Obama, 186
  and Oklahoma City bombing, 140, 142–143.
    See also Oklahoma City bombing

  photographed with, 115, 149, 223
  political acumen and approach, 112
  political and electoral legacy of, 161–172
  pragmatism of, 117
  press conference after Sandy Hook shooting,
    7, 200–203, 208
  on Protection of Lawful Commerce in
    Firearms Act, 170. *See also* Protection of
    Lawful Commerce in Firearms Act
  recruitment of Heston for NRA board and
    president, 7, 148–149
  remarks at Congressional Sandy Hook
    hearings on gun violence, 207–209
  response to Columbine shooting, 158–159
  response to Parkland shooting, 226
  response to Sandy Hook shooting, 7,
    200–203, 207–210
  on Ruby Ridge, 127
  salary, 146, 232–233
  speech to United Nations against proposed
    Arms Trade Treaty, 192–193
  "Standing Guard" column, 4, 123, 127, 134,
    135, 209–210, 235
  on success stopping gun control legislation
    after Sandy Hook, 210
  support from Hammer, Porter, 230–231. *See*
    2019 NRA annual meeting (Indianapolis)
  support from Heston, 150, 152
  tenure of, 3
  on tort reform, 170
  on 2006 midterm elections, 170
  on 2016 midterm elections, 170
  2018 speech to Conservative Political Action
    Committee, 226
  as volunteer for George W. McGovern's
    presidential campaign, 111–112
  and *The Wayne LaPierre Show* on NBC
    Radio Network, 146. *See also* NBC Radio
    Network
  and West, 29
Laredo Times, 84. *See also* Carter, Harlan B.;
  Carter, Harlon B.; and Casiano, Rámon
Law Enforcement Alliance of America (LEAA),
  162–164, 179, 187–188
Leahy, Patrick, 204
Legion of Merit, 62
Leupold scope, 73
Lexington and Concord, battle of, 134
"Lie-Ability Award," 132
Lincoln, Abraham, 17, 119, 188
Lindsay, John, 89–90
Lister, Charles Baynard "C. B.," 49, 66, 119
  American Rifleman article on "freak"
    Magnum revolver, 54–55
  background and abbreviated bylines, 48

on communist methods and goals, 58–60, 62
death of, 59–60
on disarmament and totalitarianism, 58–60
editor of *American Rifleman,* 58
elected NRA executive vice president, 59
and National Firearms Act (1934), 56
NRA acting secretary, 48
and NRA programs in support of war
    effort, 57
NRA trophy in his memory, 54
opposition to federal firearms registration,
    55, 58–59
positions on gun legislation, 48–49, 55
and Reckord, 48–49, 55–56
suffering brain cancer, 59
supporting the Federal Firearms Act (1934),
    37–38
Littlehale, P. E., 196
lobbying. *See* Institute for Legislative Action
Loesch, Dana
accusing press of profiting from Parkland
    shooting, 226
broadside attack on critical news outlets and
    journalists, 231
contract and salary with NRATV, 228, 331.
    See also Ackerman McQueen
on the fellowship of the NRA, 233
hiring as special assistant for public
    communication, 226
host of *Relentless* and other appearances on
    NRATV, 189, 231
on red flags and law enforcement, 198
threats against her and users blocked by
    Twitter, 232
2018 speech to the Conservative Political
    Action Committee, 226
use of explicitly violent language, 231–232
on use of the term Assault Weapons, 189–190
"lorem ipsum," 188
Luby's Cafeteria shooting, 130–131
Lyman, Charles, E., III, 190, 196
Lyman, David, 196
Lyman, Debbie, 196
Lyman, Remington, 196
Lyons, Kirk, 133

M1 Garand rifles, 103
M4 rifles, 191
M16 rifle, 103, 188
MacNeil, Robert, 87–89
Magnum revolver, 54–55, 78, 103, 156, 189, 210
mail-order gun sales, 75–76, 88, 115
Malcolm X, 72
Malone, Karl, 160
Manchin-Toomey, 210–211

Manifest Destiny, 30
March on Washington, 70–71, 148
Marjory Stoneman Douglas High School
    shooting, 188, 198, 215, 225–226, 228, 230.
    See also Parkland, Florida shooting
Marshall, David, 120–121
Martin, George, 101, 102–103, 104
McCain, John, 169, 174
McCain-Feingold Act, 169
McCall's, 68
McCarthyism, 59
McClure, James A., 107, 111
McClure-Volkmer Bill, 110
McDonald, Otis, 181–182
McDonald v. Chicago, 179–183
McGovern, George, 111
McVeigh, Timothy, 129–130, 140–141, 143. *See
    also* Oklahoma City bombing
Medal of Honor (Civil War), 22
Merrill, Frank, 67
Merrill's Marauders, 67
Metaksa, Tanya K.
    American Rifleman cover photo, 149
    background, 132
    debunking claims of alleged United Nations
        black helicopters, 142
    hiring by Knox as deputy lobbyist, 102
    hiring by LaPierre as chief lobbyist, 132
    hiring of LaPierre as a junior lobbyist, 102,
        112
    introducing herself to reporters, 102
    inviting press to 1997 board meeting in
        Arlington, Virginia, 147
    and Knox, 102, 111, 113, 130, 132, 147
    on Knox, 86
    meeting with Michigan Militia, 132
    and 1995 NRA annual meeting (Phoenix),
        142, 144
    NRA-ILA chief lobbyist, 130, 132, 166, 142,
        147, 149, 166
    photographed with Hammer, Heston, and
        LaPierre on *American Rifleman* cover, 149
    on presence of neo-Nazi activists at NRA
        annual meeting in Phoenix, 144. *See
        also* National Alliance; Oklahoma City
        bombing
    strategy to ally with other conservative
        groups, 130, 132
    quote on gun industry indebtedness to her in
        The Wall Street Journal, 166
Metzenbaum, Howard, 178
Mexican Expedition (against Pancho Villa)
    and Edson, 61
    and Reckord, 48
Migratory Bird Treaty Reform Act, 157

Milius, John
  disinformation techniques against Knox,
    146–147
  NRA board director, 141, 147, 203
  screenplay credits for *Dirty Harry* and
    Apocalypse Now, 147
  screenplay writer and director of *Red Dawn*,
    141
Million Mom March, 158–159
Mitchell, John N., 89
Moore, Michael, 28–29, 168
Mother Jones magazine, 212
Mumma, Morton C., 45, 46–47
Mumma, Morton C., Jr., 47
Mumma, Morton C., III, 66, 118

National Alliance
  presence at 1995 NRA annual meeting
    (Phoenix), 143–144. *See also* Oklahoma
    City bombing
  The Turner Diaries and Oklahoma City
    bombing, 140. See *also* McVeigh, Timothy,
    and Pierce, William Luther
National Association for the Advancement of
  Colored People (NAACP), 184–185
National Board for the Promotion of Rifle
  Practice, 39, 44–45, 46, 62, 65, 72
National Firearms Act (1934), 1, 50–52, 54, 56,
  78, 190
National Firearms Museum
  bronze bust of Carter, Harlon B., 83
  creation of, 145
  displays and exhibits, 156, 202
  donated firearms by Selleck, 160
  stated purpose, 156
  undisclosed, nonpublic NRA Archives, 10,
    28, 35
National Guard
  and Church, 20, 21
  and early years of NRA, 1, 15, 20, 78, 89
  and founding of NRA, 15, 16, 17, 20–22
  Idaho, 109, 126
  Maryland, 48
  mobilization of Idaho National Guard at
    Ruby Ridge, 126
  and National Board for the Promotion of
    Rifle Practice, 39
  New York, 15–16, 20, 21–22, 31, 36, 37, 39, 89
  NRA National Matches at Camp Perry, 42
  postbellum funding cuts, 37
  Texas, 86
  Utah, 89
  Vermont, 61
  Washington, 41
  and Wingate, 16, 20, 31, 39

  and Wingate's rifle practice program, 20, 36,
    37, 39
National Instant Criminal Background Check
  System (NICS), 171, 205–206, 225
National Matches (at Camp Perry), 42–43, 44,
  46–47, 60, 104, 169, 195–196
National Rifle Association (NRA)
  and at-cost purchase of government surplus
    military rifles, 46
  board of directors, 4, 6, 7, 9, 26, 27–29, 32,
    38–39, 42, 47–50, 57, 59–60, 63–64, 66–67,
    72, 85, 95–97, 100, 104–105, 107, 109–111,
    113, 115, 118–119, 122, 131, 134–141, 144,
    146–151, 155, 159–161, 165, 174, 179, 182,
    190, 196, 203, 208, 213–216, 229–230, 232
  bylaws, 4, 63–64, 97–101, 109, 112–113, 150
  centennial celebration (1971), 69–70, 79
  closed culture of, 2, 4
  drafters of certificate of incorporation, 15–24
  early funding, 21–23, 26, 37–38, 39
  embezzlement scandal (1925), 15–24, 47
  executive committee (board of directors),
    78, 138
  executive council (board of directors), 72,
    85, 118
  and Federal Firearms Act of 1938, 54–56
  first mission, 23–24
  first woman on the board of directors, 60
  founding of, 1, 15–24
  government support post–World War I,
    46–47
  and Gun Control Act of 1968, 1, 76–77, 78,
    89–90, 107–108
  Hunting Code of Ethics, 114
  "I'm the NRA" television commercial, 114
  initial goals, 20–21, 23–24, 25, 30–31, 36
  legal name (National Rifle Association of
    America), 5
  limited access for journalists and academics, 4
  membership, 1, 8
  Membership Pledge, 73
  modeled on British NRA, 25–28
  move from 192 Broadway to Temple Court
    (Manhattan), 38
  move from Washington, D.C., to Fairfax,
    VA, 145
  naming of, 25
  and National Firearms Act of 1934, 1, 50–52,
    54, 56, 78, 190
  NRA Hunter's Code of Ethics, 92–93, 114
  official journals, 8, 103, 104, 106, 241
  postwar creation of junior clubs, 60–61
  postwar growth, 21–23, 65
  U.S. presidents as members, 217
  "Weekend Massacre" (November 1976), 96

"What It Was Organized For, Who Compose It, What It Proposes To Do, and What Has It Done," 23–24

National Rifle Association oral history (unpublished, 1974), 3, 7, 51

National Rifle Association of the United Kingdom, 25–28, 34

National Service Rifle Championship, 66

National Shooting Sports Foundation, 9, 190, 196, 232

on use of the term Assault Weapons, 190

National Wildlife Federation, 114

National Women's Championship, 66

Native Americans, 29–30

American Rifleman article on Tecumseh and his British rifle, 156

NRA founders' view on, 29–30, 183

Navy Cross, 61

NBC News, 87–88, 146. See also MacNeil, Robert

Newton, Huey, 74

Newtown shooting. See Sandy Hook Elementary School shooting

New York Chronicle, 19

New Yorker, 228

New York Times, 16, 19, 23, 77, 90, 94, 98, 99, 106, 111, 122, 150, 174, 200, 206, 219, 231

disclosing opinion contributor Kopel's receipt of NRA funding (2014), 177

news story quoting Kopel without mentioning his NRA funding (2017), 220

Nixon, Richard, 89, 217

Norquist, Grover, 161

North, Oliver, 9, 29, 160, 228–230, 233

NRA. See National Rifle Association

NRA: An American Legend (second NRA authorized history), 4, 27, 95

NRA Civil Rights Defense Fund, 110, 175, 180, 203

NRA Double Distinguished National Smallbore Rifle Champions, 196

NRA Eddie Eagle gun safety program, 169

NRA Foundation, 175, 203, 214

NRA-ILA. See Institute for Legislative Action

NRATV, 189, 224, 228, 229, 231–232

Obama, Barack, 163–164, 173, 174, 186–187, 191, 210, 212, 222, 224

Oklahoma City bombing, 129–130, 140–143, 147

On Target (NRA cable show), 132

open carry laws, 74, 166

O'Reilly, Bill, 235

organized crime, 48–52

Orth, Franklin L.

background, 67

complaint of allegedly loaded questions by NBC News' Robert MacNeil, 87

Congressional testimony on gun legislation, 75

criticism of Sen. Thomas J. Dodd's first two gun control bills, 75

death of, 89

Fishing and Hunting News on his alleged betrayal of gun rights, 77

named NRA executive vice president, 67

open-minded consideration and other statements favoring gun control, 13, 75–77

President Johnson's criticism for not backing registration of firearms, 77

response to Sen. Robert Kennedy on NRA's alleged opposition to gun control, 75–76

signatory to NRA denouncing extremist groups (1964), 72–73

succeeded by Rich, 89

support for Gun Control Act of 1968, 13, 75–77, 88–89, 104

Oswald, Lee Harvey, 71, 90

Panic of 1884, 38

Parkland, Florida, shooting, 188, 198, 215, 225–226, 228, 230. See also Marjory Stoneman Douglas High School shooting

Parsons, Michael, 213–214

Partridge, John N., 22

"patriot" or militia movement (post-Waco siege), 129, 134, 148, 210

Patriots for NRA, 108

Paul, Ron, 221

Pelosi, Nancy, 212

Pence, Mike, 10, 224

Pershing, John J., 45

Peterson, Phillip, 190

Petzal, David E., 144–145

Pierce, William Luther, 140. See also National Alliance and The Turner Diaries

"Pierrepont," 19, 22

Pittsburgh Tree of Life synagogue shooting, 227–228

Planet of the Apes, 155. See also Heston, Charlton, and Ackerman McQueen

Pollock, Howard W., 113–114, 118

Popular Science, 68

Porter, Irvine C.

background, 67

elected NRA president, 67

Porter, Irvine C. (*continued*)
  his son and NRA President James W. Porter
    II's 2015 *American Rifleman* column on
    his father's role in the Cincinnati Revolt,
    99–100
  and 1978 NRA annual convention (Salt Lake
    City), 97–99
  NRA Honorary Life Membership award, 99
  presiding over 1977 annual meeting
    (Cincinnati Revolt (1977), 97–99
  signatory to NRA statement denouncing
    extremist groups (1964), 72–73
  succeeded by Schooley, 67
Porter, James W., II, 98, 99, 136–137, 140, 209
  on Bloomberg, 209
  photographed receiving Right to Bear Arms
    (Moscow) award plaque from Maria Butina
    at 2014 annual meeting (Indianapolis), 223
  and Purcell, 140
  received an award from Right to Bear Arms
    (Moscow), 212
  on the role of his father, Irvine C. Porter, in
    the Cincinnati Revolt, 99–100
  speaking out at 1994 board meeting in
    Minneapolis in favor of Tom Washington
    for president, 136–137, 140
  supporter of LaPierre at 2019 annual
    meeting (Dallas), 230–231
Pratt, Larry. *See also* Gun Owners of America
  meeting Christian Identity white
    supremacists in Branson, Missouri, 142
  meetings with Wayne LaPierre, other gun
    rights leaders in Washington, D.C., 133.
    See also Feldman, Richard
  praising NRA before white power leaders
    meeting in Estes Park, Colorado, 133–134
  protesting the Waco siege in front of FBI
    headquarters in Washington, D.C., 142–143
Presidential Unit Citation, 62
private armies and subversive activities, 73
Prohibition, 49
Protection of Lawful Commerce in Arms Act
  (2005), 170
Pulse nightclub shooting, 213
Purcell, Lee
  ambivalence on machine guns or fully
    automatic weapons, 144
  background, 138, 144
  dropped by the Nominating Committee for
    the board, 144
  and Porter II, James W. 140
  speaking out at 1994 board meeting in
    Minneapolis in favor of Tom Washington
    for president, 138
Putin, Vladimir, 212, 223

race riots, 74, 125, 136, 186–187
  "It Will Never Happen Here," Cox
    (*American Rifleman*, 2011), 186–187
  riots in London (2011), 186–187
  Rodney King riots in Los Angeles (1992),
    125, 136
  "Who Guards America's Homes?" (*American
    Rifleman*, 1967), 74
  "You Loot, We Shoot," Hammer (*American
    Rifleman*, 1992), 125
Radical Republicans (Reconstruction), 87
Reagan, Ronald
  on AK-47 rifles after the Stockton shooting,
    120, 121–122
  American Rifleman cover photo with Carter,
    Harlon B., 109
  and Arnett, 113, 114, 146
  assassination attempt, 108, 121
  and Brady Act, 121
  and Firearms Owners' Protection Act, 115,
    166, 190, 234
  first sitting president to address NRA annual
    meeting, 10, 109
  law banning open carrying of firearms in
    California, 74
  NRA endorsement of, 108, 173
  NRA member, 217
  weakening of National Firearms Act of 1934,
    51–52
  "Why I'm for the Brady Bill" (*New York
    Times*), 121–122
Reckord, Milton A., 3, 47
  appointed Maryland adjutant general, 48
  awarded Bronze Star Medal, 57
  awarded Distinguished Service Medal, 57
  awarded Medal of Honor, 57
  background, 3, 47–48
  deployed in Mexican Expedition against
    Pancho Villa, 48, 61
  on federal bill to restrict pistols and revolvers
    in District of Columbia, 48
  and Federal Firearms Act (1938), 56
  first NRA executive vice president, 3, 47,
    48–51, 55–59
  on gun control, 48–49
  interview for the oral history, 3, 51
  leave of absence from NRA during World
    War II, 3, 57
  on Magnum revolver, 55
  military career, 48
  and National Firearms Act (1934), 3, 50, 51,
    56
  opposition to federal firearms registration as
    condition of gun purchase, 55
  Provost marshal general for Europe, 57

signatory to NRA statement denouncing
    extremist groups, 72–73
succeeded by C. B. Lister, 59
supporting the Federal Firearms Act (1934),
    37–38
testified in Congress, 50
Reconstruction, 11, 15, 36
    founding of the NRA, 1
    and Grant, 39
    NRA claim that NRA allegedly stood with
        freed slaves, 10, 29
    Radical Republicans, 87
Red Dawn (film), 141, 147. *See also* Milius,
    John
Remington, Frederic, 43
Remington Arms, 22
    870 shotgun, 187
    sales, 191
    700 ADL rifle, 73
Remington Outdoor Company, 191
Revels, Hiram Rhodes, 22
Revolutionary War, 134, 152, 196
    columns on Concord Bridge battle by
        LaPierre and Kopel, 134
    Heston raising a Revolutionary War–era
        flintlock rifle at the 2000 NRA annual
        meeting (Charlotte), 152
    riflery roots in southern Connecticut dating
        back to the Revolutionary War, 196
Rich, Maxwell, 89, 91, 95–96, 98
Richardson, John, 155
Ridley, Peter S., 95
Rifle magazine (since 1969), 99
The Rifle magazine (1885–1888), 41
rifled muskets, 21
Rifleman Form! (poem), 25
Right to Bear Arms (RBA, Moscow), 212,
    222–223, 235
Right to Keep and Bear Arms (RKBA), 105,
    133, 178, 180, 221, 234
    early reference (*American Rifleman*, 1959),
        69
Rivers, J. F., 196
Robb, Inez, 72
Roberts, John, 97, 179, 187
Robinson, Mark, 215–216, 230
Rockefeller, John D., Jr., 19, 21
Rodengen, Jeffrey L., 27–28
Romney, Mitt, 174, 187, 214
Roosevelt, Franklin D., 53–54
Roosevelt, Theodore, 39, 91, 217
    and *American Rifleman*, 91
    and National Board for the Promotion of
        Rifle Practice, 39
    NRA member, 91, 217

Root, Elihu, 39
Rothstein, Arnold, 49
Roy Innis Memorial Award, 182
Ruby Ridge siege, 125–126, 129, 133–134, 140
    LaPierre's "Standing Guard" column's
        delayed response, 127
    NRA fund-raising letter signed by LaPierre
        (1995), 142
Ruger
    AR556, 225
    P89, 130
Russian Revolution, 47
Ryan, Paul, 174, 180

Salter, Stephanie, 121
Sandy Hook Elementary School shooting
    challenge for NRA, 200, 209, 210
    and gun legislation, 191, 205, 209–211
    and increased demand for assault weapons,
        191
    Lanza, Adam, 197–199
    LaPierre's press conference, 7, 200–203,
        208
    and Manchin-Toomey gun bill, 210–212
    Obama press conference, 212
Saporito, Mike, 133
Saturday night special, 90, 95, 108
Savage Mark II rifle, 197, 199
Scalia, Antonin, 178–181, 224
Schuette, Bill, 164
Schumer, Charles, 131, 159, 212
Scripps Howard News Service, 121
Seale, Bobby, 74. *See also* Black Panthers
Second Amendment, 97, 100, 116, 129, 131, 133,
        153, 158, 169, 170, 175, 180, 181, 182, 186,
        187, 190, 192, 204, 207, 208, 218, 226
    District of Columbia v. Heller, 178–181, 220
    first reference as "Second Article in the Bill
        of Rights" (1952), 62, 78
    McDonald v. Chicago, 179–183
Shaler, Alexander, 22
Shaw, George Bernard, 42
Shaw, Henry G., 26
Sheridan, Philip H., 38
Shooting and Fishing magazine, 38, 41, 42.
    See also Arms and the Man
Shoup, D. M., 57
Shotgun News, 135
Sig Sauer, 213
    MCX semiautomatic rifle, 213
    P226 semiautomatic pistol, 199
Sigel, Franz, 22
Silver Star, 89
Singleton, Marvin, 166
slob hunter, 114

Small Arms Firing School for the Instruction of Officers and Enlisted Men in Rifle and Pistol Shooting, 45
smallbore rifles, 9, 85, 161, 195–199
Smith & Wesson
    K-38 Combat Masterpiece, 95
    Magnum revolver, 54–55, 78, 103, 156, 189, 210
    MP15 AR-15 rifle, 187, 210, 225
Squire, Watson C., 22
Squire's Sharpshooters, 22
St. Valentine's Day Massacre, 49–50
Steinweis, Alan E., 219–220
Stevens, John Paul, 179
Stevens, Ted, 107
Steyer, Tom, 226
Stockton, California, elementary school shooting, 120–122, 200
Stump, Wayne H., 137
Sturm College of Law, Denver University, 204
Sugarmann, Josh, 114, 117
Sullivan, Timothy D., 43
Sullivan Act (firearms licensing law), 43, 47, 90
Sumner, Charles, 184
Sun (New York), 19, 26
Sutherland Springs First Baptist Church shooting, 163

Taft, William Howard, 217
taggants, 106–107, 129
Tanner, John, 159
Tartaro, Joe, 133
Tecumseh (Panther Across the Sky), 156. See also Native Americans
Tennyson, Alfred, 25
Texas Monthly, 160
"three strikes" laws, 130
Time magazine, 122
Toomey, Pat, 210–211
Torshin, Alexander, 212, 223
tort reform, 130, 170
Tree of Life synagogue shooting, 227–228
Trotter, Gayle, 206–207
Truman, Harry S, 58
Trump, Donald J.
    on background checks, 234
    and Butina, 224
    Kopel, David, on, 220
    LaPierre video in response to election of, 224
    lifting of donor disclosure requirements, 177
    NRA annual meeting addresses, 10, 217–218
    NRA member, 217
    NRA support for and endorsement of, 9, 217–218, 222, 224, 231
    on Second Amendment and armed resistance, 218

Turner Diaries, The, 140–141
Twain, Mark, 20

Ulysses S. Grant and the Period of National Preservation and Reconstruction, 183–184
United Nations Arms Treaty, 184–185, 192–193
United Press International (UPI) 63, 106
University of Texas tower shooting, 73–74

Vaughan, Nancy, 215
VerBruggen, Robert, 222
Vietnam War
    and Brown, 139
    McCain, prisoner of war, 174
    resettled refugees among young Stockton shooting victims, 120
    and Ridley, 95
Village Voice, 6, 139, 145
Violent Crime Control and Law Enforcement Act (1994), 6, 130–131
Virginia Tech shooting, 171–172, 212
Volkmer, Harold, 110

Waco siege, 125–127
    gives rise to the "patriot" or militia movement, 129
    McVeigh, Timothy, among motivations of, 140
    Oklahoma City bombing, second anniversary of, 130
    Pratt, Larry, leads protest at FBI headquarters, 141–142
Waldman, Michael
    on influence on American jurisprudence of NRA-funded scholars, 176
    on Justice Scalia's decision in District of Columbia v. Heller, 180–181
Walker, Mark, 215
Walker, Scott, 224
Wall Street Journal, 166. See also Kopel, David B., news story quoting Kopel without mentioning his NRA funding (2017), 220
War of 1812, 156
Warren, Francis W., 47
Washington, Tom, 136–140, 146, 149
Washington Post, 7, 77, 94, 95, 99, 132, 135, 143, 147, 231. See also Kopel, David B., news story quoting Kopel without mentioning his NRA funding (2017), 220
Watson, Kirk, 162–163
Weaver, Randy, 125–126
West, Allen, 29
    fined over mock execution in Iraq, 29
    remarks about early NRA and blacks on CNSNews.com, 182

remarks at the Roy Innis Memorial Award inauguration, 182
siding with NRA and hostile to LaPierre, 233
white power groups, 127, 129, 133, 140, 141, 143, 236, 237
Whitman, Walt, 19, 20
Whose Right to Bear Arms? (documentary), 88
Willeford, Stephen, 167
Williams, Josh, 177
Williams, Robert, 184–185
Wilson, Woodrow, 39
Winchester Bronco Buster Trophy, 43
Winchester Model 70, 157
Winchester Repeating Arms Company, 43
Wingate, George Wood, 40, 79, 157, 184, 238
    background, 17–19
    cofounding of NRA, 16–18, 20, 184, 237–238
    conservationism of, 18
    and Church, 16, 20, 23–26, 35, 36, 37, 39, 87
    and Cullen, 22
    and Creedmoor International Rifle Match of 1874, 31–33, 35
    and Creedmoor Rifle Range, 25–27
    differences with Church over labor unrest (Great Trolley Strike in Brooklyn), 31
    1878 International Military Match at Creedmoor, 36
    final years, 39
    first met Church, 20
    George W. Wingate High School (Brooklyn), 17
    hunter-conservationist ethic, 18
    "I enclose a formal obituary of the NRA" (*Shooting and Fishing*, 1892), 38
    and initial goals of NRA, 20–21, 23–24, 25, 30–31, 36, 39–40, 157
    on lack of marksmanship in the Civil War, 24
    as man of action, 18
    Manual for Rifle Practice, The, 18, 194
    meeting with Gov. Alonzo B. Cornell of New York, 37
    on the National Board for the Promotion of Rifle Practice, 44
    National Guardsman, 31, 36, 89
    on Native Americans, 29–30
    NRA president, 38
    president of the New York Public Schools Athletic League, 17
    presiding over the 1873 match with the Irish team at Creedmoor, 31–32
    promotion to sergeant in Carlisle, 17
    recollections of the 1873 match at Creedmoor, 33
    recollections of Sgt. George W. Wingate in Carlisle during the Battle of Gettysburg, 16
    recruitment of Grant for NRA president, 37–38
    report to the NRA board, January 14, 1873, 27
    rifle practice program, 35, 36–37, 194
    significance of, 37–40, 87
    skills and background, 16–18
    support for Grant's efforts to stop KKK, 183
    Through the Yellowstone Park on Horseback (Wingate, 1886), 39
    Wingate Park (Brooklyn), 17
Wingate & Cullen, 17–18
Wingate, Kearney & Cullen, LLP, 18
Winkler, Adam, 74
Woodward, John B., 26
World War I, 39–40, 41, 44–46
    Meuse-Argonne, battle of, 48
World War II, 3, 8, 16, 47, 65, 67, 114, 184, 214
    American Rifleman article (2015), 156
    the Bulge, Battle of, 89, 156
    decorated role of Rich, Maxwell, 89
    Dunkirk evacuation and NRA role, 56–57
    and Edson, Merritt A., 61–62
    and Foss, Joe, 113
    Guadalcanal, Battle of, ("Edson's Ridge") 61–62, 113
    and Reckord, Milton A., 47, 57
    and Rich, Maxwell, 89
    and Shoup, D. M., 57
    Tulagi and Gavutu–Tanambogo, Battle of, 61

ABOUT THE AUTHOR

Frank Smyth is an independent award-winning investigative journalist specializing in armed conflicts, organized crime and human rights overseas, and the gun movement and its influence at home. He is a former arms trafficking investigator for Human Rights Watch, breaking the story of France's role in arming Rwanda before the genocide there. Smyth is a global authority on journalist security and press freedom, having testified before Congress and the member states of several multilateral organizations.